XML Processing *with*
Perl, Python, *and* PHP

XML Processing *with* Perl, Python, *and* PHP

Martin C. Brown

SYBEX

San Francisco · London

Associate Publisher: Richard Mills
Acquisitions and Developmental Editor: Tom Cirtin
Editor: Gene Redding
Production Editor: Jennifer Campbell
Technical Editor: Charles Hornberger
Graphic Illustrator: Tony Jonick
Compositor: Franz Baumhackl
Proofreaders: Emily Hsuan, Nancy Riddiough
Indexer: Nancy Guenther
Cover Designer: Caryl Gorska, Gorska Design
Cover Photograph: Tony Stone

Library of Congress Card Number: 2001094603
ISBN: 0-7821-4021-1

Manufactured in the United States of America

10 9 8 7 6 5 4 3 2 1

To Sharon, always.

Acknowledgments

First, I must thank Tom Cirtin, who originally offered me the book on the basis of a brief conversation at the beginning of the year. I also need to thank Jennifer Campbell, who took over and managed the project after the initial stages. It's been a long process with occasional difficulties, but the people at Sybex were wonderful throughout the course of this project.

I also need to thank Gene Redding, who copy edited the book for me—after almost five years of writing, I'm still not as good as I could be. For the technical input, thanks go to Charles Hornberger for highlighting missed opportunities and less-than-perfect examples.

Big thanks also have to go to all the people who do the work behind the scenes and produce the modules, extensions, and examples that make up this book. This includes—but in no way is limited to—James Clarke, the folks at Late Night Software, Apple Computer, Inc., Scriptics, Larry Wall and the Perl team, Guido van Rossum, Fredrik Lundh, and the rest of the Python and PyXML teams and the folks who work on PHP, Ruby, and Rebol.

There's also a very special thanks to the people out there who helped me deal with the events of September 11, 2001, which occurred during the writing of this book. My heart goes out to anybody whose family was touched by the tragedies. Whilst neither I nor any of my family or friends were involved in the events on that day, many of the people I know and work with were. In particular, thanks and best wishes to Wendy Rinaldi, Rikke Jørgensen, and Aharon Robbins.

The penultimate thanks go to Neil Salkind and Vicki Harding, my agents, and to the rest of the team at StudioB for keeping all my contracts, negotiations, and checks in order.

Finally, the biggest thanks should go to my wife. I would be lost without her, and all too often she has to listen to my complaints and frustrations without any thanks or appreciation.

Contents at a Glance

Contents

Introduction

Almost ten years ago, my introduction to the commercial world was handling and dealing with the databases of a UK government body. We used a free text-retrieval system to store information about software products, teachers, and trainers. Although we had fields for the information, when we entered a search, we were searching the whole document, not just one field or a collection of them.

One of my jobs was to write programs that processed the information, deduced the fields, extracted compound addresses and telephone numbers, and tidied up the results to put into a new version of the database.

Access to the database was through a Sun-based Unix system, and the PCs and Macs on the network didn't talk to each other, but they did talk over Telnet to the Sun database server. You could do searches, edit information, and cut and paste, but you had no control over how the information looked without manually massaging the text you'd just copied.

Ten Years Later

Ten years later, for the most part I still do the same thing, although not with the same company or the same information. Ultimately, though, I'm still working with databases and storage systems that rely on managing and dealing with a lot of text, but in a structured way that is somehow intelligent enough to know what I'm storing but flexible enough not to restrict what it is I want to store.

The information I'm dealing with has to be accessible on a number of different platforms. In my home office alone, I've got Macs, Unix, Linux, at least five different versions of Windows, and handhelds running EPOC32 and PalmOS. They support different character sets, and I have to be able to convert the information into more usable formats, such as HTML for display, or stored in more rigid systems, like an RDBMS.

What should I use? Do I play with a free text-retrieval system again?

If I use a database system, how will I transfer my contacts from my desktop Mac to my portable Windows notebook or to Palm? If I want to view the information online, can I convert it easily? If I build an application that provides me with access to the information, how do I go about storing my preferences? How do I make the information available over the network in a format that can be accessed by all the machines that need to use it?

The Solution

The solution, if you haven't guessed it already, is that I should use XML, the Extensible Markup Language. I get all the flexibility I need without losing any capabilities. I can add new fields, structures, and layouts to the information without breaking any of the existing tools. I can use fairly standard applications to convert the XML information into a more suitable format. In fact, I can easily convert an XML document into a structured database, and I can query the database using SQL and export the records back in XML format.

Alternatively, I can store everything in XML and access, process, and update the information directly. If I want, I can even query the XML document using XQL. I can use it to exchange information between platforms and, because all the information is in a standard and easily processed format, I should be able to use the information on any platform I have access to.

The Tools

I'm not actually a firm believer in being to able to specify the "right" tool for the job. Each programming job is different and may well have a number of different solutions and possible tools that would ease the process. However, I do know that scripting languages offer one of the fastest development environments, and many offer a wider range of supported platforms (and more accessible methods) than more traditional XML processing tools based on Java or C/C++.

Python, for example, runs on MacOS, Unix, Windows and PalmOS. Rebol runs on even more. AppleScript is a standard part of every MacOS revision since 8.0 and is even included in MacOS X. Perl is supplied as standard with most Linux revisions, and even some commercial Unix installations include Perl as a standard option.

In fact, I have access to a wider range and more easily accessible set of development tools off the shelf than any Java or C/C++ development environment I know of. Furthermore, some of them are so easy to use that it's hard to understand why you would even look at another language. Did you know, for example, that you can talk to any application in MacOS with AppleScript?

Think about what you could do if only you knew how to tell Perl to convert your XML-based documents into Word documents for editing, or to HTML for viewing on the Web, or to SQL tables for storage in a database!

This Book

If you haven't already guessed, this book is all about parsing, processing, and working with ·XML using a variety of scripting languages. After a brief XML refresher, I address the languages in turn to show how each provides solutions for getting at the power of XML. Along the way, I address some of the important protocols, such as SOAP and XML-RPC, that make seamless data transfer possible. Throughout this book you'll find sample scripts. You can download the complete versions of the scripts by going to www.sybex.com and following the link to the page for this book.

XML seems to be everywhere today and used in a myriad of ways, especially in the vital and growing world of e-commerce. This book is designed to help you make the most of it. I hope that you will return to these pages often as you discover more uses for XML.

PART I

Applying XML

## CHAPTER 1

Introduction to XML

- XML Goals

- Making Data Portable

- Inside XML

- Past, Present, and Future

The storage and exchange of information has been a problem in the world of computers since they were invented. In essence, files fit into one of two categories: Either they are basic text or they are binary.

Text files are the most compatible. They use standard 8-bit characters using the ASCII system to store information. ASCII is universally accepted—from the Sinclair ZX81 to the PDP-11/73, the Commodore 64, Atari ST, to the modern PC, Mac, and Unix workstation, they all read and write ASCII data. ASCII is not without problems—different machines use different characters for line termination, for example—but these are not impossible to overcome.

However, there are problems with ASCII as a storage format for anything beyond letters, numbers and basic punctuation. One of the fundamental problems with ASCII text is that essentially we are limited to 128 different characters, consisting of the main letters (upper- and lowercase); numbers; and basic characters, such as the comma, dollar sign, and mathematical symbols.

With standard ASCII there is no way to represent anything beyond these standard characters, so accented characters and other currency symbols are missing. We don't even have access to the accent symbols, so we can't mark them up in the text so that a program such as Word will understand what we mean.

The representation issue raises the main complaint of plain text as a file. By definition, plain text is an unformatted and unstructured solution for storing information. There are solutions such as Comma Separated Values (CSV) and Tab Delimited Fields (TDF), but both of these are completely unsuitable for anything other than tabular data.

Suppose you want to store a marked-up document that uses bold and italics, different fonts, special characters and incorporates images, movies, and sound? The obvious option is to produce your own proprietary binary format. Rather than being limited to 7-bit data, you get to use 8-bit, full-width characters, and instead of relying on a text representation of what you are doing, you can format and structure your document however you like. It doesn't matter that the document isn't readable by anything other than your application. If someone wants to read your document, he can just buy a copy of your application, right?

Proprietary Data Formats

Although these proprietary formats are fine as long as you are using your application, what happens when you want to exchange that document with someone else? If you are transferring it over e-mail, then you probably need to encode it into an ASCII-based format—normally handled automatically by your e-mail software—then decode it back to its binary format.

Once your recipient gets the document, he still needs a copy of the application that created it, or at least one that is able to import or read that binary format. This presents something of a problem. There are lots of different word processors out there; if you're sending a copy of a letter that you wrote in Word, and your recipient uses AppleWorks, what do you do?

You could try saving to a compatible format. Both applications support Rich Text Format (RTF), which is actually a structured text format that retains most of the formatting for a document, but it's not infallible. Congratulations, you've just solved your first data exchange problem!

Now do the same with your latest database application. The first problem is that there's no direct equivalent of the RTF format for exchanging information. Sure, we can export the data in DIF, SYLK, or the previously mentioned CSV and TDF formats. We'll need to do that for each table in our database, and we'll need to set up the database at the other end to hold the information we need to import.

If we take a specific example, such as a contacts database, then we can be more specific. Exchanging entire tables between systems won't be a problem, but pulling out a single record can be. If the database is modeled with three different tables containing contact names, addresses, and contact numbers, then that single contact will mean taking only a few rows from each table. You'll have to import each table individually, and woe to you if your record IDs don't match!

Although transferring information between two database systems that you've created is relatively simple, trying repeating the exercise with two databases that are not identical, such as the contact DB in your e-mail software and the DB in your handheld. The field names don't match, and in all likelihood the number and type of fields don't match either.

Modifying the raw text data generated when you did the export would solve the problem, but you'd probably lose some data in the process. In addition, you would be adding a manual element to something that should really be automatic. Computers are supposed to make your life easier, right?

XML—Making Data Portable

By now you should have started to spot a trend. Exchanging data between applications, even those that you've created and written yourself, is not easy. In fact, it's often the single most frustrating process in using your application, and one of the most asked-about topics in user forums and to helpdesk managers.

Data exchange happens all the time. Everything from your latest credit card purchase to clicking on a URL in an e-mail message triggers some form of data exchange. Get more adventurous and you find that exchanging documents with your friends, importing graphics into your newsletter or catalog, doing a mail merge, or even sharing data between your desktop and your handheld all rely on the exchange of information.

The critical area in each case is how to model the data in a format that is as portable as possible and still retain the data structure. The RTF, CSV, TDF, and a myriad of other formats have all tried to fit this particularly niche. The problem is that each is targeted at solving a particular problem, which means that each essentially uses its own proprietary format. We're back to square one.

In 1974, Charles F. Goldfarb invented Standardized General Markup Language (SGML). This system represented the contents of complex documents using standard text. Tags were used to help describe the content and format of the text so that that it was possible to convert a raw SGML document and extract data from it, either to produce a final document or to extract elements. Everything from a full book to a quick reference card could be pulled from a raw SGML file, all without ever modifying or copying the contents.

In 1991, Tim Berners-Lee used the basic mechanisms provided by SGML to create a way to mark up text for formatting it on screen; he called it Hypertext Markup Language (HTML). Although the Internet was nothing new by the time it came on the scene, HTML did revolutionize the way we use the Internet and browse and exchange information.

In about 1997, it became apparent that many of the principles that applied to SGML and HTML could equally be applied for modeling data. If SGML declares document elements so that we can pick out individual paragraphs, chapters and other specific fragments and HTML defines text formatting, then Extensible Markup Language (XML) can be used to store data in a structured format.

XML enables us to mark up a text document so that we can identify different pieces of information. For example, we could mark up a contact record like this:

```
<contact>
    <name>Martin Brown</name>
    <address>The House</address>
    <town>Sometown</town>
    <postcode>AB12 3CD</postcode>
    <contact_numbers>
        <phone>01234 567890</phone>
        <mobile>09876 543210</mobile>
        <email>mc@mcslp.com</email>
    </contact_numbers>
</contact>
```

We can now pick out from this XML document the name of the contact, the address, and a list of phone numbers.

The entire document is in text, so we don't have to worry about dealing with or programming a reader for a proprietary format. The fields are easily marked up; we needn't doubt which of these fields is my phone number, and for all we know the entire record could have come from seven different tables in a database. We also haven't lost any information in the translation.

Going back to our original problem—that of exchanging data between applications—you can see that we've just solved all of the problems we had with either the binary formats or the CSV, RTF, and other text- and data-specific formats we've been using up to now.

Using our contact XML document, if we'd exported that from our e-mail application on the desktop and then transferred it over to our handheld, we'd have copied the information easily, efficiently, and without any manual intervention. If the handheld was unable to cope with mobile phone numbers, it could have ignored the field. If it used a single field to hold the address, town, and postcode information, then it could have bonded all of that together when the record was imported.

This is what XML is all about: modeling data in a structured way so that we can easily exchange information between applications. XML is a solution for making data portable.

XML Goals

Extensible Markup Language (XML) is a side-set of SGML. Although it follows most of the basic premises of the SGML system, some of the complexity has been removed in order to make it easier to use as a way of displaying and formatting information for the web. The original design goals of the World Wide Web Consortium (W3C) when developing XML were the following:

1. XML shall be straightforwardly usable over the Internet.
2. XML shall support a wide variety of applications.
3. XML shall be compatible with SGML.
4. It shall be easy to write programs to parse XML documents.
5. The number of optional features of the XML standard should be kept to an absolute minimum (preferably zero).
6. XML documents should be human-readable and reasonably clear.
7. The XML design should be prepared quickly.
8. The design of XML should be formal and concise.
8. XML documents should be easy to create.
10. Terseness in XML markup is of minimum importance.

For the most part, W3C succeeded. XML is easy to use, create, parse, and understand, even when reading it in its raw format. The XML 1.0 specification has been set in stone, with the formal ratification taking place on February 10, 1998.

XML Features

We can list the primary features that XML provides in six simple statements:

- XML enables you to store and organize information that can be tailored to your needs, rather than being controlled by the application that created the information.

- XML uses the Unicode character set, which means we are not limited to ASCII or indeed any character set for any language. XML documents can be written in English, Chinese, Gujarat, Greek, or Sanskrit.

- XML is an open standard, which means that nobody owns the standard, it's not reliant on a single company, and it's not a part of or reliant on the features of a single application.

- XML documents can be as open or strict as you like. We can check the quality of the document by examining syntax, the data content, or the document structure.

- XML is clear and easy to read. Humans can read and write XML documents, and documents can be written and modified using a standard text editor.

- XML is a system for modeling data. We can convert the data into a formatted document using style sheets, without the need to convert the data into another format.

XML: Past, Present, and Future

XML is still a relatively new technology, despite its apparent age. At the time I write this, July 2001, XML is 3.5 years old, and yet many of the features, applications, and promises made in XML's infancy have yet to be realized.

This is not in any way a criticism. HTML is just 10 years old, and even now we are only just beginning to realize its potential. Most people use, and a significant proportion of them write, HTML every day, but still there are issues surrounding how best to use the language. Compatibility issues (different browsers displaying the same HTML in different ways), tags, and where HTML fits into the whole scheme of document formatting are still topics to be decided.

XML is actually a family of technologies. The XML standard itself defines how to specify elements and their attributes within your XML documents. Behind the scenes sits the Document Type Definition (DTD), which is an optional element that defines the structure, layout, and validity of the fields and data that you can incorporate into your XML document.

Then there are extensions to the XML standard that enable you to define and specify other elements in the document, such as XLink for adding hyperlinks and XPointer and XFragments for pointing and referring to areas of an XML document. For converting the XML document into HTML for display on a web page we have Cascading Style Sheets (CSS), Extensible Stylesheet Language (XSL), and XSL Transformations (XSLT).

Finally, there are technologies for reading XML documents, such as Simple API for XML (SAX) and Document Object Model (DOM). There are the technologies that use XML, such as Resource Description Format (RDF), which is used to model metadata, RDF Site Summary (RSS), which is used to stream news information in a structured format, and remote technologies such as XML-RPC and SOAP, which use XML to exchange requests and responses with a remote server to enable you to execute functions remotely.

At the present time, XML is still in the "Let's see what we can do" stage. Standards are being discussed and agreed upon, and many companies and developers are converting their systems to use XML. Most of the topics already mentioned in this chapter are still in development, and although it's true that most things evolve over time, many of these haven't yet made it to the growing-legs and breathing-air stage.

In the future, XML will be a major part of your computing experience. Whether you are aware of this or not will depend on how it is advertised.

Other companies are creating groups that will agree on standards for communicating between systems. Already there are groups for our contact database and desktop/handheld data problem. There also are companies developing solutions for Electronic Data Interchange (EDI), a system that requires the definition of hundreds or even thousands of fields just to hold the information for an order.

You'll wake up in the morning, read the news through a set of RSS feeds, send an XML-formatted e-mail to your friends, exchange an XML document with your bank to find your latest balance, and raise orders and receive invoices from your suppliers and clients by sending them an XML document, rather than printing them out and faxing or posting them.

XML and Scripting Languages

Now that you know all about XML, where it came from, and what problems it should solve, you probably wonder where scripting languages fit into the mix. Obviously, if you want to read or write XML documents, you are going to need to do that with the language in which you write your application.

Many people will be using XML documents in rapid application development (RAD) environments, and many of these rely on scripting languages such as Perl, Python, and Tcl. Others will be using XML in their web- and Internet-based applications.

In most cases, a scripting language offers some advantages over C or C++ even when writing non-XML scripts. A scripting language is faster to write, easier to use, and generally has better text-handling features. For example, many of the scripting languages covered in this book support much better data typing systems, flexible array handling, and the complex structure building offered by combinations of strings, arrays, and the ever-present hash or dictionary.

With all these things in mind, since XML is all about processing textual information and structuring that information into a more useful format, wouldn't it make sense to use a scripting language?

Where Next

The aim of this book is to show you how we can read, write, format, and structure information in XML using Perl, Python, PHP, REBOL, Ruby, Tcl, and AppleScript. The aim isn't to show you which language is better, although we do give more attention to the top three languages.

Instead, it's a practical guide to performing a variety of XML processing and manipulation tasks in each of the different languages. With that in mind, reading the book sequentially won't be useful to you; use the following to jump to the section or chapter you want:

- If you are not already familiar with XML as a standard or how to write and use XML, then you probably want to move straight on to Chapter 2 and Chapter 3, where we look at the fundamentals of writing XML documents and DTDs, respectively.

- Regardless of your favorite scripting language, Chapter 4 provides a good background as to why you should use a scripting language for processing XML over C or C++.

- Chapter 5 covers the different technologies used when writing XML documents and how these features can be used and applied in any scripting language. In particular, we look at Unicode, how it affects XML documents, and how XML can be used to build a bridge between applications written in any language.

- If you are Perl programmer and know your XML, skip straight to Chapter 6.

- If you are Python programmer and know your XML, skip straight to Chapter 11.

- If you are PHP programmer and know your XML, skip straight to Chapter 17.

- If you are a REBOL programmer and know your XML, skip straight to Chapter 20.

- If you are a Ruby programmer and know your XML, skip straight to Chapter 21.

- If you are a Tcl programmer and know your XML, skip straight to Chapter 22.

- If you are an AppleScript programmer and know your XML, skip straight to Chapter 23.

CHAPTER 2

Fundamentals of XML

- XML Structure

- Well-Formed XML Documents

- Processing Instructions

We can't really have a book about XML processing without at least some background information on what XML is and what the different components are that make up an XML document.

In essence, XML is incredibly simple, and if you know HTML you are already more than halfway there. XML itself is just an extensible markup language; it uses the same tag style as an HTML document. Unlike HTML, which has a specific set of tags, with XML you can create your own.

The difference between HTML and XML is in the information that is contained in the eventual document. An HTML document contains text with links (hence *hyperlink*) and other embedded elements such as graphics and movies. The eventual aim is to produce a document that looks good onscreen and has links and jump points to similar documents in order to build an information source—whether that be a website, online help in an application, or an interactive info guide.

XML, on other hand, is designed to represent information in a structured and ultimately transparent and portable way. As we saw in the previous chapter, one of the problems with modern computing is that we have no portable way of transferring data, and that's what XML aims to solve. The way it does this is to use the tags and existing structure and features of HTML (actually, SGML, the precursor of HTML and XML) in a more flexible way.

In this chapter we're going to look at what makes up an XML document, what the different components are, how we can use this information to help format data, and how the different elements are identified and processed within a typical XML parser.

XML Structure

As you can see from the example below, all XML documents are made up of a number of different components. The text below is a typical XML document, in this case describing a video and some links that enable us to buy the product through Amazon UK's referral service:

```
<video>
<video_base>
<title>Alien Resurrection</title>
<subtitle>Witness the Resurrection</subtitle>
<stars>Sigourney Weaver, Winona Ryder</stars>
</video_base>
<buylinks>
```

```
<!-- The product code references go here -->
<azuk id="B00004S8GR">Buy Alien Resurrection on DVD</azuk>
<azuk id="B00004S8K7">Buy the Alien Box Set on DVD</azuk>
</buylinks>
</video>
```

The important fragments of the document are the elements (also known as *tags*), which are the portions of text between the < and > characters; the attributes within some of the tags; and the character data (the information not between the <> characters. One other piece of information that might be important is the comment text enclosed by <!-- and -->.

The whole document structure should also be noted. We start with a single element, <video>, in which all the other elements are contained, and also the fact that information in the document is divided between the XML elements and the character data.

It should be obvious from this small example that XML documents are organized so that the elements define the data we are storing, while the character data is the actual information. For example, our video contains a piece of information about its title, subtitle, and stars, and the actual data component of the title is Alien Resurrection.

You should also note that although the tags within the XML document define different fields, there is no limit to the number of tags or their structure. In our example, the video_base section includes the basic information on the video in question—the title, subtitle, and stars—and we also have a buylinks section that contains two azuk tags.

Elements and Attributes

An XML element defines an area of information within the document. In our case, our first XML element is <video> and it defines the start of the information on a video title. The end of the video title information is indicated by the </video> tag. Those familiar with HTML will recognize this structure from many tag pairs such as those used for table specifications, for example <td> and </td>.

Like HTML, XML also supports individual (that is, non-paired) tags. Single-tag elements don't define. Unlike HTML, which uses bare tags such as <hr>, XML includes a slash mark, such as <mytag/>.

Some naming rules apply to the text you use for element names. The following sidebar explains.

XML Element Naming Rules

The XML specification includes the following guidelines for tag and attribute names:

- Names are case sensitive: `<account>` and `<Account>` are treated as different tags.

- A name must start with a character or an underscore, but after that it can continue with any combination of letters, digits, underscores, or periods.

- Names beginning with `xml` (in any combination of uppercase and lowercase) are reserved for use by the XML specification and any of its associated systems.

Attributes are the additional pieces of information defined within a specific tag. For example, in our azuk elements, we included an ID number to be used when referring to the product on the Amazon UK website. Attributes can be used to give an element a unique label or to add properties to an element.

In HTML, you use attributes to include information such as the URL of a link when defining a hyperlink or the location of a graphics file when introducing an image.

Any element can have as many attributes as necessary, as long as each attribute has its own unique name (see the previous sidebar for more information on what's supported). You should also note the following:

- Individual attributes should be separated by spaces. For example, the following fragment is invalid:

```
<chapter section="1"subsection="2">
```

It should be written:

```
<chapter section="1" subsection="2">
```

- Attribute data should be enclosed in either single or double quotes. The following is an example of how *not* to quote information:

```
<chapter title=The Long and Winding Road section=1 subsection=2>
```

The problem here is that we (and therefore an XML parser) have no way of knowing where the data for the title attribute ends.

Elements are handled in a parser by accessing them either by name or by the name of an attribute being supplied to a handler function. Attributes are usually handled in the same way—with most scripting languages, the attributes are supplied as a hash, associative array, or dictionary (depending on what your language calls it).

Comments

You can introduce comments into an XML document just as you can with HTML. But, unlike HTML, where comments are used both as repositories for thoughts and as a source of additional information, XML comments are used strictly for comments. HTML comments are frequently used for everything from processing instructions (the Server Side Includes (SSI) system on the Web, for example) to adding application-specific data within tools such as ColdFusion and other HTML authoring systems.

In XML, rather than using processing instructions are handled completely differently (see the section "XML Processing Instructions," later in this chapter, for more information) and we no longer need to use an existing tag in the HTML specification to hold information—XML lets us define our own tags for that.

XML comments are formatted in the same way as HTML comments, starting with <!-- and ending with -->:

```
<!-- This is a comment -->
```

You can include as much text as you like within a comment, even XML tags:

```
<!-- Please ignore this section
<options>Rear seatbelts, heated windscreen</options>
-->
```

Most XML parsers completely ignore comments. Others allow you to read and access comments through the same mechanism as you would normally use to access XML tags and character data.

Character Data

Character data is essentially all the information within an XML document that doesn't appear within the constraints of an XML tag or its attributes. For example, in our sample XML document, the following fragment contains two pieces of information—the XML tag <title> and the character data Alien Resurrection:

```
<title>Alien Resurrection</title>
```

In the majority of XML documents, it's actually the character data that contains the real information. The tags often just define the type or field to which the character data refers.

Note that, as with XML in general, character data contents are treated verbatim—newlines, spaces, and other white space are significant. This can cause problems if you are used to building HTML documents, where white space is largely ignored. For example, this XML fragment:

```
<title>
Alien Resurrection
</title>
```

is different from this one:

```
<title>Alien Resurrection</title>
```

Different parsers handle the issue of white space in different ways. For example, some would treat the first item as three separate blocks of character data: the first newline, the actual text, and then the final newline at the end of the text. Others return any data between two tags as a single character data block, and it's then up to you to handle the information accordingly. We'll be looking at these issues when we examine the different parsers in different languages throughout the rest of this book.

XML also allows you to insert large chunks of character data that are not subject to the normal conversion and translation handled by entity references (which we'll see later). In these situations, you can insert a special CDATA block. CDATA blocks start with the prefix `<![ CDATA [` and terminate with the `]]>` character sequence. For example, the following fragment would normally fail because of the use of < and & characters:

```
<example>$a << 8; output($a && $b);</example>
```

We could resolve the problem with entity references:

```
<example>$a &lt;&lt; 8; output($a &amp;&amp; $b);</example>
```

However, not only is this difficult to read, it's also difficult to write. We can get around this by using CDATA blocks:

```
<example><[ CDATA [ $a << 8; output($a && $b); ]]></example>
```

CDATA blocks are better used in large pieces of text where the normal entity references would be difficult to use and include. For very short pieces of code, including the examples above, the use of entity references is much better.

Within most XML parsers, character data is considered to be another vital element in the processing sequence, in the same way that start and end tags are. Some also support the identity of the start and end of character data sections.

Well-Formed XML Documents

There are lots of ways to validate and verify that the structure of an XML document is correct (not least of which is the document type definition (DTD), the subject of our next chapter). However, at the basic level, all XML documents should be correctly formatted according to the rules of XML syntax. Documents that conform to this are said to be *well formed*.

It is not a requirement that a document be well formed, but many of the XML processors that we'll be using in this book will raise an error if the document is not well formed. To get the full details on the rules of well-formedness, see the W3C's XML specification at `http://www.w3.org/TR/REC-xml#sec-well-formed`.

In a nutshell, the rules are these:

- There should be one root tag (called the *parent*), from which all other tags are derived (known as *children*). Documents with more than one root tag are not well formed.

- Nested elements should be open and closed in the correct sequence. For example, the following is not well formed because the `</foo>` tag closes before the `</bar>` tag has been completed:

        <foo><bar></foo></bar>

- Child tags should be closed before their parents. For example, the following is wrong because `<bar>` has never been closed.

        <foo><bar></foo>

- Attribute values should be enclosed in double quotes. This fragment is not well formed because `hello` should be in quotes:

        <foo value=hello></foo>

Entity References

Entity references are merely ways of introducing a standard piece of text by name, rather than explicitly within the text itself. There are two reasons for using entities. The first is to get around the problem of introducing characters into character data that would otherwise be identified as special XML characters. The second is to provide an easy means for introducing repeating elements of text into your XML documents without the risk of introducing errors.

This first problem is covered in the next section, "Character Entities." The second problem is covered in the "Mixed-Content Entities" section.

There is a third entity type, the *unparsed entity*, which is used to insert binary data into an XML document. It's unparsed because including the information in the XML document would probably confuse the typical XML parser. We won't be covering or using unparsed entities in this book. See *XML Complete*, published by Sybex, for a complete discussion of entities, their types, and their definition.

Character Entities

The XML specification actually supports five standard character entities, listed in Table 2.1.

TABLE 2.1: Standard XML Character Entities

Name	Value
amp	&
apos	'
gt	>
lt	<
quot	"

To insert these entities into your XML documents, you use the form &*entity*;, where *entity* is one of the names in Table 2.1, such as in the following:

```
<condition>Where x &lt; 10</condition>
```

In addition to these standard character entities, you can also introduce characters by their numerical value. For example, to introduce the ampersand character (&) by its numerical value, we'd use &. The # sign indicates that what follows is a number and should be used as a numerical value within the Unicode table (see Chapter 5, "Data Exchange and XML," for more information on Unicode).

Finally, we can also refer to certain characters within the Unicode database by name if they've been declared within an external DTD. A DTD already exists that allows characters to be inserted by name from the Latin, Greek, Cyrillic, and Nordic scripts used in the majority of Western Europe and America.

Mixed-Content Entities

Mixed-content entities can be either internal or external. *Internal* entities are used when you want to insert the same block or section of text into an XML document. For example:

```
<?xml version="1.0"?>
<!DOCTYPE doc SYSTEM "http://www.mcwords.com/generic.dtd"
[
    <!ENTITY title "Alien Resurrection">
]>
<title>&title</title>
<review>&title is a great film, but it plays more like
a sequence of individual scenes than a connected whole.
One of the problems that you notice throughout &title;
is that the story doesn't really flow. </review>
```

Here we've used the `title` entity so that we can keep referring to the film without having to type it each time. This prevents you from entering it incorrectly; we know that each time we use `&title;` it'll appear correctly in the text.

Entities are defined as part of a DTD—the DTD in this case is defined inline within the XML document itself. The entity definition consists of the name we want to use for the entity, `title`, and the text that we want to be inserted each time the entity is referenced. The text can be anything, including more XML.

External entities can be used to insert the contents of an external file into the current XML document. You can use this to insert repeating or large chunks of data into a number of documents. For example, when writing the contents of a help document, you might want to include the same static XML fragment at the head of each XML document. That fragment would contain the generic help information, such as the product, product version, and other static information.

You specify the location of an external file by using the SYSTEM keyword within the entity declaration:

```
<?xml version="1.0"?>
<!DOCTYPE doc SYSTEM "http://www.mcwords.com/generic.dtd"
[
    <!ENTITY docheader SYSTEM "header.xml">
]>
<chapter>
&docheader;
<chapter_title>Help on Help</chapter_title>
</chapter>
```

Note that the filename following the SYSTEM keyword could just as easily be a URL to an external XML document.

Providing the parser has been configured properly, most entities should be automatically inserted into the document while it is being parsed. You normally have some flexibility over the parsing and inclusion process, including being given triggers when a parsed entity is found within a document.

XML Processing Instructions

XML itself is designed to hold data. You shouldn't use XML to hold either presentational information (such as fonts or layout) or instructions about how to handle or process the information contained within the XML document.

However, there are times when you want to be able to give an instruction to the processor to treat a piece of information in a specific way within an XML document. For example, you may want to force a particular paragraph or piece of text to be formatted in a particular way (perhaps because of style or trademark guidelines), or you may want to introduce a fixed element such as a linebreak into an otherwise freeform character data section.

Processing instructions are very simple: They follow the form <?*name data* ?>. *name* is the name used to describe the processing instruction in question; it's used in the same way as tags are to identify the instruction. *data* is any information in the form of strings or attribute/value pairs. For example, all of the following are examples of processing instructions:

```
<?font MCSLPStandard?>
<?breakline?>
<?parseasrecipe id=567 title="parsnips on parade"?>
```

Although processing instructions appear to give some information, that's not the intention. Whether you actually use processing instructions or follow them is entirely up to you when parsing the document. The result of the instruction is also up to you, although presumably you'll be defining what a process instruction does as part of the definition of the XML structure itself.

The XML Declaration

The XML declaration is a special type of processing instruction. It sits at the top of an XML document and tells the parser what the document is (XML), what version of XML is in force, what encoding system you are using to introduce text into the document, and whether the document stands alone or requires additional documents.

- version defines the version number of the XML specification to which the document applies. At the time of this writing, there is only one specification, 1.0, but it's likely that other versions will be added in the future.

- encoding specifies the character encoding used in the document. Unless you are using characters other than the standard Latin set (as used by most Western and European languages), this item is optional. Valid values depend on the Unicode standard; a quick reference to these is given in Appendix A, "Unicode Quick Reference," and we'll be covering Unicode briefly in Chapter 5.

- standalone defines whether the document is fully contained or requires other documents to be loaded to be processed properly. You would typically set this to no if there were no external entities or DTDs to the XML document and to yes if there were. You can use this value to improve performance: If the value is set to no, then processing can begin instantly. If set to yes, then you know you must first parse the document to determine what other files are needed before you can parse the document fully.

All of these properties are configured in the XML declaration just like attributes in a typical XML element. For example, all of the following are valid examples of XML declarations:

```
<?xml version="1.0"?>
<?xml version="1.0" encoding='US-ASCII'?>
<?xml version='1.0' standalone='no'?>
```

XML declarations are normally accessible through a special function as part of the XML parser, which returns the XML declaration for the XML document being processed.

Summary

XML is a language for describing data in a structured and formatted way using normal ASCII text. It uses a format similar to the HTML standard, but unlike with HTML, with XML you can define your own tags, and these tag pairs make up the information in your XML documents.

You can verify an XML document in a number of ways. You can use a Document Type Definition (DTD), which is a formal definition of an XML documents structure. You can also use simpler methods that check the validity of the tags to ensure that they match and are not nested incorrectly.

CHAPTER 3

Data Type Definitions (DTDs)

- DTD Syntax

- When to Use a DTD

- Standard DTDs

If an XML document describes data, then a Data Type Definition (DTD) describes the layout and acceptable content of an XML document. A DTD is essentially a description of the layout, structure, and in some cases the content of the character data stored within the XML document.

A DTD is more than just a method for declaring the structure of a document, however. It can also be used to declare entities, and you can use multiple DTDs within a single XML document to introduce different sets of valid XML tags and entities into a single XML document.

You specify the use of a DTD within an XML document using the DOCTYPE declaration at the head of your XML document. This consists of a name (used to indicate the root element type) and the location of the DTD that defines the structure for that element. The location should be either a file reference or a URL that points to an accessible version of the DTD. For example:

```
<!DOCTYPE account
SYSTEM "http://www.mcwords.com/XML/DTD/account.dtd">
```

In this chapter we're going to look at the major elements of the DTD syntax and also at why and how we can use the DTD to help in parsing an XML document.

DTD Syntax

The syntax of a DTD is very simple. There are two main elements that need to be covered: the Element Declaration, which defines the structure of an XML element (or tag) and the Attribute Declaration, which defines the structure and content type of attributes within an XML element. We'll also look at the Entity Declaration, which allows you to define entities to be parsed within your document.

Unlike an XML document, there doesn't need to be any prolog to a DTD as there does with an XML document. You can include an XML declaration to define the character set or XML version number.

Element Declarations

Element declarations define the name, type, and content of an XML element. The basic format is this:

```
<!ELEMENT element-name content-specification>
```

element-name should be straightforward; it's simply the name of the XML element. content-specification defines what information the element contains.

This specification defines what combination of character data and subelements can be specified within a given element, and also the order and number of repetitions and whether the sequence or elements are optional or required.

Because an XML element has the potential to be empty (such as `<tag/>`), character data, or additional tags, there are different methods for defining each of these items, all described using a series of different symbols, which are listed in Table 3.1. Many follow the same basic structure as regular expressions.

Some examples of the symbols' use are given in Table 3.2.

TABLE 3.1: Symbols Used in Element Content Specifications

Symbol	Meaning
,	Separate the elements in a required (and by order) sequence.
|	Logical OR; allows you to specify a list of alternate elements.
(`content`)	Groups a number of elements together. Parentheses can be nested to any level.
?	Marks the previous element or group as optional.
+	Requires one or more repetitions of the previous element or group.
*	Requires zero or more repetitions of the previous element or group.

TABLE 3.2: Content Specifications for XML Element Declarations

Content Specification	Description
`<!ELEMENT element (#PCDATA)>`	The element may contain parsed character data, the ordinary text enclosed within an XML element pair.
`<!ELEMENT element EMPTY>`	The element is empty (it should only be specified as `<element/>`).
`<!ELEMENT element ANY>`	The element may contain any other XML element or parsed character data.
`<!ELEMENT element a*>`	The element can contain the element a zero or more times.
`<!ELEMENT element a+>`	The element can contain the element a one or more times.
`<!ELEMENT element (a, b, c)>`	Element must contain the elements a, b, and c in that sequence.
`<!ELEMENT element (a|#PCDATA)>`	Element may contain either element a or character data.
`<!ELEMENT element (a|b|c)*>`	Element may contain zero or more repetitions of a, b, or c in any order.

The definitions that you describe apply to only a single element—you still need to provide the definition for the elements you have specified within the parent definition. For example, if you look at a simple DTD for a bank account, you can see that the content specification merely defines the other elements, which in turn also require definitions to define their content.

Also note that the content specifications themselves can be nested and structured to define the combination of elements precisely. You can see our bank account example in Listing 3.1.

Listing 3.1:   **A Sample Element-Only DTD**

```
<!ELEMENT account (name, sortcode?, accnumber, transactions)>
<!ELEMENT name #PCDATA>
<!ELEMENT  sortcode #PCDATA>
<!ELEMENT accnumber #PCDATA>
<!ELEMENT transactions (deposit, credit, adjustment)*>
<!ELEMENT deposit (date, amount)>
<!ELEMENT credit (date, amount)>
<!ELEMENT adjustment (date, amount)>
<!ELEMENT date #PCDATA>
<!ELEMENT amount #PCDATA>
```

Attribute Declarations

Attribute declarations define which attributes can be used (and what data they should contain) within a single XML element. Just as with the element declarations, the format is straightforward and simple, as you can see from this structure example:

```
<!ATTLIST element-name
attributename-1 attributetype-1 attribute-description-1
attributename-2 attributetype-2 attribute-description-2
>
```

`element-name` is the name of the element to which the attribute declarations belong. `attributename` defines the name of the attribute, `attributetype` defines the data type of the attribute in question, and `attribute-description` defines the behavior of the attribute's value. The individual lines in the layout is important only in that it acts as a distinction between the individual attribute definitions.

An attribute declaration ideally should be placed immediately after the element to which it applies, although this isn't necessary because a definition includes the name of the element to which it belongs. You can see an example of an attribute declaration here:

```
<!ELEMENT chapter (#PCDATA)>
<!ATTLIST chapter
section CDATA #REQUIRED
number CDATA #REQUIRED
type (preface|chapter|appendix) "chapter"
>
```

We look at the attribute data types and attribute behavior in more detail in the following sections.

Data Types

All attribute declarations must include information on the type of data that will be stored within the attribute itself. Some of these are fairly straightforward—for example, we have parsed character and free-form types. Others are more complex and allow relationships between elements and entities.

CDATA

The CDATA declaration indicates that the information allowed within the attribute is normal character data, which can include any normal characters, character entities, and general entities. For example, this declaration:

```
<!ATTLIST paragraph description CDATA #IMPLIED>
```

would allow any content, including this:

```
description="talks about perl, python"
description="The name of game"
description="Using a 4x2 piece of wood"
```

It would also allow the fragment:

```
<paragraph description></paragraph>
```

where the description text is implied even if not explicitly specified.

Note that the CDATA definition supports character entities, which are useful if you want to include otherwise interpreted characters, including the quotes around other XML characters.

NMTOKEN

An NMTOKEN declaration is any string sequence that starts with a letter, numbers, and certain punctuation characters. Note that the intention is for this to be a single named token (such as a single keyword, version number, or filename). Any white space in the attribute value will be removed during parsing.

For example:

```
<!ATTLIST application version NMTOKEN #REQUIRED>
```

Some examples of suitable attributes are these:

```
version="v1.2"
color="red"
genus="reptile"
```

NMTOKENS

This type is essentially identical to the NMTOKEN type except that it implies a list of tokens that should be separated by white space within the attribute's value. Most parsers will trim the white space before and after the text and also compound multiple white space characters into a single space.

An example of this specification is shown here:

```
<!ATTLIST chapter keywords NMTOKENS #REQUIRED>
```

This would support the following attributes:

```
keywords="book perl programming"
color_sequence="red orange yellow green blue brown black"
```

ID

The ID is a special type of attribute that gives an element an attribute value that is guaranteed to be unique within the document. You can use this in XML documents that support a repetition of a particular element to ensure that no two elements are treated the same, even though they may contain the same information.

For example, in a banking system, you may have multiple transactions in a document, but you would want to be able to identify each transaction individually. You'd use a declaration such as this:

```
<!ATTLIST transaction id ID #REQUIRED>
```

The actual ID itself can be any valid string—you are not limited to numerical or even alphanumeric ID numbers. For example, the following are all valid:

```
id="102738927"
sessionid="29732-7382732-827382"
product_number="video-columbia-4953VT8475"
chapter_ref="xml.scripting.1.3"
```

Note that when using ID, you must include an #IMPLIED or #REQUIRED in the attribute definition to ensure that it contains a value.

IDREF

The IDREF type is used to contain the ID reference in another element. You can use this information for cross referencing—such as when connecting given transactions to a particular account or when attaching a given word alternative to another within a thesaurus. If the identifier specified does not exist, the parser should raise an error.

During the parsing, the parser will look for an ID reference within another element that uses the same attribute name. For example, the following declaration indicates that the transaction element should have an attribute called transid, and the acctrans element has an identical transid attribute that references this value:

```
<!ATTLIST transaction transid ID #REQUIRED>
<!ATTLIST acctrans transid IDREF #REQUIRED>
```

Now we can make a connection between a transaction and a transaction within a specific account in our XML document like this:

```
<transaction transid="20010913.01">
<date>13/09/2001</date><amount>300</amount>
</transaction>
<transaction transid="20010912.04">
<date>13/09/2001</date><amount>450</amount>
</transaction>
<account>
<name>Current</name>
<acctrans transid="20010913.01"><type>Dep</type></acctrans>
<acctrans transid="20010913.01"><type>Credit</type></acctrans>
</account>
```

IDREFS

The IDREFS type is identical in principle to NMTOKENS in its relationship to NMTOKEN. Essentially, it allows you to include a list of references, again separated by white space.

ENTITY

ENTITY accepts a general entity name as a value; the string supplied should be the name of the entity you want to include. For example, with our accounts example, we might want to define the different transactions types as entities and use icons to show their types:

```
<!ENTITY deposit SYSTEM "icons/deposit.gif">
<!ENTITY withdrawal SYSTEM "icons/withdrawal.gif">
<!ATTLIST transaction icon ENTITY #REQUIRED>
```

In our XML document, we'd include the information like this:

```
<transaction icon="deposit">
```

ENTITIES

This is a list of entity names separated by spaces.

Enumerated Value List

There are times when you want an attribute to only contain one of a number of different values. For example, if your attribute is used to store a true or false value, then you know that its content should only be true or false or a similar toggle type. You can specify this by enclosing a list of values in parentheses and using the vertical bar to separate the items.

Our true or false example looks like this:

```
<!ATTLIST prefs store ( true | false ) #IMPLIED>
```

NOTATION

This type enables you to specify a list of NOTATION name tokens. We don't cover the Notation Declaration in this title, but see the W3C document on the XML standard for more information on these and other declarations.

Attribute Behavior

In addition to the specification of the data type, you can also specify the behavior of the attribute in question. Some attributes that you want to use will be optional, and others will be required. You might also want to supply a default value that should always be present.

TABLE 3.3: Attribute Behavior Alternatives

Behavior	Specification	Description
Default Value	"default"	Inserts the value default into the attribute if another value is not specified.
Optional	#IMPLIED	The attribute is marked as optional.
Required	#REQUIRED	The attribute must be specified in the element, and it must have been given a value. Not including the attribute or not supplying a value should result in a parser error.
Fixed Value	#FIXED	The attribute is given a fixed value that you must supply in quotes after the behavior definition. Using a value other than this will raise a parser error.

For example, to specify a default value from an enumerated list of possible values, you would use this:

```
<!ATTLIST week
firstday ( mon | tue | wed | thu | fri | sat | sun ) "mon">
```

General Entity Declarations

Entity declarations are the simplest of the declarations within a DTD. They allow you to specify a custom entity that can then be inserted into your document by its short name, usually with the &entityname; sequence.

For example, if you are writing a DTD that describes a book's layout, you may want to define an entity that contains the book's title so that you can maintain consistency through the document when you refer to your book. As seen in the previous chapter, entity declarations consist of just the <!ENTITY prefix, the name you want to use, and the resulting text:

```
<!ENTITY title "Scripting XML with Perl, Python and PHP">
```

Using DTDs for Modeling Data

DTDs form the link between what would be the completely free-form data stored within the XML file and a more structured format such as a formal database. The main difference with XML is that, unlike a typical database, we can model the entire record for a given information item in one document instead of spreading the information across a number of individual databases or tables.

For example, in a recipe database you would probably have a main `recipe` table that held the recipe information, a `method` table that contained a list of the steps required to make the recipe, and an `ingredients` table to hold a list of ingredients and measurements.

Within XML, we can define all this information within a single document. We don't have to worry about manually pulling together information from different sources or even making assumptions about where and how we link the information together.

The DTD describes the structure and layout of that XML document and helps you to define the tree structure of the XML document and what information it can contain.

It's therefore true to say that we can use a DTD to model information before we ever get to the point of populating an XML document. It's also possible to use a DTD as a way of defining the contents and structure of the database or system that will be used to hold the data.

Although we could use XML for this purpose, the use of XML for very large collections currently is not a good idea because searching and identifying information, especially if it contains repeating elements or complex interactions between elements, requires us to read every document that makes up the database.

When to Use a DTD

There is no requirement to use a DTD in any situation—you can write XML documents without a DTD (and you'll see lots of examples of that throughout this book). That's not to say that you can completely ignore a DTD; they provide some extra levels of error checking not otherwise available.

We looked at the basic mechanics of an XML document in the previous chapter, and we also examined "well-formedness," the basic level of checking capability that can be applied to any XML document.

The DTD provides an extra level of security and validity for a document. With a DTD, we can compare the structure of the XML document with the definition in order to determine whether it meets the requirements.

Without a DTD, the following problems may manifest themselves:

- Undisciplined structure—XML tags and data could be located anywhere with no way of verifying whether the location is valid.

- Unlimited vocabulary—The attributes or character data that the document contains could contain any information, such as alphabetic data in a field that should contain only numbers, or even character data within a XML tag pair that shouldn't have any data.

- Attribute structure—Without a DTD, an attribute could contain any information and potentially include names that would otherwise reside within the xml: namespace. Also, attribute data will be marked as character data, and therefore ID and IDREF attribute types may be difficult to match.

Of course, the use of a DTD does not automatically mean that the XML parser will support it or that the parser will either employ it or replace it with its own structure and validation routines.

Standard DTDs

It shouldn't be any surprise that with the meteoric rise of XML as a method for storing and organizing information, a number of publicly available DTDs have been produced. Of course, it is possible to declare and use more than one DTD within an XML document, and this has been used to good effect to create DTDs that define structures for different standard elements, such as dates, and also for defining standard entity declarations for different data types, including standard HTML entities and others.

Although there is no universally accepted and centralized location for finding a given DTD for a particular type of information, some standard DTDs are making the rounds already.

If you are looking for a DTD, your best approach is to talk to one of the governing bodies for the business or research sector you work in. It's highly likely that somebody has produced a DTD for modeling the information you are using. If it doesn't completely match your requirements, you can usually modify or extend it to fill your need.

If you want to look at one of the existing public DTDs, check out the DocBook DTD, which was written to allow easy production of technical documentation within a standard format. You can find more information at http://www.docbook.org.

Summary

Document Type Definitions help to define the layout and structure of an XML document. We can use a DTD both to help define the layout of an XML document and to help validate the structure of an XML document. By making comparisons between the DTD and an XML document, we can determine whether the document matches the desired structure.

DTDs themselves use a simple text-based structure to help define the XML structure. They can also be used to define other elements within the XML document, such as the element attributes and entities.

CHAPTER 4

Applying XML with Scripting Languages

- Why Use a Scripting Language?

- Scripting Language Irony

Moving on from our express introduction to XML, next you need to think about how you are going to work with that XML information. Processing XML is what the majority of this book is all about, but it's also about using the right tools for the job.

Up to now, the majority of XML processing has been demonstrated and developed using C/C++ or Java. The reasons for this are relatively obvious: C/C++ is a standard language and the obvious (and frequently only) choice for many developers.

The use of Java is also obvious. Although XML isn't a web- or even Internet-related technology, it is being seen as the obvious solution for data storage and exchange in Internet applications. In fact, Java isn't supposed to be an Internet-specific language either.

So why an alternative to these well-established, well-supported, and fast solutions to processing XML documents? The reason comes down to two very simple elements of the development process:

- Ease of use—that is, the ease with which we can process, manipulate, and work with XML documents.

- Speed of development—the speed at which we can develop the applications or reuse and retool existing application for new XML processing projects.

In this chapter, we're going to take a closer look at these issues and how we can transfer the benefits of scripting language–based development into processing XML documents.

Why Use a Scripting Language?

There are many reasons for using a scripting language, whether you are working with XML or developing the latest word processor. Scripting languages have all sorts of benefits, from the speed of code design, development, and testing to their better support of human-compatible data such as text strings.

In this section, we'll be looking at all the XML-specific and some not-so-specific benefits of using scripting languages, along with some background information on why these facilities are important for XML processing.

Text Processing

One of the most powerful features of most scripting languages (including all of those we'll be looking at in this book) is the capability to work with and process text. No matter how you look at it, when working with XML documents and information you are ultimately working with text in some form or another.

It's worth remembering that computers are ultimately designed to work with numbers, and although they are capable of working with textual information, it takes a lot more work than you might think. This is best reflected in the staple language of nearly all platforms, C and C++. Although we can manipulate strings and textual information within C/C++, it's not easy, and relatively simple tasks, such as concatenating two strings, require a reasonable amount of effort.

Perl, Python, Tcl, PHP, and many others all include the capability to create, manipulate, and access different portions of a string using relatively simple semantics. For example, in Perl we can add two strings together using a period, or split up the components of a string using `substr()` or `split()`.

In most languages, we also have access to a regular expression system. It's easier to use in some languages than in others, but they all allow you to extract, substitute, and identify different components of a string with something more flexible than fixed character sequences.

All of these become vital when working with information in an XML document. Whether you are processing the contents of an XML document and displaying or manipulating it or generating information to be written to an XML document, being able to manipulate a string quickly and easily is vital.

Data Modeling

It should be obvious from the information you've seen in the previous two chapters that processing and producing an XML document requires a certain amount of data gymnastics within the language you are using, whether you are simply processing the XML or using the XML as a storage format for an existing data type.

Whatever you are using XML for, you will probably want to hold that information within your application in some form that is more immediate and accessible than a serial data string such as the original data source. Even the XML Document Object Model (DOM)—a solution to the problem of manipulating XML documents as a whole—only solves part of the problem.

One of the major benefits of Perl, Python and many others is their flexible built-in data types and the capability to nest and structure data easily using a variety of different data types.

For example, most scripting languages support a hash or dictionary data type that allows us to access information in an array by a string or other binary identifier instead of an integer numeric value. It may sound insignificant—and indeed most programmers forget they are even using it—but it's a feature that standard C/C++ implementations don't have access to.

Even the available toolkits for supporting such a variable type don't provide the same flexibility as that offered by Perl or Python because you are ultimately still using C to work with and manipulate the variables.

Data modeling of XML and the conversion of information between internal structures and XML are topics that we'll be concentrating on in the remainder of this book.

Data Interface

XML may be touted as the next big thing in data storage, but in reality it's actually offering nothing more than a more compatible, extensible, and standardized format for holding data. In all likelihood, XML will be the format used for exchanging all types of information rather than being used as the sole solution for data storage.

For example, most companies still expect to use their SQL databases to hold tabular information, even though they may exchange individual rows and queries between applications and other companies using XML.

Access to a SQL database is not easy in C. Although it's often trivial to gain access to the required library (or access the database through Open Database Connectivity (ODBC)) and then to submit the query, it can take a long time to format and process the information once it's been extracted from the database, all for reasons already discussed in this chapter.

Java has the Java Database Connectivity extensions (JDBC), which provide easy access to many databases. The problem with JDBC and ODBC is that they rely on having access to a JDBC or ODBC component that knows how to talk to the underlying database. Even if you resolve this issue (and for most RDBMSs the problem has already been solved), you still need to process the information that you get back.

Many languages also include facilities for talking to different database systems. Perl is by far the leader here; the DBI toolkit provides a consistent interface to at least 12 different RDBMS solutions. Python, PHP, and others have similar interfaces for talking to different database systems.

Using a scripting language, we already have the data processing functionality that comes standard with the language. It's easy, for example, with a hash or dictionary to summarize information from a database automatically. We can also use the built-in data types and nested structures to model information from a number of SQL tables into a hash or array structure and then use that structure to build an XML document—or the reverse, turning an XML document back into a series of XML queries.

Memory Management

When using a scripting language, it's very easy to forget about the bane of any C/C++ programmer: memory management for the internal variables and data you are working on. It's very easy in Python, for example, to read the entire contents of an XML document into memory. The document could be 1K or 1MB in size; Python would handle the allocation of memory and also free up the memory once we'd finished using it, all without us ever worrying about what's going on behind the scenes.

Try the same in C/C++ and you have a problem. First you need to calculate how much memory you think you'll need, then you need to allocate it, start reading in the document, and then keep track of whether the amount of data is approaching the size of the block you allocated, just in case you need to extend it later. When you've finished with it, you need to free the memory; woe to you if you make a mistake and try accessing the information after you've freed it.

This may seem like a trivial process, but it isn't, but not because it's complex or particularly difficult to deal with (in most cases the interface for memory allocation hasn't changed in about 20 years). The problem is the amount of development time required to deal with the problems of managing memory. In the simple example above, things are quite straightforward, but in some applications the process of allocating, reallocating, and later freeing the memory each time can increase the size of the application considerably.

These additional steps add up to a development overhead that you could do without. From experience, I know that about 50 to 75 percent of the errors introduced into a C/C++ application will be directly related to the problem of either variable or memory management. Other programmers would rate it much higher.

With XML the problems increase, if only because we are dealing with a more flexible data storage mechanism. XML documents are essentially unlimited in size, and without a very specific DTD it's impossible to pin down the size of individual elements within an XML document. Memory management when processing an XML document is just another headache we can do without.

Development Speed

Let's take a look at the typical development cycle of a program written in C. The same rules apply to C++ and to a lesser extent Java.

1. Edit the source code.
2. Compile the code into object files.
3. Link the object files and standard library into an executable file.

4. Start the application.

5. Test its behavior.

6. Start the debugger.

7. Debug the application.

8. Stop the application.

9. Go back to step 1.

Sounds like a lot of steps, right? In reality, even for a simple program on a fast machine, you're talking about 20 seconds or more for steps 2 and 3 on a reasonable application, even when using make. Doesn't sound like much, but repeat that every 30 minutes, and during an eight-hour day you'll spend 16 minutes waiting while your application compiles.

Include the time it takes to start the application and run the debugger and you could be wasting as much as two hours each day just waiting for your application to get to where you can test its behavior.

Now let's look at a typical scripting language life cycle:

1. Start the application.

2. Test its behavior.

3. Edit program code and return to step 2.

In reality, the usual method is actually more like this:

1. Test the components.

2. Edit the program code.

3. If the unit is complete, go to step 4; otherwise, go to step 1.

4. Test the application; return to step 2.

We're still using fewer than half of the steps we used when developing a C application, and I can guarantee that you'll waste less than 30 minutes each day waiting. In my experience, it's actually difficult to waste more than about 10 minutes each day when developing with Perl.

All of this makes for a very quick development schedule, but the savings don't end there.

I can write an XML processing script in Perl, Python, or PHP to very simply dump out the XML document's contents in about 2 minutes. If you want to update to a SQL database, I can add that in about 5 minutes because all three languages have easy-to-use libraries and a very short and simple but powerful syntax. Better still, I can easily reuse what I've just written in another application within a few minutes.

Scripting languages are frequently used in Rapid Application Development (RAD) environments for this very reason. They are so quick to use and reuse that often you can cut up to 80 percent of the development time compared to a compiled language like C.

Some companies even use scripting languages to develop and investigate an application and features, intending to redevelop the same application in C/C++ once the application has matured. In many situations, the C/C++ version is never produced because it doesn't need to be.

Longevity

You have to be a very rare programmer to be one of those who actually comments and documents his work. We're all guilty of it. We're so focused on producing code that works, frequently to some kind of deadline, that we often forget to comment and document what we are doing so that other people (and often ourselves) can read the code and understand why and what we did to achieve our goal.

C/C++ is notoriously difficult; I've been programming for over 20 years, more than 12 of them in C, and even I have trouble following what I was doing, let alone somebody else, when reading C code, even if the code is only a month (sometimes just a day!) old.

Java is better, although it still suffers from the same problems as C/C++. Tracing what really happens when a function is called can be complex.

Scripting languages don't have an edge when it comes to comments and documentation (although most make the latter significantly easier), but often they do have the advantage of being easier to read. Most experienced programmers will be able to look at a Perl, Python, or other script and work out what's going on.

If you're really experienced and know the language well, you'll also start picking holes in the code, identifying areas that could be improved or optimized. If you have access to the keyboard, within a few seconds you'll be making those changes yourself.

In general, scripting languages are easier to read, with or without comments, and that makes the code much easier to use and update and manage later.

Scripting languages also have the separate advantage of being easy to extend and expand in a structured form without losing sight of what we're doing. Adding a new module or extension to an existing project is often a trivial task, and separating elements into more usable components is much more natural in Perl or Python than in C or Java.

Furthermore, converting the functions and classes that you create into a new module or extension that can then be used within another application is also easier than with C or Java. In fact, with Python there aren't even any special steps involved—you just import the module you wrote the first time and start calling the functions and classes you want to use.

All of this helps the longevity of the software you are writing. Not only will the code be easy to maintain (and therefore less likely to require replacing, rather than updating later), but it's also easy to update and if necessary reuse the code that you have already written. Reinventing the wheel is never an easy task.

There's also one final but less significant effect of the longevity angle. Update your OS to a new version and you may have to rebuild your application to ensure it works. Even updating a few libraries can require a rebuild to ensure compatibility with your new environment. With a scripting language, the chances are you won't need to change anything, even if you upgrade the interpreter. I'm still using Perl scripts I wrote five years ago without any changes. They still run, and they still do what I ask them to do. They may even do it more efficiently, but the bottom line is that I haven't edited them (or in some cases even looked at them) in all that time.

In contrast, I'm currently recompiling an application that I wrote for a client just two months ago because it now fails under the new version of Linux.

Compatibility

Unfortunately, compatibility is not an issue that crosses many people's minds. As XML becomes more standard and is used in more and more applications, it's likely to become a major issue.

Develop an application in C/C++ and you'll need to recompile it for each platform you expect it to be used on. Move from one major platform to another and you'll need to retool and develop parts of your application. Although the core C/C++ language is the same, the libraries and user interface facilities are not.

Java goes some way to reduce the effects with its "write once, run everywhere" approach. Certainly normal bugbears like the OS interface and user interface issues are resolved, but there are other problems. For a start, the truth is that Java is actually supported on fewer platforms than Perl, Python, or Rebol. Java also suffers from minor problems on different platforms and with different versions; try running a Java 1.2 spec applet on a machine that only has 1.1 and you are in trouble.

Most scripting languages—excepting the usual operating system specific foibles—are compatible out of the box on all the platforms on which the interpreter executes. For example, take a Python XML processor from a Unix machine and you can execute it without any problems on a Mac or Windows machine without modification.

Perl, Python, and others don't completely solve the problem either. There is unfortunately no universally supported user interface system. The Tk system is supported on Unix, Windows, and MacOS for example, but only Python and Tcl support development under all three. The Mac version of Perl does not work with Tk.

These compatibility issues are important because they help you to establish a wider user base without little additional effort. You don't even have to move off of Unix or Windows to appreciate how much of an issue this can be. Different versions of Linux and even commercial Unix flavors such as Solaris can break code. Linux and Solaris as execution platforms are incompatible—even though they are essentially Unix—and making a Solaris-derived application work under Linux will require more than a simple recompile.

Tools such as autoconf, automake, and the configuration scripts offered by GNU will alleviate the problems, but they don't completely solve them, either.

Moving to a whole new platform—such as Unix to Windows—is even worse. With the best planning and program structure in the world, redevelopment of an application for a new platform using C/C++ will require about 25 percent of the code to be retooled. In many situations that figure may be as high as 75 percent.

Combined with the cost of training or employing staff to cover that and the additional equipment costs required to develop and test the application, you've just doubled your development costs for supporting an additional platform. All for using a "standard" language like C.

It's at this point that you realize that the speed advantage of C/C++ in its compiled form really offers little to the developer and development-cost side of the equation.

Looking at this purely from an XML perspective, whether you use C/C++ or a scripting language should be a no-brainer decision. XML is a standard format designed to offer interoperability between platforms and applications. You may save money by using XML as your data storage format, but using C/C++ or Java for the development process may well wipe out your advantage.

Cost

Cost affects the process in two ways: cost of product and cost of development. First and foremost, most scripting languages are either completely free in their own right or free as part of a component of something else. For example, Perl, Python, Tcl, PHP, Ruby, and Rebol are all freely downloadable from the Internet (see Appendix B, "Resource Guide," for details). AppleScript as such isn't free, but it does come free with the platforms that it's compatible with: MacOS and MacOS X.

The other element is a combination of the time taken to learn the language and the time saved by using a scripting language over a traditional language such as C/C++ or Java. We've already looked at how the development speed of a scripting language is overall significantly faster than that of a compiled language.

The learning cost is low because in most instances it doesn't cost you anything more than time to learn how to write programs in a particular language. C/C++ is a great language, but learning C/C++ can be costly in terms of your time and money. To learn how to program properly in C/C++, your best approach is a formal training course or a book.

Although there are freely available compilers for C/C++ out there, they don't come with programming guides. Indeed, for C, the best programming guide in the world (*The C Programming Language*, Kernighan and Ritchie) is 23 years old and still makes it into the best sellers list each year.

Even if you find a good online guide to programming in C, it'll probably take you much longer to learn than Perl or Python, with many more pitfalls and traps. When it comes to C++, things get even more complicated because C++ is largely fragmented in terms of libraries and support across the different platforms.

Java is a slightly odd case—it's given away free by Sun, and without question the best programming guides and documentation of the language are also written and made freely available by Sun. However, you still must invest a significant amount of time to learn the language itself.

On the other hand, download a copy of Perl and you can be up and running within about 30 minutes, with the language performing some relatively complicated procedures. You don't have to worry about documentation, either, because Perl comes with some of the most extensive documentation available.

Python isn't any different; the documentation on Python is written byGuido van Rossum and the rest of the Python development team. All the others follow in a similar vein.

As if that wasn't enough, thousands of websites provide free guides, tips, hints, and all sorts of additional information on the languages, from basic training courses to advanced topics.

The Scripting Language Irony

As you go through this book, you will find that there is a strange irony to the information I've presented up to now. None of the descriptions or information given above is actually incorrect, but there is a very small issue that I've neglected to mention.

In nearly all cases, when we process an XML document within a scripting language, we are ultimately using an interface to an underlying C/C++ extension. For most basic processing needs, the library and interface we are using is Expat, an XML processor written in C by James Clark.

Perl, Python, PHP, and Tcl provide access to Expat, and most of them use Expat as the basis for all the other processing models (DOM, SAX, and others) when working with an XML document.

This is not entirely a bad thing, and it is certainly not a reason to dump scripting languages and go back to C/C++ or Java. The library is being used only to process the document; once we have the information, we still need reasonable ways of manipulating and working with the data we've extracted.

The use of extensions also has other benefits. It's definitely easier to access and work with data in a SQL database through Perl or Python than it is through C or C++, for example. Whether you are writing clients or servers, networking also tends to be easier with a scripting language than it is with C.

The other benefit of using a C/C++ extension is speed. Although Perl and Python are some of the fastest and most optimized scripting languages, they still execute code slightly slower than C or C++ (and in some circumstances Java) because the information is still being interpreted, rather than being in the raw native machine code.

Using an extension library such as Expat increases the processing time for large documents by a factor of 2 or more over an entirely interpreted solution. On the other side of the equation, scripting languages are generally faster at working with complex data structures—particularly strings—because that's what they have been optimized to work with.

Therefore, a combination of fast processing (through an extension) and fast manipulation (through the scripting languages on code) actually makes processing XML with a scripting language better than using C/C++ or Java.

Summary

Scripting languages offer a number of advantages over both Java and C/C++ applications. These include, but aren't limited to, the flexibility of the languages and their data types and their capability to work with text and textual data in a natural way.

The main two reasons for using scripting languages however, boil down to the two key reasons:

- Ease of use
- Speed of development

Perl, Python, and most other languages offer well-established, well-supported, and fast solutions for processing XML documents. Using Perl, Python, or one of the other scripting languages, we can write an XML processing application within a few lines. Moreover, we can add to the application later with ease, and we can reuse any components we developed in order to extend the functionality or solve a problem even quicker than writing the system from scratch.

CHAPTER 5

Data Exchange and XML

- Parsing XML

- Unicode

- Remote Data Exchange

It should be obvious by now that XML is all about storing information. At the simplest level, it's about modeling data in a simple and relatively efficient manner, while also making it easy to read and understand the contents without the need for special software to read the information.

At the most complex, it provides a method for exchanging information between computers and other devices without worrying about whether the destination is big- or little-endian, what character set it supports, and what type of line-termination sequence the platform uses.

In truth, XML is not a replacement for normal data storage techniques like a proper database, and it is certainly nowhere near the complexity of a full SQL-enabled RDBMS. It's also not designed to replace HTML, which is still the markup language of choice for web pages and other hyperlinked documents.

That's not to say that XML will not have its place in data storage. Many platforms and solutions are now using XML for storing preferences—Mac OS X is a case in point (see Chapter 23, "XML and AppleScript/MacOS X"). Most of the configuration of the operating system and its main components is handled in Mac OS X through the use of XML.

XML's real power is in data exchange. The capability to share information in such a portable way makes it an ideal alternative for so many different solutions. You can expect to see XML as the solution for everything from exchanging contacts between your PDA and desktop to communication between your household appliances.

In this chapter, we're going to look at the basic mechanics behind the three main components of working with XML. First we'll look at the techniques for parsing and understanding XML within any language, including the different types of parsers and existing APIs for processing XML documents.

We'll then take a brief look at Unicode, the system used to represent characters within an XML document. Unicode is a complicated subject, but we'll touch on the basics of the system and how it fits into the XML makeup.

Finally, we'll look at two of the systems that use XML for exchanging information: XML-RPC and SOAP. Both systems employ XML as a way of sending a request to a remote procedure and having the response sent back. You can use XML-RPC and SOAP to execute procedures on a remote machine—XML is used to hold the request, any arguments, and any return values.

All the information in this chapter is intended as background for the remainder of the chapters in this book. We'll be looking at different parser solutions using the different parser types, Unicode support in the different languages, and also XML-RPC and SOAP.

Parsing XML

Parsing XML by hand is full of traps and pitfalls. Although it's relatively easy for a person to read, dissecting the XML into its component parts within an application is quite difficult.

However, you don't have to worry about writing your own. There are loads of different solutions for parsing XML; all have their advantages, ranging from speed and accessibility to the interface. A parser falls into one of two categories only when it comes to accessing the XML document it has parsed.

In this section, we'll look at the two different parser types and some examples of the parser solutions available to parse and provide an interface to an XML document.

Parser Types

All XML processing tools have a basic parser mechanism. It reads the XML and identifies the tags, their attributes, and all the other components of the XML file before passing it to a separate component. The other component then does the work of modeling the information and providing an interface that allows you to access the information and, if possible, edit it.

There are many different XML parsers available for all the different languages. A quick check reveals four different systems under Python and no fewer than sixteen under Perl. Each falls into one of two groups: It provides either an event-driven interface or a tree-based interface.

Event-Driven Interface

If you split an XML document into its component parts, it's easy to identify and parse the document. As the document is processed, each particular element is treated as an *event*.

In order for the event-driven parser to work, you need to associate a particular function with the type of element that is identified in the XML document. Then, when the document is being parsed, the function is called each time a recognized element is identified. For example, each time a start tag is seen, the start tag handler function is called; each time character data is identified, the character data function is called.

This all gives rise to the term event-driven. Each time you see an element (a tag, a processing instruction, and so forth), you raise an event, which is turn processed by an event handler.

For example, given the following XML file:

```
<contact refid="23456">
<firstname>Martin</firstname>
<surname>Brown</surname>
</contact>
```

an event-based parser would raise the following events:

Found start element `contact` with attribute `refid` and value `23456`.

Found start element `firstname`.

Found character data `Martin`.

Found end element `firstname`.

Found start element `surname`.

Found character data `Brown`.

Found end element `surname`.

Found end element `/contact`.

The exact implementation will vary according to the parser you are using, but the basic sequence is there. Note, by the way, that the events only highlight that a tag has been identified; the tag name is supplied to the event handler function. This is necessary because you don't know what the tag names are in advance. It's up to the script parsing the document to make a decision about what to do with a specific tag.

Because event-driven systems read an XML document in sequence without ever holding the entire document in memory, they are generally very fast and efficient. The downside is that because you read the XML document from start to finish, you have no way of moving within the document to another position. If that's a requirement of the parsing process, you'll need to record information manually as you go along.

Event-driven parsers are ideal for processing XML data for use elsewhere, such as during conversion to HTML or when reading the data from the file for insertion into a database. Other things event-driven parsers are good at include the following:

- Document searches—You can process an XML document until you find the tag or character data you are looking for.

- Conversion—HTML is just one example, but anything that requires the raw XML to be translated into another format is generally best done with event-driven parsers because you translate the information on-the-fly to its new format.

- Minor modifications—It may seem pointless, but you can read and regenerate XML with a parser. During the parsing process, you can change minor words, character data contents, and even reform XML. Event-driven parsers are great for cleaning and reformatting an XML document.

- Simple validation—The whole document isn't in memory, so you can't do all the checks necessary to validate the information completely, but simple problems such as spelling errors and general well-formedness can be checked.

- Building an internal structure—You can use event-driven parsers to build up a complex internal representation of the XML document. In a moment, we'll look at the tree-based parser; event-driven parsers are often used to build the tree structure used by tree-based interfaces.

The downside to the event-driven parser is that because you don't hold the entire document in memory, you cannot make decisions or modifications that require you to jump around the document. For example, if you wanted to reorder or change the structure of the document, you would have to record the structure first, which kind of defeats the object of reading the XML document sequentially.

This lack also means that you can't verify the document beyond the simple checks already discussed, and you can't cross reference the contents of the document between XML elements.

Despite all of these apparent problems, event-driven parsing is the most powerful and also one of the easiest to use. It doesn't take a lot of work to get an event-driven parser working and, unless you need that cross-referencing facility, the speed and memory benefits of the event-driven parser far exceed its limitations.

Tree-Based

Logically, the individual elements of an XML document are similar to components of a tree. For example, the following extends our earlier contact example:

```
<contact refid="23456">
<name>
<firstname>Martin</firstname>
<surname>Brown</surname>
</name>
<address>
<house>29</house>
<street>The Road</street>
<town>The Town</town>
<city>The City</city>
<postcode>AB12 34CD</postcode>
<country>UK</country>
</address>
</contact>
```

The main trunk is contact; name is a branch that contains the first name and surname; address is a second branch that in turn contains further branches (or leaves, since they are at the end of a branch) containing the individual details of the address.

A tree-based parser does exactly what we've described above: It parses an XML document and turns the document into an internal representation that closely matches a tree.

If the event-driven method is sequential access, then the tree-based method is random access. Once the document has been parsed, you can access any element of the tree, change the order (grafting one branch from one position to another), and of course change the contents. For example, to change the country in our example, you just need to change the value of the country branch of the address branch of the document tree.

Scripting languages are ideally suited to the tree-based method because most support the complex structures and easy referencing and linking of information required to build a convenient tree model.

Parser Solutions

There are literally hundreds of different XML parsers and parser libraries available. In fact, long before XML actually became an official standard, there were a number of different parsers and other tools available.

It wasn't very long before it became clear that some sort of standard needed to be produced. Two standard toolkits, both originally written in Java, now exist: Simple API for XML (SAX) and Document Object Model (DOM). SAX is the standard for event-driven parsers, and DOM is the standard for tree-based parsers.

We'll also look at one other parser, Expat, which is not a standard, but is one of the most widely used parsers available for working with XML within the confines of a scripting language.

Expat

Expat was written by James Clark and is an event-driven parser for XML documents. Expat was originally written in C. As a result, it has the flexibility of being incorporated into a number of different scripting languages through their normal extension mechanisms, unlike many Java-based tools. This means that Expat is probably the most popular and widely supported of all the XML parsers that you'll be seeing in this book.

Expat lends itself well to most parsing tasks. Some solutions even use Expat as the basis of a full SAX or DOM interface.

Simple API for XML (SAX)

The Simple API for XML (SAX) really just defines the frontend interface for processing XML documents. In the background is an XML parser that is responsible for reading the information and identifying the different elements.

SAX itself is an event-driven XML parser; to actually process a document, you must first create the methods or functions that will handle the different elements of the document. The SAX standard is based on the original Java implementation, called `org.xml.sax`, and defines the names of the methods and the process behind supplying the parser with information.

In practice there is very little difference between using SAX and using any other event-driven XML parser, including Expat. However, the big difference between a SAX-compliant parser and the other solutions is that the methods you create and the XML elements that can be handled remain the same. In fact, aside from the language-specific semantics of the language you are using, migrating from SAX under one language to SAX under another should be completely painless.

Document Object Model (DOM)

The Document Object Model (DOM) is a W3C standard for a tree-based API for processing and working with XML documents. As with SAX, it was originally a Java/JavaScript solution, but it has since grown into a general specification for working with documents in tree form.

Unlike SAX, with DOM you do not define functions to be called when particular elements are found. Instead, the DOM specification requires that methods be created to enable you to modify and create branches within an XML tree structure. Most DOM implementations define a basic set of functions to do this for you.

For example, within both the Perl and Python implementations, a nested data structure is generated, with each branch having a combination of methods and properties that make up the interface for manipulating and working with the XML document in its tree form.

The minor irony with most DOM implementations is that they will often use SAX or a similar event-driven parser to build the tree before it's exposed and made available to the programmer.

Within the DOM specification, the individual elements of an XML document are identified as *nodes*; you use these nodes to access the data from the document. The different node types that should be supported by your DOM implementation are shown in Table 5.1.

TABLE 5.1: DOM Node Types

Name	Children
Document	Element (the root XML element), ProcessingInstruction, Comment, DocumentType
DocumentFragment	Element, ProcessingInstruction, Comment, Text, CDATASection, EntityReference
DocumentType	None
EntityReference	Element, ProcessingInstruction, Comment, Text, CDATASection, EntityReference
Element	Element, Text, Comment, ProcessingInstruction, CDATASection, EntityReference
Attr	Text, EntityReference
ProcessingInstruction	None
Comment	None
Text	None
CDATASection	None
Entity	Element, ProcessingInstruction, Comment, Text, CDATASection, EntityReference
Notation	None

The exact implementation and interface used are entirely dependent on the extension or module you are using. Many will class themselves as DOM-compliant if they adhere to the names and general structure as outlined in the DOM specification. Others will just identify themselves as DOM-compatible or DOM-like if they are close.

Unicode

XML documents are written using a standard text editor. If you have ever tried to exchange basic text files (rather than word processor documents) between two different platforms, you're already aware of a whole host of problems with the process.

First and foremost is line termination: Macs use the carriage return character, Unix uses linefeed, and Windows uses linefeed and carriage return. Next comes the character. Most of you will be familiar with the ASCII standard, but this defines only the first 127 characters, of which the first 31 are actually control characters such as tab and newline.

If you try to exchange more complex characters such as the British pound sign or even curly quotes, things get more complicated. After the first 127 characters, it's entirely up to the platform, and in some cases the font that you are using, which characters actually appear on the screen.

Other applications, such as Microsoft Word and to a lesser extent the Web, have gotten around these problems by inventing their own systems for marking up special characters in a portable. You can share a Word document between a Mac and a PC without too many problems (providing you have the same fonts). With HTML, some of the more common characters have their own entity sequence.

The problem is that the different systems are all incompatible with each other unless the application you are using knows how the document has been saved. For example, Word knows how to deal with HTML characters, but it can't deal with AppleWorks characters.

The problem gets even more complex when you realize that most platforms have no way to represent anything but the standard characters—the 127 ASCII characters—and most still expect characters in a document to be referred to by a single byte (8-bits), which limits you to a maximum of 256 different characters in a set. These standard characters are known as the Roman or Latin character set.

If you want to write a document that's made up of Chinese, Japanese, or Indian characters, those 256 combinations won't be enough; for basic Mandarin Chinese, for example, there are over 4000 different characters.

The Unicode Solution

The Unicode standard gets around this problem in two ways. First, it allows characters to be encoded using a multibyte format. The standard currently allows for 2-byte characters, which supports 65,536 different characters. The specification also has provision for 4-byte characters, supporting a mind-boggling 4.3 billion different characters.

This support of a multibyte format also solves the problem of mixing different characters in a document. If we can address 65,535 different characters, we should be able to choose a suitable font or character set on the local operating system to display any character properly. This assumes that everyone knows, for example, that character 947 in the Unicode table is the Greek small letter gamma character.

In essence, Unicode is really nothing more than an updated version of ASCII. The only difference is that the character table has been increased from 127 characters to 65,535, and the added slots have been filled with the different characters from a variety of different languages, both Western and Eastern, in order to support documents containing a wide variety of languages.

There are also two encoding formats, UTF-8 and UTF-16. UTF-8 is essentially the same as the ASCII format you use for most documents on Western computers. It also allows non-ASCII characters to be specified by using combinations of single-byte characters to refer to an extended character.

The UTF-16 format is the 2-byte encoding used when you need to work with a larger character set, such as that used in China, Japan, or Korea.

Unicode and XML

Unicode is not actually driven by XML; the specification was around some time before XML was finally ratified. Within the XML specification, the use of Unicode extends to everything within the document. Both character data and elements can be written in non-Roman/Latin languages. The only requirement is that the XML declaration at the top of the document must be written in Roman, and it should then also define the character set and encoding used in the document.

If this sounds very complicated, don't worry. The standard Unicode character set is Latin-1 (or ISO-8859-1), and this mirrors the ASCII table for the first 127 characters. It also mirrors the extended ASCII table (up to character 255) commonly in use on all platforms. This means that if you are using an American, British, or Western European computer, you should be able to read and write XML documents without ever worrying about Unicode.

However, if you are working with documents written in another language or using another character set, you will need to be able to understand Unicode characters within your scripts and applications. Most languages support Unicode in a transparent form; for example, Perl deals with Unicode strings natively.

The only other consideration to take into account is the specification of what you are looking for within the document. For example, looking for the word like is easy, because it's written in English and Latin-1. However, when looking for the same word in German, you must look for the Unicode string mögen.

Remote Data Exchange

No matter where you look today, you will find evidence of computers and devices exchanging information. Most of the time you never think about the process, and other times it's at the forefront of your mind. For example, requesting a document from a website is obviously an example of exchanging information with a remote machine: The client sends a request and receives the document that was requested.

Now think about logging on to computer within a network: When you type in your name and password, the information has to be checked with the network server. That exchange of data is relatively straightforward, but it still requires network communication, and in turn it requires a protocol, a method of data representation, and of course the exchange of information.

Hopefully, you've spotted a few key words there. If these systems are exchanging information and data, then they are ideal targets for the use of XML.

In practice, the web browsing example is not an ideal target for transition to XML. Currently, the act of submitting a request and getting a response is largely one-sided; a typical request will be about 100 bytes, but the response could be 2KB, 16KB, or 16MB. However, there's an argument that says this division of client and server will change as websites and services become more interactive.

The second example, that of logging in to a network, is a more likely target. You are sending very small, discrete pieces of information and getting similarly tiny responses. You're also running a remote procedure—the one that checks the user database and makes sure that what you supplied matches what's in the database. All it needs to do is return a true or false result and you've achieved your aim.

Remote procedure calls are nothing new—the Sun platform has had a system called *Remote Procedure Call* (RPC) for many years, and many of the services, from data monitoring to printer spooling, have been supported using the RPC system.

The problem with RPC is that although the system was technically cross platform, there was a substantial amount of work involved in translating the data types used in your code into an architecture-neutral format for transmission over the network. The external data representation (XDR) system was very complex, and for anything but the simplest data types you had to perform the process manually.

Using XML you get round all of this—you can convert the request, which is made up of the function or procedure you want to call and any arguments that you supply, into an XML structure. You transfer that XML document over the network to a request handler, which decodes the contents and converts it into a local function or procedure call. The whole process then works in reverse, with the return value being converted into an XML document that is then sent back.

Two such systems that provide this functionality have been produced: Simple Object Access Protocol (SOAP) and XML-RPC. Both work in a similar manner, although they are incompatible with each other.

In both cases you create a server, which can be a CGI script hosted on a web server, a dedicated network service provider (in much the same way as a web or FTP server), or in some cases an e-mail processor that reads the XML request as an attachment to an e-mail. The client then talks to the server, either through a normal HTTP request (in the case of the CGI or network service) or by bundling the request in another packet such as an e-mail, and then waits for a response.

Both SOAP and XML-RPC are easy to use, and it's likely that you will see an explosion of Internet services being supported using these systems in the future. You can already find public services for converting quantities and temperatures and doing basic calculation.

Because you're calling remote procedures, the complexity of the request and the data you transfer is not limited by the constraints of HTTP, and you don't have to worry about creating our own protocol to handle the communication side. In most instances, using the two systems is as simple as specifying the name of the function you want to call and the arguments that you want to supply. Under Perl and Python, these calls can even be as transparent as calling a local function.

The other major benefit of both solutions is that they are both platform *and* language independent. You can call a SOAP object from a Perl client when the object itself is hosted on a Python server. This interoperability means that you no longer have to worry about which language you use to provide each end of the solution.

The capability to provide mixed-language applications in this way has helped to drive Microsoft and its .NET initiative, which is in itself an attempt to blur the distinction between developing an application in one language and doing so in many.

SOAP

Simple Object Access Protocol (SOAP) was developed by a consortium of companies that included Userland, IBM, Lotus, and Microsoft. As the name suggests, SOAP was actually designed as a method for accessing and working with objects remotely.

Although you can use SOAP for the simple execution of a remote procedure, its real power is in its capability to manipulate objects, either created on the server side or created and then returned to the client. For example, you can have a server process that provides access to a customer's account through an object interface. The object and server can be written in Python, but you can create and manipulate the object from Perl or Java, or indeed Python.

SOAP's power, and its major advantage over XML-RPC, is that you can work with objects over the network. You are not dealing with a simple request and response; once the object has been created, it remains until you delete it. You can therefore use SOAP when state information is useful, such as logging in to a server or making purchases from a catalog.

Because SOAP deals with live objects, it's frequently seen as the killer application where other attempts have failed. Those with long memories will remember systems such as Common Object Request Broker Architecture (CORBA) and Microsoft's Distributed Common Object Model (DCOM). It's unlikely that we'll see these systems disappear anytime soon, but don't expect them to last forever, either.

XML-RPC

Curiously, XML-RPC actually grew out of the some of the initial work to develop the SOAP standard. However, unlike SOAP, XML-RPC was designed entirely from the procedural point of view, and rather than dealing with objects, it deals with simple requests and responses.

In fact, XML-RPC is best described simply as a method for supporting Remote Procedure Calls. Unfortunately, this makes it useful only in situations where you would normally run a function. You cannot use it for working with objects, and you can't use it for applications that require state information.

Limits

Although I've portrayed both SOAP and XML-RPC as solutions to the problem of data exchange between computers and languages, this shouldn't lead you to believe that these solutions will replace everything that requires network communication.

It's unlikely that protocols such as HTTP and FTP will be replaced. Neither SOAP nor XML-RPC is a great alternative for transferring large files, and XML itself is not ideal for storing binary data at all.

Instead, SOAP and XML-RPC will replace the sort of solutions that up until now have required either clever use of HTTP or FTP or a whole new protocol of their own.

Summary

The key power that XML provides us with is the ability to exchange information between machines and especially applications. Because the format of an XML document is standard ASCII text, we can easily process that information with a parser into a format that can be used within an application.

Two main types of parser exist: the event-driven parser, which processes each XML tag in sequence within a document and in turn triggers an event designed to handle that tag; and the tree-based parser, which converts the XML document into a complex tree structure. Examples of such parsers include the SAX system (event-driven) and DOM (tree-based).

To aid in the exchange of information, the Unicode system allows us to deal with a variety of different characters so that we can deal with foreign and even multilanguage documents without resorting to the use of special markup systems or other tricks.

For exchanging information between two different machines over a network, we can use two systems, SOAP and XML-RPC, that make use of the XML standard to exchange information between different computers and even different languages transparently.

PART II

XML and Perl

CHAPTER 6

XML Solutions in Perl

- Using *XML::Parser*

- XML Processing Using SAX

- XML Processing Using DOM

- Other XML Modules

Perl evolved over many years and is now probably the best-known and most widely used of the scripting languages available. Nearly everyone has heard of Perl, even if they don't know what it does.

Perl itself was based on some very strong string and text processing tools, including awk, sed, and sort, to form a very capable text-processing language. In addition to all of the normal text-processing facilities you would expect, there is an inline regular expression engine and a strong but flexible object modeling system that is perfect for building the complex information trees that XML documents can develop into.

In this chapter we're going to look at the core modules that make up the Perl XML processing toolset. We'll also examine some of the lesser-known tools and modules that, while not vital to your processing, may be useful.

Using *XML::Parser*

XML::Parser is built on top of the Expat XML processing library written by James Clark. XML::Parser is a vital component of XML processing under Perl because most other modules within Perl use the facilities offered by XML::Parser to support their own processing.

XML::Parser itself is an event-based parser, and because it uses the Expat libraries also offers simple validation of your XML documents for well-formedness, although it doesn't validate your documents against a DTD.

The interface to the parser is simple: You create a new XML::Parser object, a suite of functions that are called when the parser determines a start, end, or data portion in your XML document. For example, the code in Listing 6.1 builds a very simple XML parser to output the start and end tags in a document.

Listing 6.1   **A Simple XML Parser**

```
use XML::Parser;

my $parse = new XML::Parser();

$parse->setHandlers(Start => \&handler_start,
                    End => \&handler_end,);

$parse->parsefile($file);

sub handler_start
{
    my ($parser, $element, %attr) = @_;
    print "Start: $element\n";
}
```

```
sub handler_end
{
    my ($parser, $element) = @_;
    print "End: $element\n";
}
```

Running this on a simple XML document results in the following output:

```
$ perl exxmlp.pl simple.xml
Start: simple
Start: paragraph
End: paragraph
End: simple
```

As you can see, the example outputs a list of the start and end tags. Because we "register" the functions that we want to call when different elements are seen, the functions can be called anything we like.

Note as well that the functions are supplied with the name of the tag that was found and the list of attributes for a given tag. We can use this information within the parsing process to be more explicit about the information we pass on.

Using *XML::Parser* to Convert to HTML

Being an event-based parser, the XML::Parser module is ideal in situations where you need to extract or convert those elements into another form. A good example is in converting an XML document into an HTML format for display on-screen.

We're going to be looking at a CGI script that I wrote on behalf of a client who wanted to convert an XML document into HTML for displaying on its website. The documents themselves were actually a mixture of XML and some HTML components, and you can see a sample in Listing 6.2.

Listing 6.2   **A Sample Review Document**

```
<video>
<main>
<title>Alien Resurrection</title>
<para>Sigourney Weaver, Winona Ryder</para>
<title>Witness the Resurrection</title>
<para>The review...</para>
</main>
<panel>
<paneltitle>Purchase</paneltitle>
<para><b>Amazon UK</b></para>
<para><azuk id="B00004CXQ6">Buy Alien Resurrection on Video</azuk></para>
<para><azuk id="B00004S8GR">Buy Alien Resurrection on DVD</azuk></para>
```

```
<para><azuk id="B00004CXR8">Buy the Alien Box Set on Video</azuk></para>
<para><azuk id="B00004S8K7">Buy the Alien Box Set on DVD</azuk></para>
<para><b>Amazon US</b></para>
<para><azus id="787987987">Buy Alien Resurrection on Video</azus></para>
<para><azus id="787987987">Buy Alien Resurrection on DVD</azus></para>
<para><azus id="787987987">Buy the Alien Box Set on Video</azus></para>
<para><azus id="787987987">Buy the Alien Box Set on DVD</azus></para>
<paneltitle>Related Items</paneltitle>
<para><realref id="video/alien.xml">Alien</realref></para>
<para><realref id="video/aliens.xml">Aliens</realref></para>
<para><realref id="video/alien3.xml">Alien3</realref></para>
<para><realref id="video/alien_boxset.xml">Alien Legacy Box
Set</realref></para>
<para>
<b>Also see</b>: <keyref id="Sci-Fi">Sci-Fi</keyref>,
<keyref id="Horror">Horror</keyref>,
<keyref id="Action">Action</keyref>
</para>
</panel>
</video>
```

The document contains both traditional XML data and some HTML-specific link information; for example, there are links to other review files and details on the ID and host information required to link to the items available for purchase on Amazon.

The script in Listing 6.3 translates the XML document into HTML. The script works by using a single hash that contains the HTML tags and attributes to output when a specific XML tag is seen. The handler_start() function identifies the tag and then builds the equivalent HTML tag.

Listing 6.3   **An XML-to-HTML Converter**

```perl
#!/usr/local/bin/perl -w
use strict;
use XML::Parser;

# The %elements hash holds the configuration information
# for the XML tags found by the parser. The tags output
# are HTML. Because an individual XML tag can generate
# multiple HTML tags, the base key links to a list
# Within the list are individual hash references for
# each HTML tag, and the hash contains the tag and attribute
# information.
# For example, a <title> XML tag produces:
# <tr><td bgcolor="#000094" align="left">
# <font face="Arial, Helvetica" color="#ffffff"><b>
```

```perl
my %elements =
  (
    'video' => [ ],
    'title' => [{ tag => 'tr' },
              { tag => 'td',
                attr => {
                    'bgcolor' => '#000094',
                    'align' => 'left',
                },
              },
              { tag => 'font',
                attr => {
                    'face' => 'Arial,Helvetica',
                    'color' => '#ffffff',
                },
              },
              { tag => 'b' },
              ],
    'paneltitle' => [{ tag => 'tr' },
              { tag => 'td',
                attr => {
                    'bgcolor' => '#000094',
                    'align' => 'left',
                },
              },
              { tag => 'font',
                attr => {
                    'face' => 'Arial,Helvetica',
                    'color' => '#ffffff',
                },
              },
              { tag => 'b' },
              ],
    'stars' => [{ tag => 'tr' },
              { tag => 'td' },
              ],
    'description' => [{ tag => 'tr' },
              { tag => 'td',
                attr => {
                    'bgcolor' => '#000094',
                    'align' => 'left',
                },
              },
              { tag => 'font',
                attr => {
                    'face' => 'Arial,Helvetica',
                    'color' => '#ffffff',
                },
              },
              { tag => 'b' },
              ],
```

```perl
            'review' => [{ tag => 'tr' },
                         { tag => 'td' },
                         { tag => 'p' },
                         ],
            'b' => [ { tag => 'b' }
                   ],
            'br' => [ { tag => 'br' }
                    ],
            'main' => [ { tag => 'td',
                          attr => {
                              'width' => '66%',
                              'valign' => 'top',
                          },
                        },
                        { tag => 'table',
                          attr => {
                              'border' => '0',
                              'cellspacing' => '0',
                              'cellpadding' => '2',
                              'width' => '100%',
                          },
                        },
                        ],
            'para' => [ { tag => 'tr' },
                        { tag => 'td' },
                        ],
            'azus' => [ { tag => 'a',
                          href =>
'http://www.amazon.com/exec/obidos/ASIN/%%ID%%/myamzntag' },
                        ],
            'azuk' => [ { tag => 'a',
                          href =>
'http://www.amazon.co.uk/exec/obidos/ASIN/%%ID%%/myamzntag' },
                        ],
            'keyref' => [ { tag => 'a',
                            href =>
                                '/cgi/reviews.cgi?t=k&d=%%ID%%' },
                          ],
            'realref' => [ { tag => 'a',
                             href =>
                                 '/cgi/reviews.cgi?t=r&d=%%ID%%' },
                           ],
            'img' => [ { tag => 'img',
                         src => '/img/reviews/',
                         end => 0,},
                       ],
            'panel' => [{ tag => 'td',
                          attr => {
                              'width' => '34%',
                              'valign' => 'top',
                          },
```

```
            },
            { tag => 'table',
              attr => {
                    'width' => '100%',
                    'border' => '0',
                    'cellspacing' => '0',
                    'cellpadding' => '2',
              },
            },
            ],
    );

# Because this is a CGI script we output the Content-type
# http header before starting the parsing process.

print "Content-type: text/html\n\n";
show_review('alien_r.xml');

# The main show_review() function formats a review on screen
sub show_review
{
    my ($title) = @_;

# The review normally forms part of another page, so we
# embed the whole thing into a table
    print <<EOF;
<table border=0 cellspacing=0 cellpadding=0 width=100%>
<tr>
EOF

# Create the parser and pass it the XML document that
# we want to process

    my $parse = new XML::Parser();

    $parse->setHandlers(Start => \&handler_start,
                        End => \&handler_end,
                        Char => \&handler_char,);


    $parse->parsefile($title);
# Make sure we close off the table
    print "</tr></table>";

}

# the handler_start() function handles opening
# tags. Because of the %elements structure
# we need to extract the structure and parse
# %elements to work out the HTML we need to produce
```

```perl
sub handler_start
{
    my ($parser, $element, %attr) = @_;

# First, we check that the XML tag we've just
# recognized has a matching element in the %elements
# hash.
    if (defined($elements{$element}))
    {
# Work through each of the HTML tags in the embedded
# array
        foreach my $tag (@{$elements{$element}})
        {
            print '<',$tag->{'tag'}
                if (exists($tag->{'tag'}));
# If there are ID attributes in the XML and a matching
# HREF element in %elements
# If we find them then we replace %%ID%% in the HREF
# from %elements with the ID supplied by the XML tag
            if (exists($attr{'id'}) &&
                exists($tag->{'href'}))
            {
                my $url = $tag->{'href'};
                $url =~ s/%%ID%%/$attr{'id'}/;
                print " href=\"$url\"";
                delete($attr{'id'});
            }
# Check if there are any HTML attributes we need to
# generate. If so, work through the attributes to build
# an array of the attribute text, and then join them
# together with spaces to make the actual attribute text
            if (exists($tag->{'tag'}) &&
                exists($tag->{'attr'}))
            {
                my @myattrlist = ();
                foreach my $attr (keys %{$tag->{'attr'}})
                {
                    push(@myattrlist,
                        sprintf('%s="%s"',
                            $attr,
                            $tag->{'attr'}->{$attr}));
                }
                print " ", join(' ',@myattrlist);
            }
# Finally, add any other attributes defined in the XML to
# to the HTML output.
            foreach my $attr (keys %attr)
            {
                print " $attr=\"$attr{$attr}\"";
            }
```

```
# Print the closing tag
        print '>' if (exists($tag->{'tag'}));
# Output any raw elements (which appear as normal text)
# if there are any
        print $tag->{'raw'} if (exists($tag->{raw}));
    }
  }
}

# The handler_end() has to output the HTML tags from the
# %elements hash, but in opposite order (to produce valid
# HTML) and as close tags.

sub handler_end
{
    my ($parser, $element) = @_;

    if (defined($elements{$element}))
    {
        foreach my $tag (reverse @{$elements{$element}})
        {
            if (exists($tag->{'tag'}))
            {
                print '</',$tag->{'tag'},'>'
                  unless (exists($tag->{end}));
            }
        }
    }
}

# Raw character data is just output verbatim
sub handler_char
{
    my ($parser,$data) = @_;

    print $data;
}
```

In Figure 6.1, you can see the result of running the script on the review document shown in Listing 6.3. Although this was written for a specific solution, you can modify the %elements table to suit your own needs, and it'll convert your own XML documents into HTML.

An HTML version of
an XML movie review
document

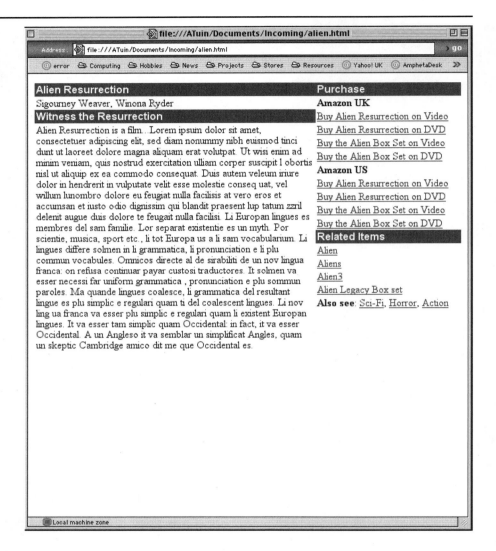

XML::Parser Traps

The Expat libraries on which XML::Parser is based have a few small traps. Because
XML::Parser is used by so many of the other modules within Perl, it's worth mentioning
these problems before we go any further:

- Errors raise exceptions: Although Expat is non-validating, it still checks the basic layout of your document to ensure that it's well formed. Unfortunately, this means that any error in the basic structure of the document raises an exception. The only way to trap this is to embed your call to the parser within `eval()`. Luckily, a further call to the parser will allow parsing to continue from the position after the last error.

- Expat supplies all data: Everything from the XML document is supplied back through one of the trigger functions you define for `XML::Parser` to use. This means that whatever function is used for handling character data must make decisions about what to do with characters beyond normal text. Expat supplies linefeed/carriage return characters, spaces, and any other characters to make the XML document more human readable.

- Data is returned in UTF-8: Although Expat isn't strictly a Unicode parser, `XML::Parser` always returns UTF-8 strings. This isn't a problem for most English-sourced documents because UTF-8 and Latin-1 character sets are the same for those first 256 characters. For other Unicode strings, especially foreign languages not supported by the Latin-1 set, you can use `Unicode::String` for this; we'll be looking at Unicode within Perl in more detail in Chapter 7, "Perl and Unicode."

- Data portions are supplied in chunks: Because Expat deals with chunks of data, you may find that data portions passed to the data handler function are incomplete. If you want to handle the data portions uniquely, you'll need to cache the information and initiate a separate handler to actually process a complete data portion. We'll be looking at some examples of this throughout the rest of this section.

Beyond these small problems, `XML::Parser` works pretty much as you would expect.

XML Processing Using SAX

Many of the parser solutions for XML in Perl support a Simple API for XML (SAX) interface to enable us to communicate between different XML processors when reading a document. SAX parsers work in the same basic fashion as `XML::Parser`; as the document is parsed and different elements within the document are discovered, a function is called to process the entity.

There are a number of different SAX parsers available, but the best is probably the `XML::Parser::PerlSAX` (PerlSAX) module. In fact, that module forms the basis of many other modules, including the `XML::Grove` module that provides a DOM-like interface for XML documents.

Unlike `XML::Parser`, which uses references to the functions that handle the entities, with PerlSAX you need to create a new class that defines the methods to use for parsing different

XML tags—suitable methods are named according to the tag you want to process. Although this sounds more complex, it does enable you to identify a number of different elements. The full SAX specification covers everything from basic document properties to specific elements.

For example, we can create a simple class to output the start and end tags from an XML document by creating a handler class like the one in Listing 6.4. We inherit from XML::Handler::Sample, which dumps the output for selected entities, and define two functions, start_element() and end_element(), which will be called when the parser identifies start and end tags in the document.

Listing 6.4   **A Simple Handler Class for SAX Parsing**

```perl
package MyHandler;

use vars qw/@ISA/;
use XML::Handler::Sample;

@ISA = qw/XML::Handler::Sample/;

sub new
{
    my $self = shift;
    my $class = ref($self) || $self;

    return bless {}, $class;
}

sub start_element
{
    my ($self, $info) = @_;

    print "Start Tag $info->{Name}\n";
}

sub end_element
{
    my ($self, $info) = @_;

    print "End Tag $info->{Name}\n";
}
```

To create the parser, we create a new instance of our handler class and then a new instance of the XML::Handler::PerlSAX class, which will do the actual processing. You can see the final parser script in Listing 6.5.

Listing 6.5   **Our *PerlSAX* Parsing Script**

```
#!/usr/local/bin/perl -w
use XML::Parser::PerlSAX;
use MyHandler;

if ($#ARGV != 0) {
    die "You must specify a file to parse";
}
$file = shift @ARGV;

$my_handler = MyHandler->new();

XML::Parser::PerlSAX->new->parse(Source =>
                       { SystemId => $file },
                        Handler => $my_handler);
```

If we run this script on a simple XML document, we get the following output:

```
$ perl perlsax-test.pl simple.xml
start_document
Start Tag simple
characters
Start Tag paragraph
characters
End Tag paragraph
characters
End Tag simple
end_document
```

SAX parsing is great for processing a document in sequence and can be useful for serializing a document into another format. We saw this with the XML::Parser solution earlier in this chapter, which converted our document to HTML. We'll see it again in Chapter 9, "Converting XML Documents Using Perl," when we'll use SAX for converting a document to and from an RDBMS.

XML Processing Using DOM

The Document Object Model (DOM) for parsing an XML document is essentially just a method of turning your XML document into an object tree. Because all XML documents are essentially built like a tree, accessing an individual element by its branch seems a logical step.

There are lots of different DOM parsers supported under Perl, including XML::DOM, XML::Simple, and XML::Twig. Of these, my personal favorite is XML::Grove, written by Ken MacLeod. XML::Grove is not strictly a DOM parser—it doesn't adhere to W3C's DOM API, but it does provide a very similar interface. For a genuine DOM parser, use the XML::DOM module.

The XML::Grove module provides an easy way to work with an entire XML document by loading an XML document into memory and then converting it into a tree of objects that can be accessed just like any other set of nested references. To demonstrate the tree format offered by XML::Grove, let's look at a sample XML document. We'll use a contact entry within an address book, a structure most people are familiar with. If we think about a single record within a contact database, then the base of the XML document will be the contact. We'll use a fictional version of me for our example, seen in Listing 6.6.

Listing 6.6   A Contact Record Written in XML

```
<contact>
  <name>Martin Brown</name>
  <address>
    <description>Main Address</description>
    <addressline>The House, The Street, The Town</addressline>
  </address>
  <address>
    <description>Holiday Chalet</description>
    <addressline>The Chalet, The Hillside, The Forest</addressline>
  </address>
</contact>
```

The grove.pl example script that comes with the XML::Grove module kit can convert this document into a textual tree. This version has been modified slightly so that it also outputs the array reference numbers of each branch. We'll need this information in a later example. The script itself is shown in Listing 6.7.

Listing 6.7   The *grove.pl XML::Grove* Sampler

```
#
# Copyright (C) 1998 Ken MacLeod
# See the file COPYING for distribution terms.
#
# $Id: grove.pl,v 1.4 1999/05/06 23:13:02 kmacleod Exp $
#

use XML::Parser::PerlSAX;
use XML::Grove;
use XML::Grove::Builder;
```

```perl
my $builder = XML::Grove::Builder->new;
my $parser = XML::Parser::PerlSAX->new(Handler => $builder);

my $doc;
foreach $doc (@ARGV) {
    my $grove = $parser->parse (Source => { SystemId => $doc });

    dump_grove ($grove);
}


sub dump_grove {
    my $grove = shift;
    my @context = ();

    _dump_contents ($grove->{Contents}, \@context);
}

sub _dump_contents {
    my $contents = shift;
    my $context = shift;

    for(my $i=0;$i<@$contents;$i++) {
        $item = $contents->[$i];
        if (ref ($item) =~ /::Element/) {
            push @$context, $item->{Name};
            my @attributes = %{$item->{Attributes}};
            print STDERR "@$context \\\\ (@attributes)\n";
            _dump_contents ($item->{Contents}, $context);
            print STDERR "@$context //\n";
            pop @$context;
        } elsif (ref ($item) =~ /::PI/) {
            my $target = $item->{Target};
            my $data = $item->{Data};
            print STDERR "@$context ?? $target($data)\n";
        } elsif (ref ($item) =~ /::Characters/) {
            my $data = $item->{Data};
            $data =~ s/([\x80-\xff])/sprintf "#x%X;", ord $1/eg;
            $data =~ s/([\t\n])/sprintf "#%d;", ord $1/eg;
            print STDERR "@$context || $data\n";
        } elsif (!ref ($item)) {
            print STDERR "@$context !! SCALAR: $item\n";
        } else {
            print STDERR "@$context !! OTHER: $item\n";
        }
    }
}
```

The script works by recursively calling the _dump_contents() function on each branch of the tree. That function works through every element within a particular branch. Through each iteration, we prefix the output with the location of the current branch. The result of running the script on our sample XML document can be seen in Listing 6.8.

Listing 6.8   A Textual XML Tree of Our Contact Document

```
0: contact \\ ()
0: contact || #10;
0: contact ||
0: contact 2: name \\ ()
0: contact 2: name || Martin Brown
0: contact 2: name //
0: contact || #10;
0: contact ||
0: contact 5: address \\ ()
0: contact 5: address || #10;
0: contact 5: address ||
0: contact 5: address 2: description \\ ()
0: contact 5: address 2: description || Main Address
0: contact 5: address 2: description //
0: contact 5: address || #10;
0: contact 5: address ||
0: contact 5: address 5: addressline \\ ()
0: contact 5: address 5: addressline || The House, The Street, The Town
0: contact 5: address 5: addressline //
0: contact 5: address || #10;
0: contact 5: address ||
0: contact 5: address //
0: contact || #10;
0: contact ||
0: contact 8: address \\ ()
0: contact 8: address || #10;
0: contact 8: address ||
0: contact 8: address 2: description \\ ()
0: contact 8: address 2: description || Holiday Chalet
0: contact 8: address 2: description //
0: contact 8: address || #10;
0: contact 8: address ||
0: contact 8: address 5: addressline \\ ()
0: contact 8: address 5: addressline || The Chalet, The Hillside, The Forest
0: contact 8: address 5: addressline //
0: contact 8: address || #10;
0: contact 8: address ||
0: contact 8: address //
0: contact || #10;
0: contact //
```

Because we can access individual tags within a DOM-parsed XML document, DOM parsers are particularly useful when we want to update the contents of an XML document. Using SAX to process the document sequentially rather than using the tree model offered by a DOM parser is far from ideal, because it means reading in the content, identifying which bits you want to change as they are triggered, and then regenerating the result.

For example, if we wanted to update my Holiday Chalet address using SAX, we'd have to read in the content, identify first that we were in the `address` branch, and then that were we in the correct `addressline` branch. Then we could replace the information in the output.

Using DOM, we parse the entire document, update the address within the branch we want to update, and then dump the XML document back out again. Updating the branch is just a case of referencing the branch's location within the DOM structure.

`XML::Grove` converts your XML document into a series of nested arrays and hashes. The arrays contain a list of elements within the current branch, and the hashes are used to supply the element type, name, and data (if applicable) for that branch. Because there are different element types, the numbers don't always match what you would normally expect.

In Listing 6.8, you'll notice the array reference numbers required to access each branch. To access the contents of a branch, you access the `Contents` element from the enclosed hash and get the data contained in a branch using the `Data` key. Finally, the `Name` key returns the tag name for a given branch, and the `Attributes` key returns the attributes for the tag.

For example, to get the data from the `name` XML tag, we'd need to access the `Data` key from branch 0 (contact), 2 (name), 0 (the data element

```
print 'Name: ',$grove->{Contents}[0]->{Contents}[2]->{Contents}->[0]->{Data},"\n";
```

Because it's an object structure, we can update my address using the following:

```
$grove->{Contents}[0]->{Contents}[8]->{Contents}->[5]->{Contents}->[0]->{Data} =
'The Shed, The Mountain, The Lakes';
```

We can output the final version of the document using the following:

```
use XML::Grove::AsCanonXML;
print $grove->as_canon_xml();
```

Generating XML

The easiest way to generate XML information within Perl is to use `print`, probably in combination with a `here` document to make the process easier.

Using `print` is an untidy solution, especially since it almost guarantees that you'll introduce errors and inconsistencies into the code that you generate, and debugging the output can be an absolute nightmare.

A much better solution is to output your XML tags by name in a structure format, just as if your were creating the XML tree yourself. We can do this using one of the modules that support DOM parsing, since DOM allows us to build the XML document branch by branch and leaf by leaf.

However, it would be much better to use a tool such as the `XML::Generator` module. Instead of building the XML tags and objects and structure ourselves, `XML::Generator` enables you to use functions to define the tag. Arguments to the functions create additional branches, leaves, and attributes.

For example, we might populate a contact file using the following:

```
use XML::Generator;
my $gen = XML::Generator->new('escape' => 'always',
                              'pretty' => 2);
print $gen->contact($gen->name('Martin C Brown'),
                    $gen->email('mc@mcwords.com'));
```

The functions don't have to be predefined: `XML::Generator` creates the functions for us on-the-fly. The previous code generates the following XML document:

```
<contact>
  <name>Martin C Brown</name>
  <email>mc@mcwords.com</email>
</contact>
```

The module generates a raw XML document. To generate a DOM tree, which we could then separately parse and process using the techniques we saw earlier in this chapter, we can use the `XML::Generator::DOM` module:

```
use XML::Generator::DOM;
my $gen = XML::Generator::DOM->new();

my $domdoc = $gen->xml($gen->contact(
                          $gen->name('Martin C Brown'),
                          $gen->email('mc@mcwords.com')));

print $domdoc->toString();
```

Other XML Modules

There is a host of other XML modules that are available on CPAN that are too numerous
to mention in any detail here, although we may go back to some of these in later chapters.
XML and Perl are developing all the time, and if you want more information about any of
the modules in Perl, check Appendix B, "Resource Guide," or the CPAN XML page at
`http://www.perl.com/CPAN-local/modules/by-module/XML/`.

DBIx::XML_RDB

Although there are lots of bits of Perl and XML that I really like, the DBIx::XML_RDB module is
one of my favorites. It simplifies one of the more complicated and often convoluted processes
when converting RDBMS information into an XML document.

The DBIx::XML_RDB module makes an SQL query submitted to any database accessible
through the DBI module into an XML document.

Using the module is straightforward—you create a new DBIx::XML_RDB object, supplying
the datasource, driver, user ID, password, and database name:

```
my $sqlxml = DBIx::XML_RDB->new($datasource, $driver,
                                $userid, $password, $dbname)
        || die "Failed to make new xmlout";
```

Submit an SQL statement:

```
$sqlxml->DoSql("SELECT * FROM $table ORDER BY 1");
```

Then print out the result:

```
print $sqlxml->GetData;
```

It's actually easier to demonstrate the effects using the sql2xml.pl and xml2sql.pl tools,
which are installed when you install the module. These convert an SQL statement into an
XML document and vice versa. For example, to dump a table containing ISBN numbers to
an XML file:

```
$ sql2xml.pl -sn books -driver mysql -uid mc -table isbn
-output hello.xml
```

You can see the resulting XML file in Listing 6.9.

Listing 6.9   **The XML Result of an SQL Query Using *DBIx::XML_RDB***

```
<?xml version="1.0"?>
<DBI driver="bookwatch">
        <RESULTSET statement="SELECT * FROM isbn ORDER BY 1">
                <ROW>
                        <isbn>0002570254</isbn>
```

```
                            <title>Sony</title>
                            <author>John Nathan</author>
                            <followref>0</followref>
                </ROW>
                <ROW>

                            <isbn>0002570807</isbn>
                            <title>'Tis</title>
                            <author>Frank McCourt</author>
                            <followref>0</followref>
                </ROW>
    ...
    </RESULTSET>
    </DBI>
```

The xml2sql.pl script obviously does the reverse, converting an XML document following the same format as that in Listing 6.9 back into a series of SQL statements.

XML::RSS

If you use the Web for reading your news and to keep up-to-date with Perl, Python, Apache, and all the other cool stuff that exists out there on the Internet, then you'll know how frustrating it is to have go to 10 or 20 different sites to pick your news.

As a solution to this problem, many sites now export their news and other regularly updated pieces through an RSS (Rich Site Summary) file. RSS files are really just XML documents conforming to a DTD that define the different news stories and how to link the original items. For example, Listing 6.10 shows a truncated version of the RSS file from CNN.com on June 29, 2001.

Listing 6.10   **A Sample RSS File from CNN.com**

```
<?xml version="1.0"?>

<!DOCTYPE rss PUBLIC "-//Netscape Communications//DTD RSS 0.91//EN"
"http://my.netscape.com/publish/formats/rss-0.91.dtd">

<rss version="0.91">

<channel>

<title>News from CNN.com</title>
<link>http://cnn.com/index.html</link>
<description>The world's news leader</description>
<language>en-us</language>
```

```
<image>
 <title>CNN.com</title>
 <url>http://cnn.com/images/1999/07/cnn.com.logo.gif</url>
 <link>http://CNN.com/index.html</link>
 <width>144</width>
 <height>34</height>
 <description>The world's news leader</description>
 </image>

<item>
 <title>Retired grocery clerk claims $141 million California lottery
 ➥ jackpot - June 29, 2001</title>
 <link>http://cnn.com/2001/US/06/29/lottery.winner.ap/index.html</link>
 </item>

<item>
 <title>Kmart pulling handgun ammunition from shelves in wake of
 ➥ protests - June 29, 2001</title>
 <link>http://cnn.com/2001/US/06/29/kmart.guns.ap/index.html</link>
 </item>
 ...
```

How does RSS make reading news easier?

Once you've downloaded the RSS files from a number of different sites, you can then combine the information in each RSS file in order to aggregate the content into a single web page. Each item in the RSS file will be a small outline of the full article. If you see something you like, you can go to the full page; otherwise, you can skip to the next story without going to multiple websites.

The XML::RSS module enables you to create and update your RSS files, usually from whatever source you use in your news service. Some people use the Slashcode (as used by slashdot.org and many other sites), and in other instances it'll be from the your news database. We can also use RSS to convert an RSS file into HTML.

To get an idea of how RSS works, you might want to try the Meerkat service offered on the O'Reilly Network (http://www.oreillynet.com/meerkat/). If you want to play around with RSS in Perl and reap the benefits of reading all your news from a single web page, then check out AmphetaDesk. Ironically, AmphetaDesk doesn't use XML::RSS, but it does download, parse, and convert RSS documents into HTML. You can see a sample of AmphetaDesk in action in Figure 6.2. The package is available for Mac, Windows, and Unix. See Appendix B for a list of RSS resources.

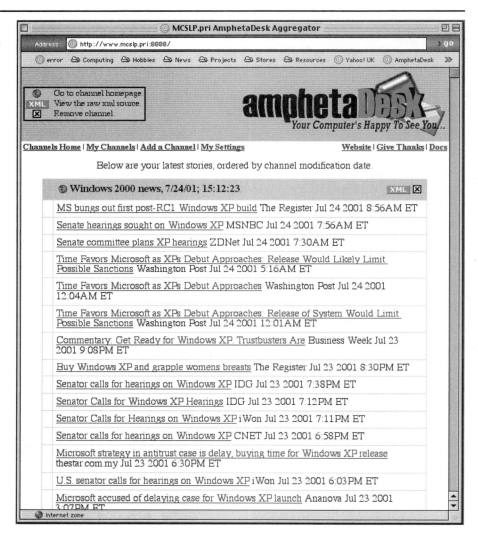

Summary

As with most problems in Perl, you can generally find a suitable solution in the CPAN
archives. XML processing is no exception—there is a whole host of different modules out
there for solving your XML processing and parsing problems using Perl.

For basic XML processing in Perl we have the `XML::Parser` module. It provides a sequential method for calling a specific function when the different elements are identified within an XML document. `XML::Parser` is an ideal solution for converting the entire content of an XML document into another format such as HTML. We saw a sample of this in this chapter.

For a more structured and ultimately expandable method of processing documents, we have the SAX interface in the form of the `XML::Parser::PerlSAX` module.

The `PerlSAX` parser also provides the basis for a number of other modules, including a DOM-like parser in the form of `XML::Grove`. The `XML::Grove` module isn't a true DOM parser, but it does enable us to manipulate an XML document as if it were a DOM tree. If you want a full DOM implementation, we also have the `XML::DOM` and `XML::Simple` modules.

As if that weren't enough, we also have a host of modules that parse and work with XML documents. The `DBIx::XML_RDB` module will convert XML documents to and from SQL statements. We can parse RSS documents for news feeds using the `XML::RSS` module.

CHAPTER 7

Perl and Unicode

- Core Support

- Specifying Unicode Characters and Sequences

- Working with Unicode Data

Perl is one of the few "old" languages that have successfully and largely transparently integrated supported for the Unicode system into the Perl language. If you wanted to, you could write your entire Perl script using ideographs and other Unicode characters for your function and variable names throughout your script—the integration is that transparent.

As we've already mentioned in Chapter 5, "Data Exchange and XML," the trick with Unicode and XML is not how to use the two together, but instead how to manipulate the Unicode when it has been extracted from an XML document in your application. In this chapter, we're going to look at the most important parts of the Perl language when working with Unicode data, including how to introduce Unicode characters into your strings and how to work with and manipulate Unicode characters once you have them in a Perl variable.

NOTE   The whole Unicode implementation within Perl is still a work in progress—at the time of this writing, Unicode support was being tidied up in the development version 5.7, with all the details of how Unicode support will work in Perl 6 still under discussion. Even with all the work, there's lots to do before all of the features and functionality within both Unicode and Perl work correctly. The best way to keep up to date is to read the Unicode documentation that comes with the latest Perl distribution, available in the `perlunicode` man page. (You might also want to look over the `unicode/Unicode3.html` document within the main Perl library directory, which contains the Unicode standard definitions used to build the internal information in Perl.)

Core Support

From Perl 5.6 it's been possible to write Perl scripts entirely in Unicode. Operators, functions, and standard variables obviously retain their U.S. English heritage, but user variables and functions can use Unicode character in their names, and we can introduce Unicode literal strings without resorting to any special techniques.

To enable full Unicode support in this fashion, you must import the `utf8` pragma. This forces Perl to accept both string literals and symbolic names that use Unicode characters. Without the `utf8` pragma in force, you can still introduce Unicode literals into your code, but you cannot use them within variable, function, and other user-definable names.

Internally, all strings are now stored in Unicode format. As a result, in addition to enabling all Perl operator functions to work with Unicode data, we can also manipulate the information character-by-character. There are no limitations in converting or combining Unicode strings into ASCII strings, because in Perl there is no such distinction.

Specifying Unicode Characters and Sequences

Perl stores all strings internally in Unicode format. That means that there is no special Unicode string datatype, and there are no complexities in mixing and matching ASCII and Unicode (which includes ASCII) characters into the same scalar value. For example, the assignment:

```
$msg = "Hello World\n";
```

is, as far as Perl is concerned, in Unicode format.

To include a Unicode character beyond the standard ASCII into your string literals, you can either do so directly, if your editor/platform supports Unicode, or through the \x{} and \N{} escape sequences in a string.

The first method, \x{}, allows you to specify the Unicode character number in hexadecimal within the braces. For example, to include the Greek lowercase Pi symbol into a string:

```
$note = "The value of \x{3a0} is 3.141592654";
```

The second format enables you to include the character by its Unicode name. This is a long name, usually specified in capitals, that describes the character according to its main character set and description. For example, the name for the letter A is LATIN CAPITAL LETTER A. To use this format, you must import the charnames pragma, which imports the necessary name/character tables.

For example, we could change the above to this:

```
use charnames ':full';
$note = "The value of \N{GREEK CAPITALLETTER  PI} ➥
    is 3.141592654";
```

Using Unicode names in this fashion is probably not the easiest way to introduce Unicode characters into your text, but it can be useful if you can remember (or work out) the description and not the corresponding number. See the charnames man page for more information on the different character classes you can import in this way.

Note that as with all other escape sequences, you actually lose the above definitions. The resulting string literal is a Unicode string, which in this case is assigned to a variable.

You can see a complete list of the Unicode character numbers and names in the file Unicode.*xxx* in the unicode directory within your Perl library directory. The *xxx* refers to the version number of the Unicode standard being used; with Perl 5.6.1, this was 3.01 (Unicode.301).

Character Numbers

The chr() and ord() functions work with Unicode values as standard. If you supply chr() with a value beyond 255, it assumes you are introducing a Unicode character and returns the value accordingly. Conversely, the ord() function translates a Unicode character back to its numerical number.

For example, this fragment introduces the ø (o with a cross) into a string:

```
$name = "Rikke J" . chr(248) . "rgensen";
```

The ord() function can be used to convert this back into a number:

```
$number = ord(substr($name, 7, 1));
```

Working with Unicode Data

The general rule to follow with Unicode in Perl is that a typical operator will now operate on characters (including multibyte Unicode ones) unless you've explicitly told it otherwise through use of the bytes pragma.

Most of the XML parsers that are supported by Perl use Expat or a derivative of a module that uses Expat. This means that all of the text you receive, both as element names and character data, will be Unicode encoded.

Care needs to be taken therefore when working with characters that are potentially non-ASCII within your XML parsing scripts. Most of these problems can be resolved fairly easily. For example, when looking for a specific character sequence, you must ensure that you are matching against the Unicode equivalent. Because Perl's support for Unicode character and mixed ASCII/Unicode strings is so transparent, this is incredibly easy.

In this section we'll look at three areas that often catch people out: case translations, regular expressions, and character- and byte-based comparisons and calculations.

Case Translations

Unless you've enabled the bytes pragma (detailed in the section "Data Size Traps," later in this chapter), Perl will automatically assume you are working with Unicode data and change the case of a string through the \U or \L character escape or the uc(), ucfirst(), and corresponding functions, according to the Unicode lookup tables.

For ASCII data, this has the expected effect. For Unicode data outside the ASCII range, it converts character or characters to their corresponding uppercase or lowercase value as defined within the language and character set in use. For example, in the following fragment, we create a variable with the lowercase PI letter, π, in it, and then use uc() to obtain the uppercase letter PI, Π.

```
$lcpi = "\x{3d6}";
$ucpi = uc("\x{3d6}");
printf("%x\n",ord($lcpi));
printf("%x\n",ord($ucpi));
```

The result should be the hexadecimal values of the characters within the Unicode table, 3D6 for the lowercase Pi letter and 3A0 for the uppercase:

```
$ perl piunicode.pl
3d6
3a0
```

Regular Expressions

By default, regular expressions work identically to regular expressions using ASCII characters. The regular expression system is completely Unicode character aware and will therefore match or substitute characters (not bytes) within source strings. There are only two areas that need special attention: the matching of non-specific Unicode characters and the use of Unicode character classes for matching.

Matching Unicode Characters

The regular expression semantics of Perl have been modified to accommodate the Unicode system so that most of the existing constructs will work with Unicode characters. For example, the period character (.) matches any Unicode (and therefore ASCII) character, as you would expect.

In addition, some new escape sequences have been introduced and existing sequences modified to handle specific Unicode and traditional instances:

- The \c sequence now matches any one-byte character, including Unicode characters that can be defined within a single byte (that is, 8-bit or ASCII only).

- The \N{NAME} sequence explicitly matches the Unicode character defined by NAME.

- The \X sequence matches any Unicode sequence that would normally make up a single character, including multibyte sequences.

This means that now you can match against a Unicode character sequence using \X and a non-Unicode character sequence using \c.

Unicode/POSIX Classes

In addition to matching against specific characters, Perl also provides methods for matching against specific character classes. Perl supports the traditional character classes, such as \d for matching any digit and \s for matching against white space, and new sequences for matching against specific properties throughout the Unicode tables.

These are defined through a series of property definitions that can be matched using \p{PROP} and its negation, \P{PROP}, to select characters according to their Unicode properties. For example, the equivalent of \d across all Unicode characters (including foreign representations of numbers outside of the Latin format) is \p{IsN}.

The full list of these properties is too large to be included here, but the basic properties (case, character, digit and non-character) are listed in Table 7.1.

TABLE 7.1: Standard Unicode Character-Class Properties

Property	Meaning
IsC	Other
IsCc	Other, control
IsCf	Other, format
IsCn	Other, not assigned
IsCo	Other, private use
IsCs	Other, surrogate
IsL	Letters (Perl defined)
IsLl	Letter, lowercase
IsLm	Letter, modifier
IsLo	Letter, other
IsLt	Letter, title case
IsLu	Letter, uppercase
IsM	Marks (Perl defined)
IsMc	Mark, combining
IsMe	Mark, enclosing
IsMn	Mark, non-spacing
IsN	Numbers (Perl defined)
IsNd	Number, decimal digit
IsNl	Number, letter
IsNo	Number, other
IsP	Punctuation (Perl defined)
IsPc	Punctuation, connector
IsPd	Punctuation, dash
IsPe	Punctuation, close
IsPf	Punctuation, final quote
IsPi	Punctuation, initial quote
IsPo	Punctuation, other

Continued on next page

TABLE 7.1 CONTINUED: Standard Unicode Character-Class Properties

Property	Meaning
IsPs	Punctuation, open
IsS	Symbols (Perl defined)
IsSc	Symbol, currency
IsSk	Symbol, modifier
IsSm	Symbol, math
IsSo	Symbol, other
IsZ	Separators (Perl defined)
IsZl	Separator, line
IsZp	Separator, paragraph
IsZs	Separator, space

In addition to these broad classes, Perl also supports more familiar composite classes through both a series of POSIX classes and Unicode properties. The POSIX classes can be used within Perl using [:*class*:]. For example, to match digits you would use [:digit:]. To match against the Unicode equivalent you would use \p{isDigit}.

The full list of POSIX character classes is given in Table 7.2. The corresponding composite Unicode properties and their POSIX equivalents are listed in Table 7.3.

TABLE 7.2: POSIX Character Classes

Class	Meaning
alnum	Any alphanumeric (equivalent to [[:alpha:][:digit:]])
alpha	Any letter (uppercase or lowercase)
ascii	Any 7-bit ASCII character (that is, those with a value between 0 and 127)
cntrl	Any control character—basically those ASCII characters with a decimal value of less than 32, including newlines, carriage returns, and tabs
digit	Any character representing a digit (0–9)
graph	Any alphanumeric or punctuation character
lower	Any lowercase letter
print	Any printable character (equivalent to [[:alnum:][:punct:][:space:]])
punct	Any punctuation character
space	Any white-space character (space, tab, newline, carriage return, and form feed)
upper	Any uppercase letter
word	Any identifier character—basically alnum and the underscore
xdigit	Any hexadecimal digit (upper- or lowercase, 0–9 plus a–f)

TABLE 7.3: Perl's Composite Unicode Properties

Property	Consists of	POSIX Equivalent
IsASCII	[\x00-\x7f]	ascii
IsAlnum	[\p{IsLl}\p{IsLu}\p{IsLt}\p{IsLo}\p{IsNd}]	alnum
IsAlpha	[\p{IsLl}\p{IsLu}\p{IsLt}\p{IsLo}]	alpha
IsCntrl	\p{IsC}	cntrl
IsDigit	\p{Nd}	digit
IsGraph	[^\pC\p{IsSpace}]	graph
IsLower	\p{IsLl}	lower
IsPrint	\P{IsC}	print
IsPunct	\p{IsP}	punct
IsSpace	[\t\n\f\r\p{IsZ}]	space
IsUpper	[\p{IsLu}\p{IsLt}]	upper
IsWord	[_\p{IsLl}\p{IsLu}\p{IsLt}\p{IsLo}\p{IsNd}]	word
IsXDigit	[0-9a-fA-F]	xdigit

For more information on the other properties supported by Perl (which are subject to constant change as new languages, character sets, and Perl composites are produced), check the Unicode documentation that comes with Perl.

Data Size Traps

One of the problems with the Unicode system is that it is possible to encode single characters into multiple bytes. This can make certain operations break if you are relying on storing information within fixed size blocks that rely on a byte, rather than a character figure.

By default, Perl now reports sizes in terms of characters where appropriate. That means that strings and other textual scalars (hash keys, for example), which are internally stored in Unicode anyway, report their length in characters when tested through the length() function.

To get the byte length of a string, as opposed to the character length, you need to use the bytes pragma. The following example imports the bytes pragma without changing the behavior of the length() function, instead to get the length in bytes we use the version in the bytes pragma:

```
use bytes (); # Loads without enforcing byte interpretation

$charlen = length($string);
$bytelen = bytes::length($string);
```

As a general rule, outside a `bytes` pragma declaration, Perl assumes you are working with characters. A more explicit list of the treatment of bytes/characters outside of a `bytes` pragma declaration is as follows:

- Strings and regular expression patterns may contain characters with values larger than 8 bits.

- Identifiers may contain alphanumeric characters, including ideographs (`utf8` pragma required).

- Regular expressions match characters, not bytes.

- Character classes in regular expressions match characters, not bytes.

- Named Unicode properties and block ranges can be used as character classes.

- The regular expression metasymbol `\X` matches any Unicode sequence.

- The `tr///` operator transliterates characters, not bytes.

- Case translation operators (`\U`, `\L` and `uc()`, `ucfirst()`, and so on) use the Unicode translation tables.

- Functions and operators that deal with position and length within a string use character, rather than byte positions. Exclusions are `pack()`, `unpack()`, and `vec()`, which traditionally work on byte- or bit-based data anyway.

- The "c" and "C" `pack()`/`unpack()` formats do not change—they still extract byte-based information. If you want to use characters use the "U" format.

- The `chr()` and `ord()` functions work on multibyte characters.

- The `reverse()` function in a scalar context reverses by character, rather than by byte.

Unicode Character Conversions

There is no convenient built-in mechanism for converting a Unicode character string into a format suitable for printing on any device. The easiest way to translate something for display on a simple (non-Unicode) capable device is probably to use `tr///` to convert anything beyond the ASCII range to a question mark:

```
tr/\0-\x{10ffff}/\0-\xff?/;
```

This is not a tidy solution, and it certainly won't help if you want to convert Unicode to Mac-Roman for example. For those situations where you have a specific destination (or source) character set in mind, the solution is to use the `Unicode::Map8` module from Gisle Aas.

In addition to supporting most of the base tables supported internally by the Unicode standard, the module also provides access to a number of other standard character tables, including Macintosh, PC code pages (starting CP, as used in DOS/Windows 3.11), and even some tables specific to certain fonts, including the Adobe Zapf Dingbat font that covers most of the ideographs available on Mac and Windows machines.

Summary

Perl supports Unicode natively, allowing you to create Unicode-compatible strings using the same methods and techniques that you would use with a normal Perl string. In addition to supporting Unicode in strings, you can also create variables, functions, and other token names using Unicode characters.

When working with Unicode strings, there is syntactically no difference to using ASCII strings, and there are methods and escape sequences for including specific Unicode characters within a given string. Other elements of Perl also support Unicode characters, and the regular expression engine even includes the capability to search and match Unicode strings for different character types, irrespective of their originating language.

The only area that needs care is when working with Unicode information. Standard Perl automatically returns all counts and other calculations within a Perl string using characters, rather than bytes. In most situations this shouldn't cause a problem, but you should be aware of the effects and how to use the `bytes` pragma to obtain size information in strict 8-bit quantities.

CHAPTER 8

Generating and Parsing XML Documents with Perl

- Using the SAX Parser

- Using a DOM Parser

P rocessing XML in Perl is mostly just a case of using the right module and calling the appropriate methods and functions to extract, convert, or manipulate the XML document. When using Perl, you have the advantage of flexible data structures that we can use to model XML documents internally and we can easily work through those structures. Furthermore you can easily integrate searching and access to that information using the existing regular expression methods.

In this chapter, we're going to take a closer look at the two main XML processing systems available in Perl: SAX and DOM. We'll also look at some of the techniques you can use to search, access, and manipulate the information.

Using the SAX Parser

The SAX system is merely an API for dealing and working with XML documents through an event-driven interface. There are many different event-driven parsers, but the benefit of SAX is that it's a standard; this makes it easy to integrate and build upon when developing parsers and parsing systems. For example, although not directly supported, it's possible to use a SAX-based C++ parser within Perl, and for a C++ application to use a Perl-based SAX parser. In fact, theoretically you could integrate a Perl SAX parser with a Python front end.

Inside SAX Processing

The XML::Parser::PerlSAX module is a PerlSAX-compliant system for XML processing. As you saw in Chapter 6, "XML Solutions in Perl," the PerlSAX system works through a class-based system in which you produce a handler that deals with the different components of an XML document as it is processed. As with most other event-based systems, the class is used to define the methods that will be called when the different XML element components are identified.

The method itself supports only three methods: new() for creating a new instance of a PerlSAX parser, parse() for actually parsing a document, and a debugging location() method to return information about the current status of the parser.

You can specify the handler for the different portions of the document using either a single handler class to handle elements, DTD and other fragments, or you can define a series of individual handlers for the different types.

The parser() and new() methods accept the options shown in Table 8.1. These should be specified in the form of key/value pairs (a hash).

TABLE 8.1: Options When Creating a New SAX Parser

Option	Description
Handler	The object instance of the handler class that will be used for processing XML events. The class will be used to handle all Document, DTD, Error, and Entity events. You can handle these with individual handlers using the options defined below.
DocumentHandler	The object instance used to handle Document events.
DTDHandler	The object instance used to handle DTD events.
ErrorHandler	The object instance used to handle Error events.
EntityResolver	The object instance used to resolve Entity references.
Locale	The locale to use when providing a localized error message.
Source	A hash containing the input source information.
UseAttributeOrder	If set to true, additional AttributeOrder and Defaulted properties are passed when an XML element is parsed. AttributeOrder will contain a list of the attributes defined in each element in the order in which they are found. Defaulted will hold the index number of the first default attribute in AttributeOrder, or the length of the array in AttributeOrder if there is no default.

The Source element is a special case. Rather than accepting a direct value, it accepts a reference to a hash that defines the source and encoding for the XML document that you want to parse. The keys and descriptions for this hash are shown in Table 8.2.

TABLE 8.2: Hash Keys for the *Source* Parameter When Parsing XML

Key	Description
PublicId	The public identifier of the document.
SystemId	The system identifier of the document.
String	A string holding the XML source text.
ByteStream	An open file handle from which the XML source will be read. Reads in bytes (handling multibyte source).
CharacterStream	An open file handle from which the XML source will be read. Reads characters, suitable for ASCII or ISO8859-1 only.
Encoding	The character encoding used in the XML stream being read.

The handler class or classes that you use to process the XML document must define certain methods in order to process the different elements of the document. As noted in Table 8.1, you can either use a single handler class, in which case you specify the class instance using the Handler option, or use individual handlers for each of the items.

In each case, as each item within the XML document is identified, the corresponding method is called and passed a single argument that will be a reference to a hash that in turn contains the information about the XML elements identified. For example, when a start tag is found, the `start_element()` method from your handler class is called and supplied with a hash reference containing the key's `Name`, which is the name of the element, and `Attributes`, a reference to another hash of attributes and their values.

Brief details on all the methods, which sub-handler they should be defined within if you are using separate handlers, and the hash keys supplied in the hash reference are shown in Table 8.3.

TABLE 8.3: Handler Methods and Supplied Information

Method	Handler	Hash Keys	Description
start_document	Document		Called when the start of an XML document is identified.
end_document	Document		Called when the end of a document is identified.
start_element	Document		Called when a start tag/element is identified.
		Name	The element name.
		Attributes	A hash of the element attributes and values.
end_element	Document		Called when an end tag/element is identified.
		Name	The element name.
characters	Document		Called when character data is found.
		Data	The character data.
processing_instruction	Document		Called when a processing instruction is identified.
		Target	The PI target.
		Data	The PI data.
comment	Document		Called when a comment is identified.
		Data	The comment text.
start_cdata	Document		Called when the start of a character data block is identified.
end_cdata	Document		Called when the end of a character data block is identified.

Continued on next page

TABLE 8.3 CONTINUED: Handler Methods and Supplied Information

Method	Handler	Hash Keys	Description
entity_reference	Document		Called when an internal entity reference is identified. If defined, internal entities are not expanded and supplied to the characters() method. If defined then internal entities are not expanded or supplied to the characters() method.
		Name	The entity reference name.
		Value	The entity reference value.
notation_decl	DTD		Called when a notation declaration is identified.
		Name	The notation name.
		PublicId	The public identifier.
		SystemId	The system identifier.
		Base	The base for resolving a relative URI.
unparsed_entity_decl	DTD		Called when an unparsed entity declaration is identified.
		Name	The unparsed entity name.
		PublicId	The public identifier.
		SystemId	The system identifier.
		Base	The base for resolving a relative URI.
entity_decl	DTD		Called when an entity declaration is identified.
		Name	The entity name.
		PublicId	The public identifier.
		SystemId	The system identifier.
		Value	The entity value.
		Notation	The notation declared for the entity.
element_decl	DTD		Called when an element declaration is identified.
		Name	The element name.
		Model	The content model.
attlist_decl	DTD		Called for each attribute in an ATTLIST declaration.
		ElementName	The element name.
		AttributeName	The attribute name.
		Type	The attribute type.
		Fixed	True if this is a fixed attribute.

Continued on next page

TABLE 8.3 CONTINUED: Handler Methods and Supplied Information

Method	Handler	Hash Keys	Description
doctype_decl	DTD		Called when a DOCTYPE declaration is identified.
		Name	The document type name.
		PublicId	The document's public identifier.
		SystemId	The document's system identifier.
		Internal	The internal subset.
xml_decl	DTD		Called when an XML declaration is identified.
		Version	The version
		Encding	The encoding string.
	Standalone	true, false, or undefined.	
resolve_entity	Entity		Called when an external entity is identified.
		Name	The unparsed entity name.
		PublicId	The public identifier.
		SystemId	The system identifier.
		Base	The base for resolving a relative URI.

For a very simple example of how to use PerlSAX and process a basic document, see Chapter 6, "XML Solutions in Perl."

Searching Documents with SAX

Because you work through an XML document sequentially with SAX (and indeed any event-based parser), you can use it for searching for information within your documents. There are two main pieces of information that you might want to search for from within an XML document:

- The name of the tag which contains a particular piece of information.
- All the information from a particular tag.

The SAX approach parses the entire document, so you know that you can search all the information you have available to pick out the items you need.

We'll look at two sample solutions. We'll be using the same basic wrapper script for both examples but two different handler classes to actually parse the content.

In fact, it's the handlers that are important here. Because you use a class to hold the information, you can use the properties of an instance of that class to help manage, store, and marshal information for output or display. For example, you can cache information about the tags, tag location, or character data that you have identified. Then you reach another target, for example when you've extracted the character data from a particular tag segment, you can write the information to a file or print the resulting text.

For our example, you're going to be working with a very simple XML document that holds contact method information for a single person. You can see the XML document in Listing 8.1.

Listing 8.1   **A Simple Contact Document**

```
<contact>
<name>Martin Brown</name>
<contactmethods>
<method><type>Phone</type>
<number>01234 567890</number></method>
<method><type>Mobile</type>
<number>09876 543210</number></method>
<method><type>Fax</type>
<number>01928 374650</number></method>
<method><type>Email</type>
<number>mc@mcslp.com</number></method>
<method><type>Email</type>
<number>mc@mcwords.com</number></method>
<method><type>Email</type>
<number>mc@whoever.com</number></method>
<method><type>Email</type>
<number>mcmcslp@aol.com</number></method>
</contactmethods>
</contact>
```

To demonstrate the two systems, you'll create two different handlers, both using the same basic wrapper script, which can be found in Listing 8.2.

Listing 8.2   **The PerlSAX Wrapper Script**

```
use XML::Parser::PerlSAX;
use TagText;

$file = shift
  or die "You must supply the name of the file to process";
```

```
$text = shift
  or die "You must supply the text you are searching for";

$my_handler = TagText->new($text);

XML::Parser::PerlSAX->new->parse(
        Source => { SystemId => $file},
        Handler => $my_handler);
```

Finding the Tag from a String

Finding a particular string within the character data and then returning the location in which you found the information relies on first recording your position within the XML document. Then you need to search the character and report the matching text.

Therefore, in your handler class, the methods that identify the start and end tags will populate a property in the class with their location, using a simple stack and push() and pop(). The method for character data does the search using a regular expression and then reports the location stored in your class instance. You can see the handler class in Listing 8.3.

Listing 8.3   **The *TagText* Search Handler Class**

```
package TagText;

sub new
{
    my $self = shift;
    my $class = ref($self) || $self;
    my $text = shift;
    my @locs;

    return bless {text => $text,
                  loc => \@locs,
                  }, $class;
                        ^

}

sub start_element
{
    my ($self, $info) = @_;
    push @{$self->{loc}},$info->{Name};
}

sub end_element
{
    my ($self, $info) = @_;
    pop @{$self->{loc}};
```

```
}

sub characters
{
    my ($self, $info) = @_;

    if ($info->{Data} =~ m/$self->{text}/i)
    {
        print("Matched $info->{Data} in ",
            join(' -> ', @{$self->{loc}}),"\n");
    }
}

1;
```

You can now use your wrapper script to search for a given piece of text:

```
$ perl tagfromtext.pl contact.xml mcslp
Matched mcslp in contact -> contactmethods -> method -> number
Matched mcslp in contact -> contactmethods -> method -> number
```

You can see from the result that you've found the text mcslp within the number element within your list of contact methods.

In this simple example, you searched only for a simple piece of text, but because you're using regular expressions to do the actual match process, you could have supplied a regular expression. You could, for example, extract only e-mail addresses by using a suitable expression, rather than making decisions based on the method type defined in the XML:

```
$ perl tagfromtext.pl contact.xml "[a-zA-Z0-9][a-zA-Z0-9_\.\-]\@[a-zA-Z0-9\.\-]"
Matched mc@mcslp.com in contact -> contactmethods -> method -> number
Matched mc@mcwords.com in contact -> contactmethods -> method -> number
Matched mc@whoever.com in contact -> contactmethods -> method -> number
Matched mcmcslp@aol.com in contact -> contactmethods -> method -> number
```

Finding the Information from a Particular Tag

If you want to extract all of the information from a particular tag, you can do so easily using PerlSAX by dumping the character data in a specific tag element. For example, if you want to list all of the numbers for a given contact, you need to access all the character data within the number tag.

The way to do this is with a very simple change of logic in your handler class. You need to record the *current* tag. You also need to remember if you are in the tag you are searching for and also within a tag within that tag. You can do this with a simple counter. You also need to record any character data within your desired tag, and you need to output this information when you see the end of the tag element.

The handler class for this is in Listing 8.4.

Listing 8.4   **The *TextInTag* Search Handler Class**

```perl
package TextInTag;

sub new
{
    my $self = shift;
    my $class = ref($self) || $self;
    my $tag = shift;
    my @locs;

    return bless {tag => $tag,
                  intag => 0,
                  text => '',
                  loc => \@locs,}, $class;
                          ^
}

sub start_element
{
    my ($self, $info) = @_;

    if ($self->{intag} >= 1)
    {
        $self->{intag}++;
    }
    else
    {
        if ($info->{Name} eq $self->{tag})
        {
            $self->{intag} = 1;
        }
    }
}

sub end_element
{
    my ($self, $info) = @_;

    if ($self->{intag} > 1)
    {
        $self->{intag}--;
    }
    else
    {
```

```
        if ($info->{Name} eq $self->{tag})
        {
            print "$info->{Name} -> $self->{text}\n";
            $self->{intag} = 0;
            $self->{text} = '';
        }
    }
}

sub characters
{
    my ($self, $info) = @_;

    $self->{text} .= $info->{Data} if ($self->{intag} == 1);
}

1;
```

Now you can use this to dump all of the contact numbers from a given contact's XML document:

```
$ perl textintags.pl contact.xml number
number -> 01234 567890
number -> 09876 543210
number -> 01928 374650
number -> mc@mcslp.com
number -> mc@mcwords.com
number -> mc@whoever.com
number -> mcmcslp@aol.com
```

Incidentally, if you already know the names and locations of the data that you are searching for, you can use a DOM system such as XML::DOM or XML::Grove to process the document. You also can use the XPath or XQL system to search and move within a particular document. See the section "Inside XML::DOM Processing," later in this chapter, for more information.

XQL and XPath both allow you to access tags by their name (and location, if there are repeating elements) or to search for all the nodes with a specific tags or path. For example, you could access all of the number tags in your phone number document by using the specification method/number/* in an XPath query.

Of the two, only XPath is currently an agreed standard, and you can find XPath systems for most different implementations, including Java, C/C++, and less-used languages such as Ruby (see Chapter 21, "XML and Ruby"). A Perl version is supported through the XML::XPath module. The XQL standard is still being considered, and the XML::XQL module is one of the better implementations.

For more information, check out your local CPAN mirror for the modules—both come with a number of good samples. Also, check my website, `http://www.mcwords.com`, where you'll find some other examples based on XQL, a query language similar in principle to SQL, for searching XML documents. XQL uses a DOM-parsed XML document to do the searching.

Using SAX for Conversions

In the majority of cases, if you have an XML document that you want to convert then the chances are you want to translate the entire document, or at least significant proportions of it, into another format. The benefit of SAX here is that you can parse the entire document, using the individual methods within a handler class to set the different display or formatting options.

You've already seen an example of an event-based parser that converts an XML document into HTML format, albeit using the basic `XML::Parser` module rather than PerlSAX. The process is the same in each case: You determine the tag (and any attributes) and how you want that information to appear in the destination format, and then you output the character data and do the whole process in reverse.

I've successfully used this for all sorts of conversions and translations, but my favorite tool that makes use of this is the subject of Chapter 9, "Converting XML Documents Using Perl." It's a system for extracting and importing information from a database. Rather than just concentrating on the data, the system will dump and work with the database structure, allowing you to move an entire project, DB spec and data, from one SQL RDBMS to another.

Using a DOM Parser

DOM parsers convert an XML document into an easily traversable tree. Unlike SAX and other event-based parsers, this means you can access information within your XML document in a random access fashion; you don't need to process the document manually to find or update a particular a piece of information. You can just go straight to it.

There are a number of different DOM- and tree-like systems that process documents, and you looked at `XML::Grove` in Chapter 6. The main DOM implementation in Perl, however, is `XML::DOM`. In addition to the normal access methods, you can also search and traverse the branches in your XML tree and search for specific tags by name, moving directly to a particular branch in each case.

In this section we're going to look at how you can use the DOM model to work with and parse XML documents. Although the scripts and samples you'll be using are XML::DOM-specific, most of the basic principles used in this section can also be applied to any DOM- or tree-like implementation.

Inside *XML::DOM* Processing

To open and parse a document into a DOM tree using XML::DOM, all you have to do is create a new XML::DOM object, which you can do directly from a file by using the `parsefile()` method to an XML::DOM::Parser instance:

```
use XML::DOM;

my $parser = new XML::DOM::Parser;
my $doc = $parser->parsefile("faq.xml");
```

The resultant $doc is the root object from which you can start to process and manipulate the document. From there, accessing and processing the document requires traversal through the nodes of the XML document.

Access "By Node"

When using XML::DOM, the most import thing to remember is that you are accessing a tree. If you look at a sample XML document in the form of an FAQ for this book (see Listing 8.5), you can see the basic layout.

Listing 8.5   **A Sample FAQ XML Document**

```
<faq>
<description>
Simple FAQ for working with the Scripting XML book
</description>
<section title="Chapters">
<topic>
<question>
How many chapters are there in the book?
</question>
<answer>
There are 23 chapters and 2 appendixes split
into 5 different sections.
</answer>
</topic>

<topic>
<question>
How many chapters are there on Perl/Python/PHP?
```

```
</question>
<answer>
The Perl section has 5 chapters, the Python section
6 and the PHP section 3 chapters
</answer>
</topic>

</section>
<section title="Author">
<topic>
<question>Who is the author?</question>
<answer>Martin C Brown</answer>
</topic>

<topic>
<question>What does he do for a living?</question>
<answer>Writer and web programmer/consultant</answer>
</topic>
</section>
</faq>
```

Each XML tag within the document is called a *node* in XML::DOM (others such as XML::Grove take the branch/leaf *root*). Each node can contain sub-data, including the node's attributes and any character data it contains, in addition to a list of child nodes, which are all the XML tags within that node. For example, each topic node contains a question and answer node.

In addition, it's important to know that each of the subelements is itself a node. For example, the character data between a pair of question tags is described in a node, and if that character data includes an entity reference, then each entity reference is also a node. This subdivision of information continues throughout the description of the XML document. To give you an idea of far the system goes, see Table 8.4, which lists the main modules that support the different node types in the XML::DOM package.

TABLE 8.4 CONTINUED: Modules Supporting Different Node Structures in XML::DOM

Module	Description
XML::DOM::Node	Superclass for the individual node types.
XML::DOM::Document	The root of the entire XML document structure.
XML::DOM::DocumentType	Describes the <!DOCTYPE...> declaration.
XML::DOM::Element	Describes an individual XML element (or tag).
XML::DOM::Attr	Describes an XML element attribute.
XML::DOM::CharacterData	Superclass for character data (including comments and CDATA).

Continued on next page

TABLE 8.4 CONTINUED: Modules Supporting Different Node Structures in XML::DOM

Module	Description
XML::DOM::Text	The text within an XML element pair.
XML::DOM::CDATASection	Describes a CDATA section.
XML::DOM::Comment	Describes XML comment.
XML::DOM::EntityReference	Describes an XML entity.
XML::DOM::Entity	Describes an XML entity definition.
XML::DOM::ProcessingInstruction	Describes a processing instruction.
XML::DOM::DocumentFragment	Holds a "light" version of a document fragment suitable for copying and pasting between segments.
XML::DOM::Notation	Describes a notation definition.

Armed with this information, you can search for a list of matching nodes, modify the details about a node, and ultimately modify the XML document on which your node structure was based.

Extracting Information

The XML::DOM module relies on you traversing through the structure of nodes in order to get information. Every node supports a number of basic methods that will tell you information about the node, including its type and its name (if applicable) and a list of all the child nodes. Table 8.5 lists some but not all of the methods available in each.

TABLE 8.5: Methods Supported by Most Node Types

Method	Description
getNodeType	Gets the node type; you can check the return value against one of the constants from XML::DOM (see Table 8.6).
getNodeName	Gets the node's name; this is the tag or attribute name for suitable nodes. Other node classes return different information.
getNodeValue	Returns the node's value. Note that for element nodes it returns undef because the text in a tag pair is stored in its own Text node.
setNodeValue(value)	Sets the node's value; useful for setting the text in Text or Attr node.
getParentNode	Returns a reference to the node's parent.
setParentNode(node)	Sets the node's parent to node.
getChildNodes	Returns a list of the child nodes.
getFirstChild	Returns the first child node for the current node.

Continued on next page

TABLE 8.5 CONTINUED: Methods Supported by Most Node Types

Method	Description
getLastChild	Returns the last child node for the current node.
getPreviousSibling	Returns the previous sibling node.
getNextSibling	Returns the next sibling node.
getAttributes	Returns a list of Attr nodes for an Element node in the form of a NamedNodeMap.
insertBefore(new, ref)	Inserts the node new before the node ref.
replaceChild(new, old)	Replaces the node new with the node old.
removeChild(old)	Removes the child node old.
appendChild(new)	Appends the node new to the list of nodes for the current child.

A list of constants exported by XML::DOM to help you identify different node types is shown in Table 8.6.

TABLE 8.6: XML::DOM Constants

Constant	Numeric	Corresponding type
UNKNOWN_NODE	0	Unknown
ELEMENT_NODE	1	Element
ATTRIBUTE_NODE	2	Attribute
TEXT_NODE	3	Text node
CDATA_SECTION_NODE	4	CDATA section
ENTITY_REFERENCE_NODE	5	Entity reference
ENTITY_NODE	6	Entity
PROCESSING_INSTRUCTION_NODE	7	Processing instruction
COMMENT_NODE	8	Comment
DOCUMENT_NODE	9	Document
DOCUMENT_TYPE_NODE	10	Document type
DOCUMENT_FRAGMENT_NODE	11	Document fragment
NOTATION_NODE	12	Notation

Armed with this information, you can dump out the basic structure of your FAQ document with the script shown in Listing 8.6.

Listing 8.6   **Dumping a DOM Document Structure**

```perl
use XML::DOM;

my $parser = new XML::DOM::Parser;
my $doc = $parser->parsefile("faq.xml");

dumpnodes($doc,0);

sub dumpnodes
{
    my ($node, $level) = @_;

    foreach my $subnode ($node->getChildNodes)
    {
        if ($subnode->getNodeType eq ELEMENT_NODE)
        {
            print(' ' x $level, $subnode->getNodeName,"\n");
            dumpnodes($subnode,$level+4);
        }
    }
}
```

The script uses a recursive function to continually get a list of child nodes and then to dump the node name to the screen. The resulting output is shown here:

```
faq
    description
    section
        topic
            question
            answer
        topic
            question
            answer
    section
        topic
            question
            answer
        topic
            question
            answer
```

All further processing with a DOM-parsed document works in the same basic way—you get a node, access a list of subnodes, and then print or work on the information.

Of course, doing a node-by-node walkthrough like this is not particularly efficient. The benefit of DOM is the immediate access to different elements (and therefore nodes within the document).

Accessing Elements More Specifically

To make the process of updating and finding the specific tags you are interested in easier, you can obtain a list of nodes according to their tag names. From this you can start to process the information in the document much more explicitly. The starting point for this getElements-ByTagName() method is your base XML document object. This returns a list of the XML elements matching the supplied string.

For example, Listing 8.7 shows a script that extracts a list of the XML elements matching the section element from which you can extract the title attribute and therefore dump the basic FAQ structure.

Listing 8.7   Getting a List of Nodes by Tag Name

```
use XML::DOM;

my $parser = new XML::DOM::Parser;
my $doc = $parser->parsefile("faq.xml");

my $nodes = $doc->getElementsByTagName("section");
my $nodelength = $nodes->getLength();

for my $i (0..($nodelength-1))
{
    my $node = $nodes->item($i);
    my $title =
        $node->getAttributeNode("title")->getValue();
    print "$title\n";
}
```

To take the process one stage further, you can generate a formatted FAQ by using further getChildNodes() and getElementsByTagName() methods to traverse farther down your node tree. You can see an example of this in Listing 8.8.

Listing 8.8   Getting the *Full* FAQ

```
use XML::DOM;

my $parser = new XML::DOM::Parser;
my $doc = $parser->parsefile("faq.xml");
```

```
my $nodes = $doc->getElementsByTagName("section");
my $nodelength = $nodes->getLength();

for my $i (0..($nodelength-1))
{
    my $node = $nodes->item($i);
    my $title =
        $node->getAttributeNode("title")->getValue();
    print "Section $title\n";
    foreach my $topicnode
        ($node->getElementsByTagName("topic"))
    {
        foreach my $subnode ($topicnode->getChildNodes)
        {
            if ($subnode->getNodeType eq ELEMENT_NODE)
            {
                print "Question: "
                    if ($subnode->getNodeName eq
                        'question');
                print "Answer: \n"
                    if ($subnode->getNodeName eq
                        'answer');
                my @textnodes = $subnode->getChildNodes;
                foreach my $textnode (@textnodes)
                {
                    print $textnode->getNodeValue
                        if ($textnode->getNodeType eq
                            TEXT_NODE);
                }
                print "\n\n";
            }
        }
    }
}
```

You can also access specific nodes within a list of nodes by using the item() method. For example, if you want to examine the first node within the list of topic nodes immediately, you can use this:

```
$firstopicnode
    = $doc->getElementsByTagName('topic')->item(0)
```

You can use the same basic techniques to extract the different elements from a document to perform updates or to extract information. For example, you could insert a simple match so that you output only the questions in each section or a match that generates only the questions within a particular section, all without traversing the entire node tree.

Modifying Structures and Data

Beyond the easier access to specific areas of an XML document, the other benefit with DOM is that you can very easily manipulate the internal DOM structure in order to add new nodes or to add information to existing nodes.

You can create a new element node using the `createElement()` method. You can also add text to an element by calling the `addText()` method on the new element node. You can then manipulate the XML structure using the methods you saw earlier in Table 8.6.

For example, to create a new question, answer, and topic, you would use:

```
my $topic = $doc->createElement ("topic");
my $question = $doc->createElement("question");
my $answer = $doc->createElement("answer");
$question->addText("How long is the book?");
$answer->addText("About 440 pages");
$topic->appendChild($question);
$topic->appendChild($answer);
```

In turn, you could easily add this to one of the sections:

```
$section = $doc->getElementsByTagName('section')->item(0);
$section->appendChild($topic);
```

When adding attributes you have two possible choices—either you set the attribute directly using the `setAttribute()` method for a node:

```
my $section = $doc->createElement("section");
$section->setAttribute("title", "Scripts");
```

Alternatively, we can create an attribute node that we then append to the list of children for the element that you want to set the attribute in:

```
my $section = $doc->createElement("section");
my $attribute = $doc->createAttr("title", "Scripts");
$section->appendChild($attribute);
```

Regenerating XML from a DOM Tree

Using the XML::DOM module, this process is probably the easiest of all the procedures for DOM processing. Assuming you have a root XML::DOM document object, you can get the string version of an XML document using this:

```
$myxml = $doc->toString;
```

or you can print the document straight out to a file using this:

```
$doc->printToFile ("newfile.xml");
```

Summary

Perl has two primary methods for working with XML documents. The PerlSAX system allows for sequential and complete parsing of an XML document. The DOM system allows for selective access to different parts of an XML document without the need to work through the entire document beforehand.

We can use the sequential features of SAX to search for text in an XML document and we can use this either to identify the tag in which the tag is located, or we can do the reverse, identifying the text within a particular tag by name.

The DOM system is better suited to situations where we need to pull out information from an XML document by its element name but don't want to traverse and parse the entire document to extract the information. DOM has the added benefit that we can also modify and update the character data and structure of the document and then dump this structure back out to an XML file.

## CHAPTER 9

Converting XML Documents Using Perl

- Database Management

- Converting Database Content to XML

You saw in the last chapter that you can use XML as a storage format for some databases. Although it works as a flexible format for storing and working with data, particularly complex types, its limitation is the searching and retrieval of information.

If you think about a typical company using XML to store customer records, then it's not unlikely to find 20,000 or more records in its database, even within a relatively small company. In a larger company you could be talking about millions of records. Now consider the process for searching or updating that information.

Dealing with searching first, you run into the same problems that you would encounter if you were working with a flat file text-delimited database. In order to find a single record, you have to search through a large number of records to find what you want. With small datasets, this is not an issue; computers and hard disks are so fast now that even searching 10,000 or more files takes little more a few seconds. Extend that to a few million records and it's turned into minutes and is beginning to approach major fractions of an hour to search the dataset.

You can get round this by using a separate file with an index to other documents, and you can improve the overall speed by storing all the records within a single file. Using a single file, you can make educated jumps through the document to find the information. However, you are introducing extra levels of complexity—building and updating an index of even 10,000 records is a mammoth task, especially if you use XML for the index data.

Turning to the updating process, updating single records stored in single files (assuming you can find them) is not a problem. If you decide to use a single file for your entire data set, then making a modification becomes a major project. If you use SAX, you need to deconstruct and rebuild the XML document each time. If you use DOM, you'll need to work with a huge file in memory, which will be slow and very resource hungry.

In all likelihood, therefore, you won't be using XML for all your data storage needs. Instead, you'll be using it as an exchange format to enable you to exchange information between different applications. That means that you will need to be able to export your information from your SQL database into XML format and the reverse, export XML back into your database.

We'll be looking at that process in this chapter, including some tricks that will make the whole process easier. Before we get there, however, I'd like to take a look at some XML-based solutions for managing the databases on which you store the data.

Database Management

Although transferring information between applications, and even between entire databases, is a problem, I've always found managing the databases at the outset more of a complication.

The problems arise in particular when you develop a database on one machine but deploy the database and associated application on another. For me, the problem occurs because my websites are hosted with a hosting service called Dreamhost (http://www.dreamhost.com), but all the development and updating occur on one of the servers in my office. Although updating and uploading any script changes or HTML is easy, handling the database is more complex.

What happens, for example, if I create a new table within the database to hold some information? What is needed is some way of recording database structure in a format that makes it easy to update, extended, and modify the structure without requiring me to edit SQL statements directly or execute SQL statements directly on a SQL database system.

Traditional Solution

My solution a number of years ago was to build a hash structure that contained a list of the tables as the keys and then a nested hash that contained the database information, including a short name and description, which included another nested array of field definitions.

Because this information was internally useful, I placed the entire specification into a new module in Perl and then created suitable class methods to extract the information into a hash that can be used by other parts of the application. For example, using the database structure in this way, I could easily create a hash structure of a table record—because I know the field names—and use it to validate a hash supplied to a function that writes the data to a record.

The result is a module such as the one shown in Listing 9.1, which shows a slightly reduced version of the table structure for a new version of the MCwords.com website, which will be launched at the end of 2001. Not shown here are all the tables or the index specification.

Listing 9.1   **Class Holding the Database Specification**

```
package Database;

# Class for supplying back database configuration

# Main database configuration

my %tablespec
    = (
# Tablespecs for core MCSLP functionality
        'mcslp_user' =>
        {
            'short' => 'Users',
            'description' => 'Public user logins',
            'fields' =>
```

```
            [
              {
                field => 'userid',
                type => 'char',
                size => '255',
                opt => 'NOT NULL',
              },
              {
                field => 'password',
                type => 'char',
                size => '20',
                opt => 'NOT NULL',
              },
              {
                field => 'type',
                type => 'char',
                size => '1',
                opt => 'NOT NULL',
              },
              {
                field => 'usergroup',
                type => 'char',
                size => '20',
                opt => 'NOT NULL',
              },
            ],
      },
      'mcslp_sessionid' =>
      {
          'short' => 'User Sessions',
          'description' => 'Session IDs for logged logged in/cookie users',
          'fields' =>
            [
              {
                field => 'session',
                type => 'char',
                size => '30',
              },
              {
                field => 'userid',
                type => 'char',
                size => '255',
              },
              {
                field => 'expires',
                type => 'int',
              },
            ],
      },
      'mcwords_books' =>
      {
```

```
        'short' => 'Books',
        'description' => 'Books in the database',
        'fields' =>
            [
            {
                field => 'isbn',
                type => 'char',
                size => '20',
                opt => 'NOT NULL',
            },
            {
                field => 'code',
                type => 'char',
                size => '20',
                opt => 'NOT NULL',
            },
            {
                field => 'title',
                type => 'char',
                size => '255',
                opt => 'NOT NULL',
            },
            {
                field => 'releasedate',
                type => 'char',
                size => '8',
            },
            ],
    },
    'mcwords_books_contents' =>
    {
        'short' => 'Book Contents',
        'description' => 'Content data for individual books',
        'fields' =>
            [
            {
                field => 'isbn',
                type => 'char',
                size => '20',
                opt => 'NOT NULL',
            },
            {
                field => 'chapter',
                type => 'int',
                opt => 'NOT NULL',
            },
            {
                field => 'sublevel',
                type => 'int',
                opt => 'NOT NULL',
            },
```

```
                {
                    field => 'subsublevel',
                    type => 'int',
                    opt => 'NOT NULL',
                },
                {
                    field => 'subsubsublevel',
                    type => 'int',
                    opt => 'NOT NULL',
                },
                {
                    field => 'description',
                    type => 'char',
                    size => '255',
                    opt => 'NOT NULL',
                },
                {
                    field => 'pagestart',
                    type => 'int',
                    opt => 'NOT NULL',
                },
                {
                    field => 'pageend',
                    type => 'int',
                    opt => 'NOT NULL',
                },
                ],
        },
        'mcwords_books_index' =>
        {
            'short' => 'Book Index',
            'description' => 'Index entries for individual books',
            'fields' =>
                [
                {
                    field => 'isbn',
                    type => 'char',
                    size => '20',
                    opt => 'NOT NULL',
                },
                {
                    field => 'description',
                    type => 'char',
                    size => '255',
                    opt => 'NOT NULL',
                },
                {
                    field => 'page',
                    type => 'int',
                    opt => 'NOT NULL',
                },
```

```
                    ],
            },
        'mcwords_books_errata' =>
        {
            'short' => 'Book Errata',
            'description' => 'Book errata entries',
            'fields' =>
                [
                    {
                        field => 'isbn',
                        type => 'char',
                        size => '20',
                        opt => 'NOT NULL',
                    },
                    {
                        field => 'page',
                        type => 'int',
                        opt => 'NOT NULL',
                    },
                    {
                        field => 'description',
                        type => 'blob',
                    },
                    ],
        }
);

sub new
{
    my $self = shift;
    my $class = ref($self) || $self;

    bless {},$self;
}

sub tables
{
    my $self = shift;
    return %tablespec;
}

1;
```

Now you can get the entire database structure from within a calling script using this:

```
my $dbspec = new Database();

my %tablespec = $dbspec->tables();
```

Although it's not shown here, you could also get the definition of the indexes for the tables using this:

```
my %indexspec = $dbspec->indexes();
```

You can use this information to build the tables for the database using a simple script that traverses the hash structure and extracts the table name and field definition and creates a suitable set of SQL statements to create the table on the desired database system.

The SQL statement for creating a new table looks this:

```
create table TABLENAME (FIELD TYPE[(SIZE] FIELDOPTS, …)
```

For example, to create the mcslp_sessionid table, you'd use this:

```
create table mcslp_sessionid (session char(30),
                              userid char(255),
                              expires int)
```

The script in Listing 9.2 does exactly this, creating the tables and executing the statements based on the database specification.

Listing 9.2   Creation Script for Tables

```perl
#!/usr/local/bin/perl -w

use Database;
use DBI;

my $dbname = shift or die "You must supply a database name";

my $dbh = DBI->connect("DBI:mysql:$dbname");

my $dbspec = new Database();

my %tablespec = $dbspec->tables();

create_tables(0,0,keys %tablespec);

sub create_tables
{
    my ($dummy, $drop, @tables) = @_;
    foreach my $table (sort @tables)
    {
        if ($drop)
        {
            print "Dropping table $table...";
            unless ($dummy)
            {
                $result = $dbh->do("drop table $table");
                print "Error: ",$dbh->{dbh}->errstr(),"\n"
```

```
                    unless ($result);
        }
        print "Dropped\n";
    }
    my $query = "create table $table ";
    my @fieldspec;
    foreach my $fieldkey
        (@{$tablespec{$table}->{fields}})
    {
        my $fielddef;
        $fielddef = sprintf("%s %s",
                            $fieldkey->{field},
                            $fieldkey->{type});
        $fielddef .= "($fieldkey->{size})"
            if (exists($fieldkey->{size}));
        $fielddef .= " $fieldkey->{opt}"
            if (exists($fieldkey->{opt}));
        push(@fieldspec,$fielddef);
    }
    $query .= sprintf("(%s)",join(',',@fieldspec));
    print "Creating table $table...";
    unless ($dummy)
    {
        $result = $dbh->do($query);
        print "Error: ",$dbh->errstr(),"\n"
            unless($result);
    }
    print "Done\n";
}
}
```

Although there are no problems with this method, I have come across a few instances where the location of the definition caused a problem. I've used the same system on a number of different applications now, and on the whole it works very well. However, as always there are some little problems with the solution, which are summarized here:

- Because the definition is wrapped up within a Perl module, making changes requires Perl knowledge (in case you miss a quote or bracket). Although this didn't affect me, it did occasionally affect a client installation where the people dealing with the system wanted to modify the structure but didn't know Perl.

- Being a Perl module, any script that wants access to the structure has to import the module first, and that requires additional overhead. You could solve this by using the Auto-Loader system or by creating a super class that inherits the definitions for individual tables from other modules dynamically.

- Documenting and otherwise annotating the information requires use of either Perl documentation tools or comments or just exporting the structure to another format, such as a line-by-line field definition for importing into a word processor.

- Migrating the database structure to another platform means having to use Perl on that platform. Although this is not necessarily a problem for Unix and Windows, I didn't always have a Perl installation available.

These problems lead to a decision to move from an internal hash structure into an XML format. Using XML, you gain these things:

- Easier modification and extension.

- Easier documentation and incorporation in other systems.

- Easier processing and conversion to other formats.

- External storage of the structure, so it could be loaded on demand.

- Database specification can be parsed and understood by any XML parser, which then translates to any format, including creating the database on an available RDBMS.

- An easier method for adding new fields and metadata about the tables and fields, without increasing the load within the Perl scripts and without adding further layers of nested structures to hold the information.

It also means the development of new tools, first to convert the existing structure to XML, and then new tools for taking the XML structure and creating a database from it. While I was going through that process, I also developed a set of scripts that would dump an existing database structure into XML format when modifying an existing database installation from a client.

Most of these tools are covered in the rest of this section of this chapter.

Dumping the Hash to XML

The first job was to dump the existing hash structure to an XML document. The structure of the XML required for this is fairly straightforward. You use a tag to hold the table data, another to hold the field data, and tags to hold the field name, type, size, and constraints (options) for a given field. The basic format looks like this:

```
<dbspec>
<table>
    <tablename>mcwords_books</tablename>
    <short>Books</short>
    <description>Books in the database</description>
    <field>
```

```
        <fieldname>isbn</fieldname>
        <fieldtype>char</fieldtype>
        <fieldsize>20</fieldsize>
        <fieldopts>NOT NULL</fieldopts>
    </field>
  </table>
  </dbspec>
```

As a further expansion, you could separate individual constraints into their own elements, for example:

```
<fieldopts>
    <fieldopt>NOT NULL</fieldopt>
    <fieldopt>UNIQUE</fieldopt>
    <fieldopt>DEFAULT = 0</fieldopt>
</fieldopts>
```

The process to convert the hash structure into something you can use is just a modification of the code that created the database tables straight from the hash itself. You could have used one of the XML generator modules, but it's easier in this instance just to use `print()` statements to dump the XML tags and data. You can see the script in Listing 9.3.

Listing 9.3   Script for Dumping the Hash Structure to XML

```perl
#!/usr/local/bin/perl -w

use Database;

my $dbspec = new Database();
my %tablespec = $dbspec->tables();

print "<dbspec>\n";

my @tablelist;

if (@ARGV)
{
  @tablelist = @ARGV;
}
else
{
  @tablelist = keys %tablespec;
}

foreach my $table (map { $_ = lc($_) } @tablelist)
{
```

```perl
      print STDERR "Dumping $table\n";
      my $xmltable = dump_table($table);
      print $xmltable;
    }

    print "</dbspec>\n";

    sub dump_table
    {
      my ($table) = @_;
      my $xmlout;
      if (exists($tablespec{$table}))
      {
        $xmlout =
          "<table>\n\t<tablename>$table</tablename>\n";
        foreach my $dbinf (qw/short description/)
        {
          $xmlout .=
            "\t<$dbinf>" .
            "$tablespec{$table}->{$dbinf}" .
            "</$dbinf>\n";
        }
        my @fieldspec;
        foreach my $fieldkey
          (@{$tablespec{$table}->{fields}})
        {
          my $fielddef;
          $fielddef =
            sprintf("\t\t<fieldname>%s</fieldname>" .
                    "\n\t\t<fieldtype>%s</fieldtype>\n",
                    $fieldkey->{field},$fieldkey->{type});
          $fielddef .=
            "\t\t<fieldsize>$fieldkey->{size}</fieldsize>\n"
              if (exists($fieldkey->{size}));
          $fielddef .=
            "\t\t<fieldopts>$fieldkey->{opt}</fieldopts>\n"
              if (exists($fieldkey->{opt}));
          push(@fieldspec,"\t<field>\n$fielddef\t</field>\n");
        }
        $xmlout .= join('',@fieldspec);
        $xmlout .= "</table>\n";
      }
      return $xmlout;
    }
```

When run, the script will dump any structure as defined in the example (Listing 9.1) to the standard output, while describing its process through the standard error. The result from the sample looks like Listing 9.4.

Listing 9.4   **The Resulting XML Structure**

```
<dbspec>
<table>
    <tablename>mcwords_books</tablename>
    <short>Books</short>
    <description>Books in the database</description>
    <field>
        <fieldname>isbn</fieldname>
        <fieldtype>char</fieldtype>
        <fieldsize>20</fieldsize>
        <fieldopts>NOT NULL</fieldopts>
    </field>
    <field>
        <fieldname>code</fieldname>
        <fieldtype>char</fieldtype>
        <fieldsize>20</fieldsize>
        <fieldopts>NOT NULL</fieldopts>
    </field>
    <field>
        <fieldname>title</fieldname>
        <fieldtype>char</fieldtype>
        <fieldsize>255</fieldsize>
        <fieldopts>NOT NULL</fieldopts>
    </field>
    <field>
        <fieldname>releasedate</fieldname>
        <fieldtype>char</fieldtype>
        <fieldsize>8</fieldsize>
    </field>
</table>
<table>
    <tablename>mcwords_books_errata</tablename>
    <short>Book Errata</short>
    <description>Book errata entries</description>
    <field>
        <fieldname>isbn</fieldname>
        <fieldtype>char</fieldtype>
        <fieldsize>20</fieldsize>
        <fieldopts>NOT NULL</fieldopts>
    </field>
    <field>
        <fieldname>page</fieldname>
        <fieldtype>int</fieldtype>
        <fieldopts>NOT NULL</fieldopts>
    </field>
```

```
      <field>
          <fieldname>description</fieldname>
          <fieldtype>blob</fieldtype>
      </field>
  </table>
  ...</dbspec>
```

The result, as you can see, is a nice handy XML-formatted version of the database structure. Included are the description and other information, as well as the field descriptions. You could have shortened the output through the use of attributes, such as this:

```
<field type="char" size="255" opts="not null">userid</field>
```

This would certainly make parsing easier, but I find that it confuses many people who are using the system for managing their databases, so I returned to the longer explicit XML version.

Creating the Database from the XML

With the database specification in XML, you need to be able to convert the XML description of the tables in the database into a series of SQL statements that can then be executed to build the tables within the database system.

There are a number of ways you could do this, including using a DOM parser to extract individual table definitions from the XML and build the necessary expression. However, since you'll be using this in a sequential form to build up a series of queries from an XML database specification, you can more easily use SAX to parse the content.

The main wrapper for the SAX parser is shown in Listing 9.5. This just extracts the name of the database name in which you want to create the tables and the name of the file that contains the database specification. It also extracts a username and password from the command line to allow you to connect to a secure database to perform the database creation.

Listing 9.5   **The XML Processing Wrapper Script**

```perl
#!/usr/local/bin/perl -w

use XMLDBHandler;
use XML::Parser::PerlSAX;

my $dbname = shift or die "No database name supplied";
my $xmlspec = shift or die "No filename supplied";
my $my_handler;

if (@ARGV)
{
    my ($user,$pw) = @ARGV;
```

```
        $my_handler = XMLDBHandler->new($dbname, $user, $pw);
}
else
{
        $my_handler = XMLDBHandler->new($dbname, '', '');
}

XML::Parser::PerlSAX->new->parse(
        Source => { SystemId => $xmlspec },
        Handler => $my_handler);
$my_handler->{dbh}->disconnect();
```

The script uses the XMLDBHandler class to process the XML file using SAX methods. The class itself is defined in Listing 9.6.

Listing 9.6   The SAX Handler Class for Processing the XML

```
package XMLDBHandler;

use DBI;

sub new
{
    my $self = shift;
    my $class = ref($self) || $self;

    my ($dbname,$user,$pw) = @_;

    my $dbh = DBI->connect("DBI:mysql:$dbname", $user, $pw);

    unless(defined($dbh))
    {
        die "Couldn't open connection to database\n";
    }

    my @fields = ();

    return bless {table => '',
                  in => '',
                  field => '',
                  fieldtype => '',
                  fieldsize => '',
                  fieldopts => '',
                  fields => \@fields,
                  dbh => $dbh,
                  }, $class;
}

sub start_element
```

```perl
{
    my ($self, $info) = @_;

    $self->{in} = lc($info->{Name});
}

sub end_element
{
    my ($self, $info) = @_;

    my $element = lc($info->{Name});

    if ($element eq 'table')
    {
        my $query = sprintf("create table %s (%s)",
                            $self->{table},
                            join(', ', @{$self->{fields}}));
        print "Creating table $self->{table}\n";
        $self->{dbh}->do($query);
        @{$self->{fields}} = ();
        $self->{table} = '';
    }
    elsif ($element eq 'field')
    {
        my $fielddef;
        $fielddef = sprintf("%s %s",
                            $self->{field},
                            $self->{fieldtype});
        if ($self->{fieldsize} =~ /^\d+$/)
        {
            $fielddef .= "($self->{fieldsize})";
        }
        else
        {
            die "Data in <fieldsize> " .
                ($self->{fieldsize}) .
                " should be numeric";
        }
        if ($self->{fieldopts} =~ /[a-zA-Z0-9]+/)
        {
            $fielddef .= " $self->{fieldopts}";
        }
        else
        {
            die "Data in <fieldopts> " .
                ($self->{fieldopts}) .
                " should be alphanumeric";
        }
        push @{$self->{fields}}, $fielddef;
        $self->{field} = '';
        $self->{fieldtype} = '';
```

```
        $self->{fieldsize} = '';
        $self->{fieldopts} = '';
    }
    $self->{in} = ''
}

sub characters
{
    my ($self, $info) = @_;

    my $data = $info->{Data};
    $data =~ s/[\r\n]//g;
    $data =~ s/[\t ]+/ /g;

    if ($self->{in} eq 'tablename')
    {
        $self->{table} .= $data;
    }
    elsif ($self->{in} eq 'fieldname')
    {
        $self->{field} .= $data;
    }
    elsif ($self->{in} eq 'fieldtype')
    {
        $self->{fieldtype} .= $data;
    }
    elsif ($self->{in} eq 'fieldsize')
    {
        $self->{fieldsize} .= $data;
    }
    elsif ($self->{in} eq 'fieldopts')
    {
        $self->{fieldopts} .= $data;
    }
}

1;
```

An instance of the class has a number of different properties. The in property holds the name of the current tag you are processing so that you know what to do with the character data when you receive it. The table property holds the name of the current table, and the field* properties hold the field name and others. The fields property is a list that contains the SQL definition for creating each field. Finally, you also hold a reference to the database handle—the connection is made when the instance is created.

The start_element() function just records the name of the element you are in. You're not interested in the element name, just where you are within the document, so you record the information in the `in` property. Note that you record a lowercase version of the element name to make testing of element names easier.

The `end_element()` function is more extensive. It creates a field definition when you find the `</field>` end tag, pushing the resulting string onto the `fields` property. Note that because you are continually adding text to the `field*` properties when you process character data, you also have to make sure that the `field*` properties are emptied once the field definition has been created. You use an array here, rather than a hash, because the order of the fields is important, especially if you update the tables in your scripts without using explicit fieldnames, for example using `insert into table values(…)`.

Once you reach the end of a single table definition, you create the full SQL statement required to create the table and then execute the statement to create the table in the database. Again, you must empty both the table name and the list of field definitions; otherwise you end up with compound table names and tables that contain all the fields specified in the database specification.

The `characters()` method collects all the character data and appends it to the corresponding object property. The information in these properties is used to build the SQL statements.

To create the databases using the XML specification file you created earlier, you just need to type:

```
$ xmlspectodb.pl mcslp mcslpdbspec.xml
```

Easy!

You can use exactly the same principle with just about any database that you need to define in any way, and because you have the information in a nice portable XML format, you can also the database specification that you've created here in any other language to create the tables. For example, I have a similar Perl script that creates the tables on a Windows platform, and another in Python that can create the tables within a Gadfly database for use in Python scripts and Zope.

Dumping any SQL Database Structure to XML

The first time I went to a new client and was asked to modify and redevelop part of their database, I found myself more or less back at square one. Although they had documented the database structure, it wasn't in a convenient machine-readable format, so to transfer the database to my own machine for development and testing would have meant manually creating the XML for the database specification.

The solution to this time-consuming process was to create the database specification in XML from the database as it stood within the RDBMS.

For this to work, you need to know how to access the information itself and how to parse the information returned through the DBI interface into the XML specification.

For example, we can use the MySQL utility to submit SQL queries directly into a database. The SQL statement for displaying a list of tables within a given database is show tables:

```
mysql> show tables;
+-----------------------+
| Tables_in_test        |
+-----------------------+
| mcslp_sessionid       |
| mcslp_user            |
| mcwords_books         |
| mcwords_books_contents |
| mcwords_books_errata  |
| mcwords_books_index   |
+-----------------------+
6 rows in set (0.00 sec)
```

When using fetchrow_hashref() and an active statement handle, the hashref will contain a single field name, Tables_in_*DBNAME* where *DBNAME* is the name of the database you are connected to. The value of the element is the table name.

To get a specific table setup, you use describe TABLENAME to describe the fields within a given table:

```
mysql> describe mcwords_books;
+-------------+-----------+------+-----+---------+-------+
| Field       | Type      | Null | Key | Default | Extra |
+-------------+-----------+------+-----+---------+-------+
| isbn        | char(20)  |      |     |         |       |
| code        | char(20)  |      |     |         |       |
| title       | char(255) |      |     |         |       |
| releasedate | char(8)   | YES  |     | NULL    |       |
+-------------+-----------+------+-----+---------+-------+
4 rows in set (0.02 sec)
```

The corresponding field names from a fetchrow_hashref() call are shown as the headings to each column of the table. Field and Type should be self explanatory; the remainder hold the individual field options. Null defines whether the field can be empty when data is inserted. Key specifies whether the field is a primary key for use with a table index, and Default describes the default value. Finally the Extra field holds additional options such as auto incrementation.

Armed with this information, you can write a script, shown in Listing 9.7, that will dump the database table definition from any database to an XML file.

Listing 9.7   **The MySQL-to-XML Database Structure Dumper**

```perl
#!/usr/local/bin/perl -w

use strict;
use DBI;

my $dbname = shift;

my $dbh = DBI->connect("DBI:mysql:$dbname");

my @tables = ();

my ($sth) = $dbh->prepare("show tables");
$sth->execute();
while (my $row = $sth->fetchrow_hashref())
{
    push @tables, $row->{"Tables_in_$dbname"};
}
$sth->finish();

foreach my $table (@tables)
{
    print "<table>\n\t<tablename>$table</tablename>\n";
    my ($sth) = $dbh->prepare("describe $table");
    $sth->execute();
    while (my $row = $sth->fetchrow_hashref())
    {
        my @opts;
        print "\t<field>\n";
        print "\t\t<fieldname>$row->{Field}</fieldname>\n";
        my ($type) = ($row->{Type} =~ m/([a-zA-Z0-9]+)/);
        my $size = 0;
        ($size) = ($row->{Type} =~ m/\(([0-9]+)\)/);
        print "\t\t<fieldtype>$type</fieldtype>\n";
        print "\t\t<fieldsize>$size</fieldsize>\n"
            if ($size);

        push @opts, "primary key"
            if ($row->{Key} eq 'PRI');
        push @opts, "not null"
            unless ($row->{Null} eq 'YES');
        push @opts, $row->{Extra}
            if ($row->{Extra} =~ /\S+/);

        print("\t\t<fieldopts>",
            join(' ', @opts),
            "</fieldopts>\n") if (@opts);
        print "\t</field>\n";
```

```
    }
    $sth->finish();
    print "</table>\n";
  }
$dbh->disconnect()
```

To use the script, just supply the database name on the command line for the database you want to dump to XML:

```
$ sqldbtoxml.pl mcslp
```

The XML is printed to standard output, so you'll need to capture the output to store the file. If you've been using the scripts in this chapter and choose to dump out the database specification created by the script in Listing 9.5, you should get back an XML file that is almost identical to the one you used to create it in the first place.

There will be a few differences. There will be no short name or description, for example. This information was originally generated from the hash specification, but the table names, field names, and field options should be the same.

Converting Database Content to XML

There are a few decisions that you need to make about how you are going to dump your information to XML. First and foremost, you must think about why you are dumping the data to XML format:

- What you are extracting. Is it the entire content of a given table or a "record" of information with individual rows from a number of tables?

- The layout of the information that you generate. If you are working to an existing XML DTD, then you obviously have something to work to, but if you are just dumping the data for your own purposes, then consider what you will do with it once it's been dumped.

- If you expect to use the XML directly, then consider using a DTD and some of the XML-specific features such as ID attributes to identify different records in the XML file.

- How you want your information represented in XML. Are you going to use attributes to hold field data, or will you use XML tag pairs to hold all the information?

These questions can't be answered easily, and certainly it's beyond the scope of this book to answer these questions for you, but we will be looking at some of the issues as we examine the process of converting data to XML format.

A Traditional Dumping Approach

If you are trying to dump out the information for transfer from one system to another, there are better and ultimately more straightforward ways of dumping the information to a file that can later be processed and imported into another database system. Personally, I use a script that writes out the information in the form of SQL statements. Then, to import on any system, all I need to do is read each line from the file and execute the statement. For reference and utility, I've included the script that I use for this in Listing 9.8.

Listing 9.8   A Simple Script for Dumping Database Contents

```perl
#!/usr/local/bin/perl -w

use strict;
use DBI;

my $dbname = shift;

my $dbh = DBI->connect("DBI:mysql:$dbname");

my @tables = ();

my ($sth) = $dbh->prepare("show tables");
$sth->execute();
while (my $row = $sth->fetchrow_hashref())
{
    push @tables, $row->{"Tables_in_$dbname"};
}
$sth->finish();

foreach my $table (@tables)
{
    $sth = $dbh->prepare("select * from $table");
    $sth->execute();
    while(my $row = $sth->fetchrow_hashref())
    {
        my $query = "insert into $table set ";
        foreach my $field (keys %{$row})
        {
            $query .= "$field=" .
                $dbh->quote($row->{$field}) . ',';
        }
        chop $query;
        print "$query\n";
    }
}
```

When executed, the script dumps the content of every table as a SQL statement. Rather than dumping the fields in sequence, what you actually do is write the information with field-by-field specifications. You can see the sample output here:

```
insert into mcwords_books
    set releasedate='20010601',
    code='cdr',
    title='CD Recordable Solutions',
    isbn='1929685114'
insert into mcwords_books
    set releasedate='20011006',
    code='cdr',
    title='Python: The Complete Reference',
    isbn='007212718'
```

This way, the script protects you from a situation in which a table is re-created with the same fields but in a different order, or when you add new fields to the table definition. When the SQL is executed, it updates the information, ignoring the table field order, thereby retaining the information irrespective of the current table definition.

NOTE   If your SQL implementation doesn't support the `insert into … set field=value` format, you can easily change the script to use `insert into … (field1, field2, …) values (value1, value2, …)`.

Again, for reference, Listing 9.9 includes a simple script for inserting the information back into a database from the SQL statements.

Listing 9.9   Inserting Raw SQL Statements into the Database

```perl
#!/usr/local/bin/perl -w

use strict;
use DBI;

my $dbname = shift;

my $dbh = DBI->connect("DBI:mysql:$dbname");

my $linecount = 0;
open(DATA,$ARGV[0]);
while(<DATA>)
{
    $linecount++;
}
close(DATA);
```

```perl
my $counter = 0;
open(DATA,$ARGV[0]);
while(<DATA>)
{
    chomp;
    $dbh->do($_);
    $counter++;
    printf ("$counter/$linecount (%0.1f%%)\r",
            ($counter/$linecount)*100);
}
print "\n";
```

The XML Dump Approach

Although I don't recommend XML for database dumping, there are still occasions when it's useful. You've already seen an off the shelf tool in Chapter 6, "XML Solutions in Perl," under the guise of the DBIx::XML_RDB module. This generates an XML file using the table name and field names of the table you have selected to build the data file.

In fact, we can modify the script in Listing 9.10 to do what you want quite simply, just by changing the outer foreach loop to dump XML instead of SQL statements.

Listing 9.10   **Inserting the Data Back into the Database**

```perl
foreach my $table (@tables)
{
    print "<table>\n<tablename>$table</tablename>\n";
    $sth = $dbh->prepare("select * from $table");
    $sth->execute();
    while(my $row = $sth->fetchrow_hashref())
    {
        print "<record>\n";
        foreach my $field (keys %{$row})
        {
            print "<$field>$row->{$field}</$field>\n";
        }
        print "</record>\n";
    }
    print "</table>\n";
}
```

Using the test data, this produces the following output:

```
<table>
<tablename>mcwords_books</tablename>
<record>
```

```
<releasedate>20010601</releasedate>
<code>cdr</code>
<title>CD Recordable Solutions</title>
<isbn>1929685114</isbn>
</record>
<record>
<releasedate>20011006</releasedate>
<code>cdr</code>
<title>Python: The Complete Reference</title>
<isbn>007212718</isbn>
</record>
</table>
```

Generating More Complex XML Documents

Generating more complex XML records when you are collecting the information from a number of tables is really just an extension of the basic principles already discussed. You select the data you want to extract from your database and then build the XML document accordingly.

There are those who believe that the best way to build a document from a database is to use XML::Generator or alternatively to construct the document using a DOM model and then to dump the DOM model in serial form to your XML document. In my experience, I've never found the need to build an XML document in this way when extracting data straight from a database.

For an example of the sort of XML document you might produce from a database, let's go back to the sample database structure that holds information about the books on the MCwords.com website. Suppose you want to generate an XML document containing all of the errata for a given book, including all the book information.

To do this, you first need to dump the book data, followed by all of the errata records for that book. You'll end up with a document that looks roughly like this:

```
<bookerrata>
<book>
<isbn>1929685114</isbn>
<code>cdr</code>
<title>CD Recordable Solutions</title>
<releasedate>20010601</releasedate>
</book>
<errata>
<erratum>
<page>23</page><description>Some error</description>
</erratum>
```

```
<erratum>
<page>35</page><description>Some other error</description>
</erratum>
</errata>
</bookerrata>
```

You can now use this to produce an HTML document or indeed any other document you want.

Since you already know the basics, we won't look at an example of how to produce this document; instead, let's concentrate on some of the benefits and situations you may want to work with and handle using the scripting facilities of a language such as Perl or Python when generating XML from another data source:

- Use attributes where necessary. For example, if you are exporting data that uses a unique ID code or serial number that is not part of the data itself, then consider storing this in an attribute against each record, rather than an element pair. That way, you can compare notes easily between XML files and also between the XML and database.

- Modifying the representation of the information in your XML document. For example, you want to represent dates in your database in International format (YYYYMMDD), but in your XML document in U.S. (MMDDYYYY) or European (DDMMYYYY) format. You can use a regular expression to make the change quite easily:

  ```
  $date =~ s/(\d{4})(\d{2})(\d{2})/$2$3$1/;
  ```

  Again, it might be a good idea to store the original date string in an attribute, just to make processing easier.

- Modifying the structure. In the previous example, you created an XML file that conveniently ignores the ISBN information for the errata list—you don't need it because you already know you are dumping information about a specific book. You could also have changed the output to store the errata incidental data such as page number in an attribute, while placing the main content in the body of the element.

- You can make light work of multiple records and element groups within Perl and other languages. The nested structures supported by most scripting languages and the capability to walk easily through these structures—especially arrays and hashes—make the process even easier. Anything you can model in a nested structure in a scripting language can be dumped to XML.

- Most scripting languages can act as glue between another data source and XML. For example, using the DBI toolkit in Perl, you can communicate with Oracle, mSQL/mySQL, Informix, PostgreSQL, SQL Server, and even Excel spreadsheets and Comma Separated Values (CSV) text files.

XML to Database

Converting an XML structure back into records in a database is merely a matter of parsing the content and from that building a SQL or other database statement. You've already seen a number of different examples in this chapter that use this method to build queries into something that you can send to a SQL-compliant database.

The most important aspect of the process is taking the information and identifying the elements that should be transferred to the database. For example, with the book errata example, there are potentially two tables you could create from the data: the book table and the errata table. The two tables are also linked, in this case by ISBN number, which means adding further information to the errata entries. From the information you're given, you need to create three statements:

- The book data, which has the following basic template in SQL:

```
insert into mcslp_books values(isbn, code,
    title, releasedate)
```

- The two errata entries, including the ISBN number, producing a SQL statement that looks like this:

```
insert into mcslp_book_errata values(isbn,
    page, description)
```

For a more complex document, for example a contacts record in XML format, you'd end up with a number of different sequences of statements that would need to be created, including information about the addresses the person uses, phone, e-mail and other information, and any comments or notes for that person. All of these need to be linked, based on the information in the XML document.

The issues to look out for when converting XML documents back to a database are these:

- Get a record of any auto-generated ID numbers so that you can use those numbers to add other linked records to the database. When converting a contact document, for example, you'll want to create a unique ID for the contact, and you'll need that to add the other information for the contact to the database.

- Use regular expressions or other tricks to convert your XML tag data into the format required by your database.

- Remember when parsing that the order of fields in your XML data will not necessarily match the sequence defined in your database. Either cache the information and output it in the correct order or explicitly define field names and their data in your queries.

- Remember to quote the character data and attributes when posting. Using the DBI system, the `$dbh->quote()` function will automatically quote any data in the correct format for insertion into the database according to the DBD driver you are using.

Summary

XML is frequently seen as a method of storing data in an architecture- and platform-neutral format, but the focus often stays on data, not data about data. Everybody that uses a database of any kind will be familiar with the problem of recording the database structure.

You can use XML to store the database structure in an easy-to-use format that makes building the database on any platform much easier. First of all, you might need to turn an existing internal structure of arrays and hashes into an XML document. The same principles can be applied to any nested structure that you want to convert into XML easily.

Once you have the XML document that defines the database structure, a different tool can then be used to convert that XML structure into a series of statements used to create the tables in your database. The same principles can be used to convert an XML document into any other format, just by processing the document with a SAX parser.

You can use similar processes to convert a database description into XML format, and you can also convert a series of records within the individual tables into XML format.

CHAPTER 10

Applying SOAP/XML-RPC in Perl

As you already know if you've read the introductory material in Chapter 5, "Data Exchange and XML," XML-Remote Procedure Calls (XML-RPC) and Simple Object Access Protocol (SOAP) aren't really XML technologies, nor do we need to know how to parse or extract elements from XML documents to use them.

Instead, XML-RPC and SOAP are XML applications: They convert a function call on a client into a function call on a remote machine by using XML to describe the request to the server. Once the function has been executed, the whole process works in reverse, translating the response by the server into another XML document, in order to return the value to the client.

Remote procedures are nothing new; Unix has had RPC capability for years. More recently, many object technologies such as Common Object Request Broker Architecture (CORBA) and Distributed Common Object Model (DCOM) have also provided remote (or distributed) function calls. The difference is a common standard for making these operations work; both XML-RPC and SOAP are cross-platform and language compatible.

NOTE   Chapter 5 contains generic information on how XML-RPC and SOAP work and how they can support distributed services irrespective of the platform and language.

The Perl SOAP::Lite module provides both SOAP and XML-RPC functionality in the same module and hides all of the complexity of the technology behind a set of very simple functions. The Lite in the module's name refers to its ease of use and not its capabilities.

The module itself provides support for HTTP, HTTPS, CGI, TCP, FTP, SMTP, POP3, e-mail parsing, and traditional file-based transport methods for communicating remote requests. The module also provides methods for operating as a stand-alone network service, a CGI interface for providing info through an existing web server, and a mod_soap module to enable SOAP requests to be handled transparently through Apache and mod_perl extensions.

In this chapter were going to look at how to use SOAP::Lite to provide a distributed solution, using some of the XML technologies we've already seen elsewhere in this part of the book.

Introducing *SOAP::Lite*

All SOAP systems work on the same basic principle—you have a SOAP server, which replies to requests, mapping the function called by the client to a function within another module. You also have a SOAP client that makes the request in the first place.

With SOAP::Lite, the server side sets up a script that accepts the request over a given transport. That script then calls the function defined within a particular package—either internal or external to the server handler script—before supplying the return value from the function back to the caller.

For example, Listing 10.1 shows a very simple CGI-based server.

Listing 10.1   A Simple *SOAP::Lite* Server

```
#!/usr/local/bin/perl

use SOAP::Transport::HTTP;

SOAP::Transport::HTTP::CGI
    ->dispatch_to('/export/http/webs/test/','SOAP::Demo')
    ->handle();
```

The main line creates a new server handler object. The dispatch_to() method first specifies the location of the module tree that will be used to handle the client requests, and the second argument defines the name of the module that we'll accept and handle from the client. Finally, the handle() method passes off the processing to the module, calling the function requested by the client.

Note the name of the module that we've explicitly defined as being available to clients. The module is SOAP::Demo, and the handler will actually try to load the module /export/http/webs/test/SOAP/Demo.pm.

The client, shown in Listing 10.2, is equally brief.

Listing 10.2   A Simple *SOAP::Lite* Client

```
use SOAP::Lite;

print SOAP::Lite
    ->uri('http://test.mchome.pri/SOAP/Demo')
    ->proxy('http://test.mchome.pri/SOAP/request.cgi')
    ->getmessage()
    ->result;
```

The client creates a new SOAP::Lite object, calls the uri() method, the proxy() method, and the getmessage() method, and then accesses the result attribute of the object. Because this is part of a call to print, we'll be printing out the result.

The different components here are important, and we'll look at each item in detail:

- The uri() method defines the namespace. The namespace is the location of the module that provides us with the functions that we want to call. In this case, the URI refers to a remote machine (using HTTP) and the SOAP/Demo namespace. Observant readers will have noticed the similarity here with the name of the module defined in the server handler script.

- The proxy() method specifies the actual URL that will be used to send the request to the remote server. In this case, we're calling a script called request.cgi in the SOAP directory within the same server as our object.

- The getmessage() method is actually the name of the function on the remote server that we want to execute. The function is called within the confines of the remote namespace, which we already know is SOAP/Demo—therefore, the full expansion of the function that is called is SOAP::Demo::getmessage().

- The result is the return value from the remote function. The result attribute is actually an object and includes result and error information (if an error occurred). In this instance, we're going to assume that everything is working OK.

The final part of the puzzle is the module that provides the actual getmessage() function. The module is called Demo, and it's installed within the SOAP directory on our web server. You can see the module in Listing 10.3.

Listing 10.3   Our Remote Module

```
package SOAP::Demo;

sub getmessage
{
    return "Hello, world!\n";
}

1;
```

The module defines just a single function—the function getmessage(), which we know we want to call remotely. The package specification again is important here—it's SOAP::Demo, the same as the namespace we requested in the URI we requested in the client and also the same as the name of the module that we specified as available in the request handler.

To install these scripts on your own server:

1. Create a directory on your web server called SOAP.

2. Copy the request handler (seen in Listing 10.1) into the SOAP directory using the name request.cgi. Modify the directory argument to the dispatch_to() function to point to the Demo module.

3. Copy the remote module (seen in Listing 10.3) into the SOAP directory using the name Demo.pm.

4. Now modify the client (seen in Listing 10.2) to reflect the name of your server in both the uri() and proxy() methods.

TIP I use the .pri domain name extension on my servers to indicate the address is private (for example, the domain mchome.pri is unique to my LAN). The .pri extension is not officially recognized, but it is generally accepted as an alternative for use on internal networks that are not available on the Internet. The host could be public and available on the Internet, on your intranet with an official name, or as I've specified it here.

Once you've made all the modifications, you're ready to go. Execute the client and you should get a message:

```
% perl client.pl
Hello, world!
```

Success!

If the script doesn't appear to work, see the "Diagnosing Problems" section, later in this chapter.

How *SOAP::Lite* Works

If you've read Chapter 5, you'll already know how SOAP itself works. To recap, SOAP converts your request to execute a specific function within a specific module into an XML document. The document is then transferred over the transport mechanism to a remote request handler (in our case a request to a CGI handler on a website).

The XML document that is created makes up the SOAP request and contains the namespace, the function to be called, and any supplied parameters. In our case, it turns the request to execute `getmessage` into the SOAP envelope, shown in Listing 10.4.

Listing 10.4   **An XML-Encoded SOAP Envelope**

```
<?xml version="1.0" encoding="UTF-8"?>
   <SOAP-ENV:Envelope xmlns:SOAP-ENC =
              "http://schemas.xmlsoap.org/soap/encoding/"
   SOAP-ENV:encodingStyle =
              "http://schemas.xmlsoap.org/soap/encoding/"
   xmlns:xsi="http://www.w3.org/1999/XMLSchema-instance"
   xmlns:SOAP-ENV =
              "http://schemas.xmlsoap.org/soap/envelope/"
   xmlns:xsd="http://www.w3.org/1999/XMLSchema">
   <SOAP-ENV:Body>
      <namesp1:getmessage xmlns:namesp1 =
              "http: //test.mchome.pri/SOAP/Demo"/>
   </SOAP-ENV:Body>
</SOAP-ENV:Envelope>
```

In this example we were using standard CGI, so SOAP::Lite sends a POST request to the URL specified by the proxy() method in the client script.

The server CGI script extracts the XML document that was sent as part of the POST request and extracts the information it needs to execute the function. The value of the uri() method is encoded in the SOAP envelope body; this tells the request handler which module it should be looking for, along with the name of the function that we want to call.

SOAP::Lite then looks for the module/function (assuming that the request handler has been configured to accept the module and function combination), executes the function, and then serializes the response into another SOAP envelope to send back to the client.

SOAP Client Programming

SOAP is not limited to calling a simple function; you can pass arguments through to the remote function the same as you would call the function within a normal script. For example, we could change our getmessage() function so that we supply the name of the person we are greeting, as shown in this code:

```
my $request = SOAP::Lite
    ->uri('http://foodies.mchome.com/Foodies/Conversion')
    ->proxy('http://foodies.mchome.pri/request.cgi')
    ->greet('Martin');
```

You can also configure the client to automatically pass on calls to functions not identified locally to a remote request handler. In addition, we can use SOAP to access remote objects and their methods.

Explicit Calls

We've already seen examples of explicit calls, such as that in Listing 10.2. The example shows how to access a remote function directly by an explicit name. Explicit calls are great for scripts in which you call only one function.

Automatic Calls

SOAP::Lite also supports a facility called *autodispatch*. This mode uses the autoload mechanism to call a remote procedure automatically when the function name cannot otherwise be resolved. For example, we could change our explicit example from Listing 10.2 into an autodispatching client using the code in Listing 10.5.

Listing 10.5   **An Autodispatch Client**

```
use SOAP::Lite +autodispatch =>
    uri => 'http://test.mchome.com/SOAP/Demo',
    proxy => 'http://test.mchome.com/SOAP/request.cgi';

print getmessage();
```

The first benefit of autodispatch is that we can call remote functions just as if they were local. The second is that we can obtain their return values just as easily.

Autodispatch is also useful when you want to call a number of different remote functions within your code. The only problem with autodispatch is that if you get the function name wrong, you will be unable to trap that information in the script. See the section "Debugging *SOAP::Lite*," later in this chapter, for information on how to find and debug errors in your SOAP code.

Getting Multiple Return Values

When calling a function that returns multiple values, you need to extract the information differently. The `result()` method returns only the first value returned by the remote function. Further return values are accessible through the `paramsout()` method.

Because the return values are split across these two method calls, care needs to be taken when extracting the information. For example, the `convert_qty()` function accepts three arguments: the quantity, the measurement, and the destination measurement group (metric, imperial) that you want the value converted to. The function returns the converted quantity and measurement. You can see a modified client to handle multiple return values in Listing 10.6.

Listing 10.6   **A Client to Handle Multiple Return Values**

```
use SOAP::Lite;

my $request = SOAP::Lite
    ->uri('http://test.mchome.pri/SOAP/Conversion')
    ->proxy('http://test.mchome.pri/SOAP/request.cgi')
    ->convert_qty(1.5,'Kg','Imperial');

@res = $request->paramsout;
$result = $request->result;

if ($request->fault)
{
    printf("SOAP Error: %s: %s\n\t%s\n",
           $request->faultcode,
           $request->faultstring,
```

```
                $request->faultdetail);
}
else
{
    print "Result is: $result\n";
    print "Params are: ",join(', ',@res), "\n";
}
```

Because of this difference, you might want to standardize on returning a success value in the first argument and then returning the proper argument list in the remaining arguments that are accessible through the `paramsout()` attribute. That way you can always check the function/method return status with `result()` and all the real arguments from `paramsout()`.

The other alternative to handling multiple return values is to return an array or hash reference that then contains all the real values. For example:

```
sub getcontact
{
    # get contact information
    my $result = {'status' => 1,
                  'name' => 'Martin Brown',
                  'email' => 'mc@mcwords.com',
                  ...
                  };
    return $result;
}
```

Now when we get the return value from the `result()` method call, we have all the information we need without needing to call `paramsout()`.

Using Objects and Methods

SOAP was designed as an object access protocol to replace the many different distributed objects standards out there, so it seems a shame not to mention how we can use it to access objects.

Actually, object access is easy, especially if we use autodispatch. Listing 10.7 shows a request handler (with built-in support module) supporting an accounting system.

Listing 10.7   A SOAP Accounting Server

```
#!/usr/local/bin/perl

use SOAP::Transport::HTTP;

SOAP::Transport::HTTP::CGI
    ->dispatch_to('Account')
    ->handle();
```

```perl
package Account;

sub new
{
    my ($self,$name,$balance) = @_;
    my $class = ref($self) || $self;
    bless { balance => $balance,
            name => $name }, $class;
}

sub balance
{
    my $self = shift;

    return $self->{balance};
}

sub deposit
{
    my $self = shift;

    $self->{balance} += shift;
    return $self->{balance};
}

sub withdraw
{
    my $self = shift;

    $self->{balance} -= shift;
    return $self->{balance};
}
```

The client is shown in Listing 10.8. Note that, because we are using autodispatch, execution is identical to what we would normally use in a standard Perl script if using the module locally.

Listing 10.8   A SOAP Object Client

```perl
#!/usr/local/bin/perl
use SOAP::Lite +autodispatch =>
    uri => 'http://test.mchome.pri/Account',
    proxy => 'http://test.mchome.pri/accrequest.cgi';

my $current = Account->new('Current',1000);

print $current->deposit(1000);
```

Creating SOAP Servers

The `SOAP::Lite` module hides all of the complexity of building servers. It handles all of the communication, the serialization of your request into a SOAP envelope and, in the case of a request handler, the job of deserializing the envelope back into the information required to execute your desired function. As such, the request handlers are limited to controlling the location and/or definition of the module that the client is requesting to execute. However, that doesn't mean that we can't be flexible.

Dispatch Methods

The dispatch method passes off control to a function within a given package, but the location of the package does not have to be external, as in the examples we've already seen. You can pass control to an internal package.

The `dispatch_to()` method controls this interaction between what the client requests and which module is actually loaded and used (if necessary) and also acts as a control mechanism. The `dispatch_to()` method accepts any number of arguments, which can be in one of three forms:

- A directory, which is used to populate the `@INC` variable when importing external modules.

- A module name, which restricts client requests to any function within the specified module.

- A module and function definition, which restricts client requests to a specific function in a specific module. Alternatively you can specify a directory and a module name which restricts the request to specific module in a specific directory.

All three help to control access to a given module or function as requested by a client. For example, specifying the name of a module limits client requests to functions within that module. In practical terms, it leads to three main dispatch methods: the static internal, the static external, and the dynamic request handler. We can also create a mixture of those solutions by using a combination of those arguments.

Static Internal

The static internal form relies on creating a new package within your request handler. Static internal handlers are useful for stand-alone solutions when you need to support a SOAP service, but within a single file and without reliance on an external module. You can see a modified version of our simple Hello World script in Listing 10.9.

> **Listing 10.9**   **A Static Internal SOAP Request Handler**

```perl
#!/usr/local/bin/perl

use SOAP::Transport::HTTP;

SOAP::Transport::HTTP::CGI
    ->dispatch_to('SOAP::Demo')
    ->handle();

package SOAP::Demo;

sub getmessage
{
    return "Hello, world!\n";
}

1;
```

Static External

Static external handlers use dispatch_to to pass control to an external but named module
that is imported by the request handler explicitly via a normal use statement. An example is
shown in Listing 10.10.

> **Listing 10.10**   **A Static External SOAP Request Handler**

```perl
#!/usr/local/bin/perl

use SOAP::Transport::HTTP;

use SOAP::Demo;

SOAP::Transport::HTTP::CGI
    ->dispatch_to('SOAP::Demo')
    ->handle();
```

Static external request handlers are most useful when you want to restrict access to a particular external module that can be loaded safely from a generic location through the normal
@INC array of directories.

Dynamic

The dynamic model enables the client to specify the name of the module to be loaded
(through the uri method). It's up to the request handler only to define the location of the

modules that can be dynamically loaded to handle the client's requests. This allows a single request handler to support the requests for a number of clients using different modules. We've already seen an example of this; all that's required is to specify the directory location in the dispatch_to method, as shown in Listing 10.11.

Listing 10.11   **A Dynamic Request Handler**

```
#!/usr/local/bin/perl

use SOAP::Transport::HTTP;

SOAP::Transport::HTTP::CGI
    ->dispatch_to('/usr/local/lib/SOAP')
    ->handle();
```

Obviously the dynamic format passes the responsibility of calling the correct module on to the client; it also reduces the security aspect. The request handler has to a large extent been given free reign to the client to request any module available in the directory you configure. This has its advantages because we can use a single request handler to cope with all the requests for a multitude of different modules without ever needing to change the request handler.

NOTE   Dynamic dispatch actually zeros the content of @INC, replacing it entirely with the list of directories that you supply.

Mixed

The mixed format enables you to dynamically load modules from a specific directory and to explicitly preload external modules from the normal @INC variable. For example, the code in Listing 10.12 will dynamically load modules from /usr/local/lib/SOAP while loading the Contacts module from a directory in @INC.

Listing 10.12   **Mixed Mode Dispatching**

```
#!/usr/local/bin/perl

use SOAP::Transport::HTTP;

SOAP::Transport::HTTP::CGI
    ->dispatch_to('/usr/local/lib/SOAP','Contacts')
    ->handle();
```

SOAP Support Modules

The backend of any SOAP application and request handler is the module or function that it calls. Although there are not many differences between writing traditional modules, there are a few changes that you may need to make, along with some traps that you might want to watch out for:

- Modules do not need to export the functions explicitly. You do not need the services of Exporter, nor do you need to populate @EXPORT to provide access to the functions. Calls are made by the dispatcher using the explicit module and function/method name.

- All functions are called with at least one argument—the package (or namespace) used when the request was received from the client. For example, our greet() function is supplied with a single argument: SOAP::Demo.

- All further arguments to a function are supplied just as they are received from the client. For example, from the client call to the module Conversion and the function convert_qty(1.5, 'kg'), the server function receives ('Conversion', 1.5, 'kg').

- Return values from the server-side function remain the same. No additional information is added, but make sure that your client knows how to extract multiple-argument return values (see the section "Getting Multiple Return Values," earlier in this chapter).

In all other respects, any modules that you specifically create for use with SOAP can follow any of the traditional formats and rules that you probably are already using.

Migrating Existing Modules

The majority of modules and functions should be directly compatible with SOAP without too many modifications—after all, we are dealing only with functions that accept arguments and return values. However, therein lies a small trap: Functions called by a SOAP handler accept the class or module in which they were called as their first argument.

This extra initial argument leads to a small problem. If your module is one that you are already using in another local application, then the modifications that you make must be nondestructive.

There are two ways around this. The first is to modify your scripts to silently ignore the first argument if it contains the name of the module from a SOAP client. This is easy for some functions because they accept a specific number of arguments, and you can identify when there is one too many.

A more complex but much more practical solution is to create a glue module that supports the same functions but strips the first element. You use the glue module with the SOAP client. For example, to support an existing module called `Conversion` that provides a function `convert_qty()`, you'd create a glue module such as the one shown in Listing 10.13.

Listing 10.13   A Glue Module for Providing Access to an Existing Module

```perl
package SOAP::Conversion;

use Conversion;

sub convert_qty
{
    my $class = shift;
    return Conversion::convert_qty(@_);
}
```

Using a glue module not only solves the problems of that additional function argument, it will also enable you to customize the arguments you accept and the return structure, all without making any modifications to your existing module.

Debugging *SOAP::Lite*

Unfortunately, because of the complexity of the SOAP system, problems are notoriously difficult to diagnose and isolate. The problem could be related to how the function was called, how the server and dispatcher were configured, or a transport problem completely unrelated to the operation of SOAP itself. Something as simple as the wrong hostname could cause your SOAP client to fail.

Avoiding Problems

Prevention is always better than cure, so it's worth taking some time to look at the potential problems (and solutions) that many SOAP::Lite programmers encounter.

With SOAP::Lite, the important elements in the client and server process are

- The uri() method (as part of the client initialization), which defines the name of the module (including any parent modules/directories) that contains the function we want to execute.

- The proxy() method (as part of the client initialization), which defines the name of the request handler that will actually broker the function call.

- The dispatch_to() function and its arguments (in the request handler), which define the location of the modules to be called and the optional list of modules and functions that the handler is willing to process.

- The location and name of the module that you want to call as defined on the server side.

If any one of these elements is incorrect, your SOAP system will fail. In particular, make sure that you've correctly aligned the URI, the module registration in the request handler, and the name of the module itself.

For example, in our example system, the URI ends with SOAP/Demo, the package is SOAP::Demo, and the request handler accepts requests for the SOAP::Demo module. Requesting simply Demo in the client would cause the request to fail. If you execute the client program and don't get a valid response from the remote function, then it probably means one of these elements is wrong.

Diagnosing Problems

There are two possible solutions available for diagnosing. The first and most obvious is to use the facilities offered by SOAP::Lite to identify and highlight errors as part of any normal error-checking procedure. By default, all clients will die with a suitable message when an error occurs due to the transport, but they will do nothing if the function and/or module that you have called does not exist.

The second solution is to use the interactive SOAP shell to communicate with your remote proxy handler and submit requests to a remote function interactively.

Adding Error Checking

Error-handling information is held within the return value sent back by the remote function. The return value from the remote function call is actually an object that contains additional information about the success or failure of the result, as well as the actual result from the remote function. Up to now we've accessed only the actual function result, which is held in the result attribute.

If you change the client script shown in Listing 10.2 so that we access the object rather than the result directly, you can get more information about why the operation failed. You can see a modified version of the script in Listing 10.14.

Listing 10.14   **A Client Script with Error Checking**

```
use SOAP::Lite;

my $request = SOAP::Lite
    ->uri('http://test.mchome.pri/SOAP/Demo')
    ->proxy('http://test.mchome.pri/SOAP/request.cgi');

$result = $request->getmessage();

if ($result->fault)
{
    printf("SOAP Error: %s: %s\n\t%s\n",
            $result->faultcode,
            $result->faultstring,
            $result->faultdetail);
}
else
{
    print $result->result,"\n";
}
```

The `faultcode` always starts with a probable location for the error, such as `Client`, `Server`, and so on. The two most common problems are

- **Client: Failed to locate method (%s) in class (%s)**—You've tried to call a method that the request handler can't find in the module you've requested. This usually points to a typographical error in your client code.

- **Client: Failed to access class (%s)**—The class you've specified can't be found. Check that the URI the client has requested is valid and that the request handler has the correct directory configured for the class you are trying to access.

Because transport errors are raised by calling `die`, the only way to trap them reliably is to embed your remote function call in an `eval()`. The actual error message raised when the problem occurs will be that raised by the transport—when using HTTP or CGI transport, for example, you will have HTTP error codes returned. A full list of the different error codes can usually be found with your web server.

Examples of error codes include a 404, which indicates that you've probably specified the wrong `proxy` address, and a 403, which may indicate either a permission problem or incorrect permissions on the request handler. An HTTP error code 500 probably means that there's an error in the request handler—try running the handler locally.

The SOAP Shell

The SOAP shell is installed by SOAP::Lite and provides a shell-like interface to a SOAP request handler. The basic format of the command is

```
SOAPsh.pl proxy [uri [commands...]]
```

For example, we can try using our demo function by using

```
$ SOAPsh.pl http://test.mchome.pri/SOAP/request.cgi
➥http://test.mchome.pri/SOAP/Demo
Usage: method[(parameters)]
> getmessage()
--- SOAP RESULT ---
'Hello, world'


>
```

We could deliberately break our request handler by changing the dispatch location:

```
> getmessage
--- SOAP FAULT ---
SOAP-ENV:Client
Failed to access class (SOAP::Demo): Can't locate SOAP/Demo.pm in @INC
➥(@INC contains: /export/http/webs/test/OtherEx) at (eval 5) line 3.
```

Using XML-RPC

The SOAP::Lite package includes support for XML-RPC through the XMLRPC::Lite package. Users familiar with how SOAP::Lite works shouldn't have any difficulties developing XML-RPC–compliant clients and servers. As an example, Listing 10.15 shows an XML-RPC client.

Listing 10.15   An XML-RPC Client

```
use XMLRPC::Lite;

$remote =  XMLRPC::Lite
    -> proxy('http://test.mchome.pri/xml.cgi');

print $remote->call('greet', { username => 'Martin' })
    -> result;

print $remote->call('goodbye', 'Brown')
    -> result;
```

In essence, the mechanics of the two systems are identical. XMLRPC::Lite attempts to hide the complexities of XML-RPC as much as SOAP::Lite tries to hide the complexities of SOAP.

The proxy method specifies the URL that we want to use to send the request. In this instance, we're using a CGI host, but we can also use an HTTP daemon—just remove the reference to the CGI script. Also note that the URL is strictly the location of a server-side handling script—it bears no relation to any module at the receiving end.

Note as well that we use the call() method to specify the function to be called (the first argument, in this case greet) rather than naming the function directly as part of the call. This is less straightforward than the SOAP method, but it may be more practical when you know the function by its name and don't want to use soft references to execute the function.

The server script that will handle the requests is shown in Listing 10.16.

Listing 10.16   An XML-RPC Server Handle

```perl
#!/usr/local/bin/perl

use XMLRPC::Transport::HTTP;

my $server = XMLRPC::Transport::HTTP::CGI
    -> dispatch_to('methodName')
    -> handle;

BEGIN { @main::ISA = 'XMLRPC::Server::Parameters' }

sub methodName
{
    my $self = shift;
    my $method = $_[-1]->method;

    return $self->$method(@_);
}

sub greet
{
    shift if UNIVERSAL::isa($_[0] => __PACKAGE__);

    my ($params) = shift;

    $username = $params->{username};

    return "Hello $username";
}

sub goodbye
{
    shift if UNIVERSAL::isa($_[0] => __PACKAGE__);
```

```
    pop @_;

    return "Goodbye @_";
}
```

The most important point to notice from the server script is that the `dispatch()` method sends the request to a single, local function. In this case it's called `methodName`, but it could be any function. It's up to the `methodName` function to handle the requests, first extracting the name of the method that was called by the client, which is available in the `method` attribute of the supplied parameters. We then pass off control to the called function.

The second point to note is that we are not—indirectly or otherwise—passing control to an external module. The Perl SOAP implementation is designed to work with external modules; when a function is called, the handler executes the function from an external module. This is because the SOAP protocol itself was designed to work with classes and objects, which in Perl are better organized in separate modules. XML-RPC, on the other hand, is designed to execute a remote procedure, which could be defined locally or in an external module.

Where Next with *SOAP::Lite* and XML-RPC

SOAP and XML-RPC are XML applications—they use XML to exchange information between servers and clients about the remote function and arguments and to supply the return values. You can use XML-RPC and SOAP in any situation where you need to communicate with a remote server but don't want to produce your own protocol or rely on the features of another protocol.

We've only scratched the surface just to show you what SOAP and XML-RPC are capable of and, more importantly, what we can achieve using XML above and beyond the examples that we've already seen.

SOAP and XML-RPC projects and services are popping up all over the Internet right now, and it's easy to see that in a few years we'll be using the distributed offerings of SOAP and XML-RPC in the same way as we use traditional client/server solutions now. It'll certainly put an end to incompatibility problems when exchanging data between remote machines—part of the main focus of the XML protocol as a whole.

Check out the resources in Appendix B, "Resource Guide," for some examples of Internet-based SOAP and XML-RPC services. For compatibility with some of the examples we've seen in this chapter, check the other chapters that contain SOAP and XML-RPC examples in other languages.

Summary

We can communicate remotely with a Perl script by hosting it on a web server and sending and receiving requests. We could also do so through the use of a communications system such as Graham Barr's libnet bundle. However, neither method provides a simple solution to calling a remote function or object method over a network.

The SOAP and XML-RPC systems provide a more elegant solution to the problem. The SOAP::Lite module is one of the easiest to use of all the solutions we'll see in this book. It provides an almost transparent interface between a remote server and the client. In fact, when using the autodispatch mode, once you've specified in the client what server to communicate with, you'll never have to worry about explicitly executing a remote function again.

On the server side, SOAP::Lite also enables you to support access to all the modules in a directory, specific modules, and even specific functions. The system also supports the creation of objects and calling methods.

A less object-oriented approach, but one that is nonetheless still useful, is the XML-RPC solution supported by the XMLRPC module. The module provides support for both client and server XML-RPC solutions, but it requires much more care when setting up the client and server sides of the solution.

PART III

XML and Python

CHAPTER 11

XML Solutions in Python

- The *xmllib* Module

- Parsing Using Expat

- Parsing Using SAX

- Parsing Using DOM

Python's XML support is probably one of the most complex of the different solutions available, largely because of the way in which the different XML parsers have been developed. The original XML parsing system provided with Python 1.5.2 is called xmllib, and it comes as standard with all Python distributions. xmllib was developed on the same basis as the sgmllib module, which provides SGML parsing tools.

The xmllib parser is both a simple validation parser and an event-driven data parser that provides the base methods for you to use to parse an XML document. To use it, you need to create a new class that inherits from the xmllib module, providing the necessary methods to trap start and end tags, data sections, and entities.

Python 2.0 introduced a completely new hierarchy of modules and packages for developing with XML. The base xml package now includes xml.dom for processing using the DOM, xml.sax for providing an event-driven parser, and xml.parsers.expat for an interface to the generic Expat parser used by many other languages. In addition, the xmllib module is still available as part of the standard Python library, but its use and support have been deprecated in favor of the superior xml.sax package.

We'll be having a look at each of these systems briefly before we take a closer look at specific solutions in later chapters in this part of the book.

The *xmllib* Module

Python has had a long history of supporting parsers for HTML and SGML. Some four years ago a developer I know was using sgmllib in combination with a suite of custom tools to manage the technical documentation for QNX, Inc., a company that develops a real-time Unix-like operating system.

The only problem with Python's SGML support is that it is somewhat limited. In fact, the sgmllib module was designed to be able to support only enough of the SGML standard to be able to handle HTML. This prevented the use of document type definitions (DTDs) and many of the extensions used in SGML that make it attractive. However, it was possible to subclass the sgmllib parser to support the extensions and facilities needed.

The xmllib module is actually quite advanced—it tries to support the entire XML standard and while reading the document performs basic checks on the document structure. These include the basics of checking that the tags balance and that the document is based entirely on a single top-level element.

Unfortunately, xmllib has now been pushed aside in favor of xml.sax, which provides a more standardized event-drive method for parsing XML documents. This doesn't mean that xmllib is now useless, but you should probably avoid using it for production systems because it will no longer be updated in future Python releases.

For us, it's going to form the basis of understanding XML processing with Python before we concentrate on the Expat, SAX, and DOM solutions now recommended. They all work in a largely similar fashion, and xmllib's simplicity will help you understand how the other systems work.

Understanding *XMLParser*

The main part of xmllib is the XMLParser class. The class contains all of the methods required to parse a document, in addition to a series of methods designed to handle different XML content.

To create your own parser, you create a new class based on the XMLParser class, overloading the methods that identify the different elements you want to extract. For example, if you wanted to parse an XML document and identify start and end tags and any raw data, you would overload the unknown_starttag and unknown_endtag methods.

You can see a sample of a basic parser class in Listing 11.1. The resulting script parses the first XML document on the command line. Because we haven't defined any of the other methods, this script merely allows the xmllib parser to check the validity of the XML it's supplied.

Listing 11.1   **An Example of *XMLParser***

```
import xmllib,sys

# Create a new class from which we'll inherit the base
# methods and parser system we need
class MyParser(xmllib.XMLParser):

    # The instance creator - we need to manually
    # call the initiator for the parent class
    def __init__(self, filename=None):
        xmllib.XMLParser.__init__(self)
        if filename:
            self.loadfile(filename)

    # Load a file, based on the supplied filename
    # feeding the information to the XML parser
    def loadfile(self, filename):
        xmlfile = open(filename)
        while 1:
            data = xmlfile.read(1024)
            if not data:
                break
            self.feed(data)
        self.close()
```

```
# Get the first argument from the command line
try:
    filename = sys.argv[1]
except IndexError:
    print "You must supply a filename"
    sys.exit(1)

# Create a new MyParser instance and parse the
# file supplied on the command line
# We ignore EOFError's, which just indicate the
# end of file
# The xmllib.Error exception is raised by xmllib's
# parser when an error occurs
try:
    parser = MyParser(sys.argv[1])
except EOFError:
    pass
except xmllib.Error,data:
    print "There was an error in the XML:",data
    sys.exit(1)
except:
    print "Something went wrong"
    sys.exit(1)

# Assuming we haven't trapped an exception, then the
# XML has been validated
print "Everything appears to be fine"
```

The script works very simply: The `loadfile()` method opens a file and reads the contents, supplying each batch of information to the `feed()` method defined within the `xmllib` `.XMLParser` class. The `feed()` method passes on information directly to the actual parsing engine. The parsing engine uses regular expressions to extract XML tags and information from the source data stream.

Because we haven't overloaded any of the methods responsible for handling XML tags and data, nothing happens—although they are defined within the `XMLParser` class, their default operation is to do nothing.

Supply the script with a valid XML document and we get a message to the effect that everything is OK:

```
$ python exxmllib.py alien_r.xml
Everything seems fine
```

However, supply it with a badly formatted XML document and we get an error, trapped through the `xmllib.Error` exception raised by the parser:

```
$ python exxmllib.py faulty.xml
There was an error in the XML: Syntax error at line 3: missing end tags
```

Identifying XML Elements

To change the script to identify the different elements, we just need to overload the unknown_starttag() and unknown_endtag() methods for the start and end tags and the handle_data() method to handle the bare text data within the XML document. You can see an example of this in Listing 11.2.

Listing 11.2   **A Simple XML Parser Using** *xmllib*

```
import xmllib,sys

# Create a new class from which we'll inherit the base
# methods and parser system we need
class MyParser(xmllib.XMLParser):

    # The instance creator - we need to manually
    # call the initiator for the parent class
    def __init__(self, filename=None):
        xmllib.XMLParser.__init__(self)
        if filename:
            self.loadfile(filename)

    # Load a file, based on the supplied filename
    # feeding the information to the XML parser
    def loadfile(self, filename):
        xmlfile = open(filename)
        while 1:
            data = xmlfile.read(1024)
            if not data:
                break
            self.feed(data)
        self.close()

    # Called when a start tag is found
    def unknown_starttag(self, tag, attrs):
        print "Start: ",tag, attrs

    # Called when an end tag is found
    def unknown_endtag(self, tag):
        print "End:   ",tag

    # Called when raw data is found
    def handle_data(self, data):
        print "Data:  ",data

# Get the first argument from the command line
try:
    filename = sys.argv[1]
except IndexError:
    print "You must supply a filename"
    sys.exit(1)
```

```
# Create a new MyParser instance and parse the
# file supplied on the command line
# We ignore EOFError's, which just indicate the
# end of file
# The xmllib.Error exception is raised by xmllib's
# parser when an error occurs
try:
    parser = MyParser(sys.argv[1])
except EOFError:
    pass
except xmllib.Error,data:
    print "There was an error in the XML:",data
    sys.exit(1)
except:
    print "Something went wrong"
    sys.exit(1)

print "Everything seems fine"
```

Now, each time the parser identifies either a start tag, an end tag, or raw data, it calls the corresponding method. In our case, the methods just print out the information received (tag, attributes, or data). Now if we execute the script and supply it with an XML document, we get the following:

```
$ python exxmllib2.py simple.xml
Start:  simple {}
Data:

Start:  paragraph {}
Data:   and some data
End:    paragraph
Data:

End:    simple
Everything seems fine
```

Beyond *xmllib*

This concludes our brief look at xmllib. We probably won't be using xmllib again, but the basic principles shown here can also be followed for the Expat and SAX implementations we will be using. Use of xmllib is now deprecated in favor of the other systems.

However, the basics described here apply to the other solutions available in Python because they follow the same basic structure. The xmllib module is also a useful fallback if you need to support XML on production systems currently using Python 1.5.2 or 1.6.

Parsing Using Expat

Expat, as we've already seen in Chapter 6, "XML Solutions in Perl," is a non-validating XML parser written in C by James Clark. Like xmllib (and SAX), it's event driven, parsing individual XML constructs and using callbacks to initiate the processing of individual start and end tags and data portions.

To use Expat in Python, we need to import the xml.parsers.expat module. The module supports one main function, ParserCreate(), which creates an instance of the Expat parser that we can use to parse XML documents.

It's probably easiest to create a new class into which you put all the methods you need to use, including those that will be triggered when different XML constructs are seen. It's not a requirement, but it does keep the system nice and tidy. Unlike xmllib, however, we don't inherit the methods from the parent class but use them directly. Rather than overloading the methods to handle the different XML elements, we register the functions to the base parser.

For example, Listing 11.3 is a script that mimics our second xmllib example.

Listing 11.3   **An Expat Version of Our Simple XML Parser**

```
import xml.parsers.expat
import sys

# Create a new class to hold all the methods that
# we want to use when parsing an XML document
class MyParser:

    # Instance constructor. We create a new parser instance
    # which we hold locally in parser, then we register
    # the different methods which will handle the
    # XML elements
    def __init__(self, filename):
        self.parser = xml.parsers.expat.ParserCreate()
        self.parser.StartElementHandler = self.starttag_handler
        self.parser.EndElementHandler = self.endtag_handler
        self.parser.CharacterDataHandler = self.data_handler
        if filename:
            self.loadfile(filename)

    # Kills off and deletes the parser instance once the
    # processing of a given XML file is complete
    # To ensure we get rid of circular references we must
    # delete the parser reference
    def close(self):
        if self.parser:
            self.parser.Parse('',1)
            del self.parser
```

```
        # Hand off some data to the parser
        def feed(self, data):
            self.parser.Parse(data, 0)

        # Called when a start tag is found
        def starttag_handler(self, tag, attrs):
            print 'Start: ',repr(tag), attrs

        # Called when an end tag is found
        def endtag_handler(self, tag):
            print 'End:   ',repr(tag)

        # Called when a data portion is found
        def data_handler(self, data):
            print 'Data:  ',repr(data)

        # Load a file and supply the info to the parser
        def loadfile(self, filename):
            xmlfile = open(filename)
            while 1:
                data = xmlfile.read(1024)
                if not data:
                    break
                self.feed(data)
            self.close()


try:
    filename = sys.argv[1]
except IndexError:
    print "You must supply a filename"
    sys.exit(1)

try:
    parser = MyParser(sys.argv[1])
except xml.parsers.expat.ExpatError:
    print "Error in XML"
except:
    print "Some other error occurred"
```

If we use this on our sample document, we should get output similar to that in the xmllib example:

```
$ python exexpat.py simple.xml
Start:  u'simple' {}
Data:   u'\n'
Start:  u'paragraph' {}
Data:   u'and some data'
End:    u'paragraph'
Data:   u'\n'
End:    u'simple'
```

NOTE   The output differs slightly from that given by xmllib; that's because the Expat parser works with Unicode strings, rather than ASCII strings. We'll be looking more closely at how Python works with Unicode and how to encode and decode between Unicode strings and other types in Chapter 12, "Python and Unicode."

Parsing Using SAX

The Simple API for XML (SAX) interface was originally developed under Java, although interfaces now exist under most languages. Python 2 supports SAX version 2 (or more simply SAX2), and the interface is extensive. Python provides the basic interface to the SAX parser, an exception-handling system, a set of base classes for creating SAX handlers, and a low-level interface to the SAX system for building your own low-level SAX-based parsers.

SAX works by accepting a content handler class that you have previously created to handle the different elements. The method is similar in principle to Expat, except that the class you create is entirely devoted to supporting the handler methods for the different elements. SAX handles all of the data reading and feeding of the information to the parser.

Keeping with the basic theme for the moment, Listing 11.4 is a script that uses SAX to output the start and end tags from a sample file.

Listing 11.4   A Simple SAX Parser

```python
from xml.sax import make_parser
from xml.sax.handler import ContentHandler

# Define a new content handler class, the defined methods
# will be triggered when the individual elements
# are found in the XML document
class FindStartEnd(ContentHandler):
    def __init__(self):
        pass
    def startElement(self, name, attrs):
        print 'Start: ', name, attrs
    def endElement(self, name):
        print 'End:   ', name

# Make a new parser
parser = make_parser()
```

```
# Create a new handler instance based on our class
sehandler = FindStartEnd()

# Set up the content handler for using our handler
parser.setContentHandler(sehandler)

import sys

try:
    xmlfile = open(sys.argv[1])
except:
    print "You must supply the name of the file to parse"
    sys.exit(1)

# We pass off the name of the file to the parsing engine
parser.parse(xmlfile)
```

Aside from not printing out our data sections, the output from this script is identical to the previous examples. Also note that we no longer have to supply the data in discrete segments to the parser: The SAX interface opens a file by name and handles all of the reading internally.

Because of the way SAX works, it's ideally suited to situations where we want to pick out specific elements while processing a document. For example, we can install triggers to identify specific tags and/or data sections in a simpler way than offered by the DOM techniques we'll see in the next portion of this chapter.

SAX can also be a great way of serializing documents into another format because we can act on each element as it's extracted from the original XML source. We'll be looking at some examples of using SAX in this way in Chapter 14 and again in Chapter 15, "Applying SOAP/XML-RPC in Python," as part of our look at the Python SOAP and XML-RPC solutions.

Parsing Using DOM

The Document Object Model (DOM) allows you to model an XML document as a tree structure. In fact, the entire document is accessible as a series of objects, and by following the branches of the tree, you can traverse the entire document. Because we are representing the XML document in one piece, we can use DOM both to parse existing documents and to create new documents.

The only problem with using DOM is that it stores the entire document in memory. For the small documents we're working with here, this won't be a problem, but a 512KB document may require up to five times that amount when it's stored internally as a DOM object.

Of course, in Python we don't have to worry about allocating the memory, but that also means that we run the risk of using large quantities of memory without realizing it.

Under Python the DOM interface is based on the IDL version of the specification released by W3C. The standard Python 2.x distribution comes with a basic DOM parsing system, called `minidom`, and a more complex `pulldom` system that extracts individual elements from a DOM tree without having to read the entire XML document into memory.

Because of Python's flexible object system, it's very easy to create an equivalent of the tree structure that an XML document mirrors within a Python object. Coupled with the easy object-handling features (especially when working with dictionaries and lists), we have a good platform for handling XML documents.

Using *minidom*

To parse an existing XML document into a DOM object using `minidom`, you need to call either the `parse()` method, which accepts a filename or file object and processes the contents, or `parseString()`, which parses a bare string of information that you may have read separately from a file or network connection. In fact, it's as easy as this:

```
from xml.dom.minidom import parse, parseString

# Parse a bare string as XML

stringdoc = parseString('<para>Some text</para>')

# Parse a file object

xmlfile1 = open('myfile.xml')
filedoc = parse(xmlfile1)

# Parse a file directly

filedoc = parse('myfile.xml')
```

Once you've converted the XML stream into a DOM object, you can then access the individual tags by name. For example, suppose that we've modeled a client's bank accounts in XML, as shown in Listing 11.5.

Listing 11.5   **A Sample Account Record**

```
<client>
<clientname>Martin Brown</clientname>
<account>
    <accname>Checking</accname>
    <provider>HSBC</provider>
```

```
<balance>$4567.00</balance>
<transaction>
    <payee>Rent</payee>
    <amount>$280.00</amount>
    <freq>Monthly</freq>
</transaction>
<transaction>
    <payee>Time Subscription</payee>
    <amount>$26.00</amount>
    <freq>Quarterly</freq>
</transaction>
</account>

<account>
    <accname>VISA</accname>
    <provider>Morgan Dean Stanley Witter</provider>
    <balance>$-3485.00</balance>
    <transaction>
        <payee>Supermarket</payee>
        <amount>$-450.00</amount>
    </transaction>
    <transaction>
        <payee>Gas Station</payee>
        <amount>$-18.00</amount>
    </transaction>
</account>
</client>
```

The document could be represented as a tree structure, as shown in Figure 11.1. We'll be using this diagram to help us understand how Python's DOM implementation works.

FIGURE 11.1:

An XML tree

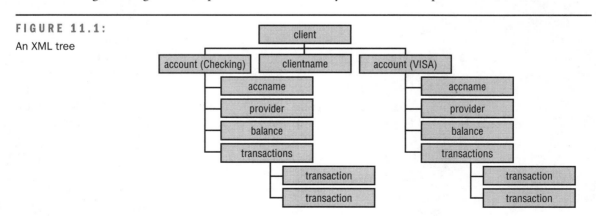

We could get the name of the client who owns the account information using Listing 11.6.

Listing 11.6   **Extracting Content from an XML Document Using** *minidom*

```
from xml.dom.minidom import parse

# Create a function to get the data between XML tags
# Information is held in nodes (discrete blocks)
# which we'll need to concatenate together to get the
# full picture. We only need to add text nodes to the
# string
def getdata(nodes):
    rc = ''
    for node in nodes:
        if node.nodeType == node.TEXT_NODE:
            rc = rc + node.data
    return rc

# Parse the document
client = parse('client.xml')

# Get the first clientname tag from the document
clientname = client.getElementsByTagName("clientname")[0]

# Print out the data contained within the tags
# using getdata to extract the text from the nodes
# defined within the element
print 'Client name is', getdata(clientname.childNodes)
```

The getElementsByTagName() method returns a list of *all* the tag elements with the supplied name. The resulting objects contain the information about the tag, including any attributes if supplied, and a set of nodes that make up the data contained within the tags.

Note that the object returned by getElementsByTagName() is a branch (or leaf) of the tree structure shown in Figure 11.1. The root of the tree is the first (root) tag within the document—so to access all the elements within the XML document, we'd have to access the client branch. From that base, we can then access the other elements. For example, to extract the data from the clientname branch, we must refer to the branch in reference to its parent, the client branch. Further branches and leaves are referenced in the same way, relative to their parent branches.

Had we used this:

```
accounts = client.getElementsByTagName("account")
```

The accounts object would now be a list containing the two account branches. Each element would refer to one of the account branches in our diagram. To get a list of the transactions within the checking account, we could have used this:

```
checking = accounts[0]
trans = checking.getElementsByTagName("transaction")
```

Now `trans` would contain the information in the two transactions in our account. Each element would be one of the transaction branches.

DOM in Action

To put all of this into practice, Listing 11.7 is a script that uses DOM to generate a simple list of accounts and transactions for a given client. The script is actually a good example of a tree-based XML parser in Python. Because we're not following the tree sequentially, we can be a little less restrictive about how we extract information: We don't have to worry about recording states or determining whether the output format should change because we've reach a particular end tag.

Listing 11.7   **Using _minidom_ to Summarize an XML Document**

```python
from xml.dom.minidom import parse

def getdata(nodes):
    rc = ''
    for node in nodes:
        if node.nodeType == node.TEXT_NODE:
            rc = rc + node.data
    return rc

def handleclient(client):
    clientname = client.getElementsByTagName("clientname")[0]
    print 'Client:', getdata(clientname.childNodes)
    accounts = client.getElementsByTagName("account")
    handleaccounts(accounts)

def handleaccounts(accounts):
    print 'Accounts:'
    for account in accounts:
        handleaccount(account)

def handleaccount(account):
    accname = account.getElementsByTagName("accname")[0]
    provider = account.getElementsByTagName("provider")[0]
    print ' ' * 4, '%s (%s)' % (getdata(accname.childNodes),
                                getdata(provider.childNodes))
    print ' ' * 4, 'Transactions:'
    trans = account.getElementsByTagName("transaction")
    for transaction in trans:
        handletransaction(transaction)
    balance = account.getElementsByTagName("balance")[0]
    print ' ' * 9, '%-40s %s' % ('', '======')
    print ' ' * 9, '%-40s %s' % ('', getdata(balance.childNodes))
    print ''
```

```
def handletransaction(transaction):
    payee = transaction.getElementsByTagName("payee")[0]
    amount = transaction.getElementsByTagName("amount")[0]
    print ' ' * 9, '%-40s %s' % (getdata(payee.childNodes),
                                  getdata(amount.childNodes))

client = parse('client.xml')

handleclient(client)
```

If we run this script on our client XML document, we get the following output:

```
$ python exdom2.py
Client: Martin Brown
Accounts:
        Checking (HSBC)
        Transactions:
                Rent                                    $280.00
                Time Subscription                       $26.00
                                                        ======
                                                        $4567.00


        VISA (Morgan Dean Stanley Witter)
        Transactions:
                Supermarket                             $-450.00
                Gas Station                             $-18.00
                                                        ======
                                                        $-3485.00
```

We could have just as easily converted this document into HTML or XHTML or extracted the information easily for writing into the individual tables of a database.

Building XML Documents with DOM

You can write XML documents just by including the necessary `print` or similar statement in your script, but it relies on generating the tags in the correct order and structure and ensuring that they are matched up. Although this is not an impossible task, it does add extra levels of complexity to the process.

Simple serialization from one format into XML is easy if the information is in sequence and you convert directly into an XML document following the same structure. But what happens if you need to add new branches within the existing structure, or the definition of the XML document requires you to organize the information into a given structure that doesn't match your source material?

The immediately obvious solution is either to separately model the incoming data into a more suitable format before translating it to XML or to cache information into one or more objects and dump them at appropriate times. Neither solution is infallible, and both are entirely reliant on getting the information correctly and in the order you expect in the first place.

A much better solution is at hand, though. The Document Object Model specification is really just a method for modeling XML documents within the confines of a programming language or other system. Up to now, we've used the system only to model an external XML document into an internal tree to extract information.

We can also use DOM to build an XML document by creating the branches and leaves of the document. Because DOM is not a sequential system such as SAX or Expat, we can add new branches and leaves to any part of the document without making modifications to the XML document in its raw text format.

The `xml.dom.minidom` module supports a very simple interface for adding new XML tags and data to an XML document. For a quick example, see Listing 11.8, which adds both a text block and a tag to a previously parsed XML string.

Listing 11.8 **Rebuilding an XML Document**

```
from xml.dom.minidom import parseString

dom = parseString('<title></title>')
root = dom.documentElement
nelem = dom.createElement("separator")

root.insertBefore(nelem, None)
cdata = dom.createTextNode("The New Avengers")
root.insertBefore(cdata, nelem)
print root.toxml()
```

The start of the process is to create the equivalent of the blank root document as a DOM object by using the `parseString()` function to parse a string in XML format into an object.

Then we get the root of the document and create a new element, "separator." The `insert-Before()` method in our document then inserts the element according to its reference location. In this case, we're inserting the element with reference to `None`, which will insert the tag between the root `title` tags in our original XML string. The `createTextNode()` method creates a new block of text that we'll insert before the element we just created.

Finally, the `toxml()` method returns the entire DOM structure as an XML string that we print out. Executing the script gives us a very simple document in return:

```
$ python dombuild.py
<title>The New Avengers<separator/></title>
```

Although this is simplistic, it demonstrates how easy it is to insert new tags and text data anywhere within a given DOM tree. The process of converting XML data to or from an alternative source will be a recurring topic. XML is not the ideal format for all situations, so we'll be returning to the DOM system in Python in later chapters.

Summary

XML processing in Python is relatively easy. Once you've selected the type of processing that you want to use, it's then a simple case of importing, or in some cases inheriting from, the supporting module. From then on, sequential parsing involves handing off the XML document data and supplying it to the data input of the class we're using.

The `xmllib` module is not the ideal module any longer, but it is the only solution available if you want to guarantee support for older versions of the Python interpreter. For the ultimate in XML parsing in a sequential format, the best solution is the Expat parser, a standard part of the Python distribution since version 2. Expat offers a familiar event-based interface that is supported by a number of different languages.

For more advanced event-based parsing, you should use the SAX parser. Python's SAX module works identically to the Expat and `xmllib` systems, so migration to SAX should not be difficult. The benefit of SAX is that it is a standard agreed upon by the XML standards group, so we can pass information and events both to Python and other language interfaces.

The more flexible option is to use the DOM system. This uses SAX as the base parser to build the DOM object, but once we have the XML document in DOM format, we have more freedom about how to access the tags and data within. We can access elements in the document by name, and if necessary we can also replace and even rebuild parts of the document without having to manipulate any text.

## CHAPTER 12

Python and Unicode

- Creating Unicode Strings

- Translating Unicode

- Accessing the Unicode Database

As part of the major update that brought much wider support for XML—including a native interface to the Expat parser—Python 2.0 also brought extensive Unicode support. In addition to the capability to introduce Unicode and raw Unicode strings, Python now also includes facilities for encoding and decoding Unicode and the translation of Unicode characters.

In addition, most of the core modules are also Unicode compliant, so you can execute regular expressions, character manipulations, and other translations using Unicode character strings without needing to resort to a special collection of Unicode functions.

In this chapter we're going to look at how to work with Unicode strings in Python, including creating Unicode and translating it between different formats, as well as methods for looking up Unicode characters and even creating your own Unicode encoder. Armed with this information, you should be able to handle Unicode data within Python and know how to format and encode the information for display or storage.

Creating Unicode Strings

Rather than supporting Unicode strings natively—as supported by Perl—Python instead supports a new data type: Unicode strings. You can create a new Unicode object by prefixing a string with the letter u, in the same way that you introduce raw strings. For example:

```
>>> u'Hello World'
u'Hello World'
>>> u'Hello\0020World'
u'Hello World'
```

To include special (non-native) characters into the Unicode object, use the Unicode escape, \u. This introduces the character according to the supplied hexadecimal value. In the previous example, we introduced the Unicode character with the hexadecimal value of 20—the space character, which as you can see has been interpreted accordingly in our example. Here's another example, this time inserting a lower case *o* with a stroke or slash (in other words, ø) into a Unicode string:

```
message = u'J\u00f8rgensen'
```

All other characters are converted according to the Latin-1 encoding. See the section "Translating Unicode," later in this chapter, for information on translating a Unicode string to another format. Note that on platforms and systems that support it, the Unicode string conversion will also translate non-ASCII characters into Unicode. For example, on a Mac, introducing accented and other foreign characters is a built-in part of the operating system, so we can insert these characters directly into a u-prefixed string:

```
>>> u'øåé'
u'\xbf\x8c\x8e'
```

To introduce a raw Unicode string, use the ur prefix when creating the Unicode object. For example:

```
>>> ur'Rikke\u0020J\u00f8rgensen'
u'Rikke J\u00f8rgensen'
```

Raw Unicode strings work in the same way as their raw string cousins—they exist to enable us to introduce strings that may contain information that we don't want translated or interpreted. As with raw strings, this is especially useful when using Unicode strings within regular expressions. In these instances, Unicode escape sequences are interpreted only when there is an off number of backslashes in front of a small u character. You can see this more clearly in the following:

```
>>> ur'\\u0020'
u'\\\\u0020'
>>> ur'\u0020'
u' '
>>> u'\\\u0020'
u'\\\\ '
```

Obviously, as we've already seen, the old xmllib module in Python extracts only raw text—it's not Unicode compliant. However, the new SAX, DOM, and Expat interfaces all support Unicode extraction. In the case of Expat and SAX, the information is returned in the form of Unicode objects.

Translating Unicode

Most of the time, you'll probably be parsing content in Unicode. It's unlikely that you'll want to deal with Unicode objects all of the time when working with data from an XML document.

At the most basic level, you can mix and match Unicode and normal Python string sequences, but the result will always be another Unicode object. For example:

```
>>> 'Hello ' + u'Miss J\u00f8rgensen'
u'Hello Miss J\xf8rgensen'
```

To convert a Unicode object back into a normal ASCII (7-bit) string, use the built-in str() function:

```
>>> str(u'Hello World')
'Hello World'
```

Be careful, however, with Unicode strings that are not ASCII compatible. The str() function will raise an error if you try to convert a string that contains non-ASCII characters. For example:

```
>>> greet=u'Miss J\u00f8rgensen'
>>> str(greet)
Traceback (most recent call last):
  File "<stdin>", line 1, in ?
UnicodeError: ASCII encoding error: ordinal not in range(128)
```

Note that this applies however you access the string, even when extracting characters from a Unicode string individually. For example, the following code will still raise an error:

```
for char in u'Miss J\u00f8rgensen':
    print char,
```

NOTE   Errors in encoding and/or decoding strings raise a UnicodeError exception, which can be trapped in the same way as any other exception. The exception supplies the error message as the only argument.

Encoding to Unicode Formats

ASCII is not the most useful of formats. You can translate a Unicode string into one of a number of different using encode(). encode() changes the encoding used to represent the Unicode object directly into another character set, such as Latin-1 or UTF-8. The method takes a single argument—the encoding type that you want to translate the Unicode string to. In fact, the encode() method is what is called when the str() built-in function is used on a Unicode object, supplying the encoding type as ASCII.

Latin-1 encoding, which supports the first 256 characters provided in the 8-bit ASCII table, can be used for most string representations, such as our earlier example:

```
>>> greet = u'Rikke J\u00f8rgensen'
>>> greet.encode('latin-1')
'Rikke Jørgensen'
```

Reproduction of that onscreen will of course rely on you having a font, application, and OS that adhere to the Unicode standard!

A classic example here is the Mac OS, which doesn't directly support the Unicode standard. To get the same effect when writing to a standard Mac document or to the screen, you'll need to use mac-roman encoding.

The `encode()` method can also be used to encode your Unicode object into one of the native Unicode encoding formats, such as UTF-8 or UTF-16. For example, to encode our sample string, you'd use the following:

```
>>> greet.encode('utf-8')
'Rikke J\xc3\xb8rgensen'
>>> greet.encode('utf-16')
'\xfe\xff\x00R\x00i\x00k\x00k\x00e\x00
~CA\x00J\x00\xf8\x00r\x00g\x00e\x00n\x00s\x00e\x00n'
```

Decoding to Unicode Formats

To translate an encoded string back into its Unicode format (that is, to reverse `encode()`), you need to use the built-in `unicode()` function. This was introduced with Python 2.0. The function accepts two basic arguments: The first is the bytestream that you want to decode, and the second is the format that you want it decoded into. For example, we can decode `Rikke Jørgensen` from Mac-Roman format into a Unicode string using the following:

```
>>> unicode('Jørgensen','mac-roman')
u'J\xf8rgensen'
```

The return type is a Unicode object. Be aware that `unicode()` decodes a string object into its Unicode version using the format you supply—use the wrong format and you end up with the wrong Unicode object. For example, decode `Jørgensen`, sourced from a Mac document using Latin-1 encoding, and you get a different Unicode string:

```
>>> unicode('Jørgensen','latin-1')
u'J\xbfrgensen'
```

We can also use `unicode()` to translate directly from one encoding into another. The UTF-8 stream of `Jørgensen`, for example, can be translated straight into UTF-16 using this:

```
>>> unicode('Miss J\xc3\xb8rgensen','utf-16')
```

The error string is used by the codecs to translate Unicode characters to determine how the encoding and errors should be handled. The actual error strings and their effects are dependent on the codec that you are using, but there are some standard strings supported by the translation system.

Using `strict` causes the translation to fail, irrespective of what the problem was. Using `ignore` allows the translation to continue, removing any special characters within encoded string, such as the following:

```
>>> unicode('Jørgensen','utf-8','ignore')
u'Jrgensen'
```

In this case the 'ø' character cannot be translated from the local character set (`mac-roman` in this case) to `utf-8`. The `'ignore'` tells the Unicode system to ignore any characters that it can't convert, essentially deleting the character from the resulting string.

To replace an unknown character with a character that the codec thinks may be suitable, use an error string of `replace`. Python will use the official \uFFFD replacement character as defined by the codec being used.

Unicode and XML in Python

The most important consideration to make when working with an XML document is that the extracted data will be in Unicode format. The basic `xmllib` module that we've already seen does not support Unicode strings. But the new SAX and DOM interfaces for XML parsing do.

Unicode support in XML affects everything from the tag and attribute names to character data. In particular you'll need to take care when comparing strings hard-coded within your scripts—such as within a dictionary when formatting or translating an XML document—and when used within regular expressions.

For example, when using a dictionary that contains a tag name, make sure that the name is specified as a Unicode string using `u''`. This will ensure that when a comparison is made, the comparison is between two Unicode strings and not a normal string and the `str()` representation of the Unicode extracted from the XML file.

Also remember if you are displaying XML information on-screen that you almost certainly need to convert the string using the `encode()` method into a suitable online version. Most displays support either the Latin-1 or Mac-Roman format. See Appendix A for a list of the different formats.

Remember as well that the process goes both ways—when storing information that has been entered by the user, it'll need to be converted into a UTF-8 or UTF-16 format for storage in an XML file.

Translating Character Numbers

The `ord()` built-in function will return the number that represents a particular character. The function is Unicode aware, so we can get the Unicode number for a character like this:

```
>>> ord('ø')
191
```

To translate that back into a Unicode character, however, we need to use the `unichr()` function rather than the `chr()` function:

```
>>> unichr(191)
u'\xbf'
```

As you can see, this returns a single-character Unicode object.

Accessing the Unicode Database

Occasionally you may want to access a character in the Unicode database with a description, rather than with a character number. This can be particularly useful if you want to introduce a particular character from its on-screen encoding into its Unicode format from within an application.

The `unicodedata` module provides a direct interface to the Unicode database as defined by the data file released by the Unicode consortium.

To look up a Unicode character by its description, use the `lookup()` function. For example, to determine the Unicode character for the Greek capital letter pi (Π):

```
>>> import unicodedata
>>> unicodedata.lookup('Greek capital letter pi')
u'\u03a0'
```

To get the Unicode name for a specific Unicode character, use the `name()` function:

```
>>> unicodedata.name(u'\u03a0')
'GREEK CAPITAL LETTER PI'
```

Writing Your Own Codec

The `unicode()` function and the `encode()` method use the `codecs` module, which is part of the standard library. The `codecs` module provides the base classes required to translate between the different formats, but a separate set of modules within the `encodings` directory in the Python standard library does the actual work.

For example, when you select to translate to Mac-Roman format, it's the `mac_roman` module within the `encodings` directory that does the actual work.

Python comes with a standard set of codecs for working with the majority of encoding formats supported by Python. However, there may be times when you want to add an encoding system to support a new language or format. We can also use the encoding system to provide custom encodings, which can be useful if you want to convert specific characters to your own sequences when displaying Unicode strings on-screen.

You can write your own codec by creating a new module. It needs to import the `codecs` module, and you then need to define a `Codec` class that should inherit from the `codecs.Codec` class. The `Codec` class should include two methods: `encode()` and `decode()`. The easiest way to implement these two methods is to use the `charmap_encode()` function and `charmap_decode()` functions within the `codecs` module.

Both these accept a character map—a dictionary that maps the character to encode or decode to or from. For example, look at the following extract from the `mac_roman.py` module.

```
{
    0x0080: 0x00c4, # LATIN CAPITAL LETTER A WITH DIAERESIS
    0x0081: 0x00c5, # LATIN CAPITAL LETTER A WITH RING ABOVE
    0x0082: 0x00c7, # LATIN CAPITAL LETTER C WITH CEDILLA
    0x0083: 0x00c9, # LATIN CAPITAL LETTER E WITH ACUTE
    0x0084: 0x00d1, # LATIN CAPITAL LETTER N WITH TILDE
    0x0085: 0x00d6, # LATIN CAPITAL LETTER O WITH DIAERESIS
    0x0086: 0x00dc, # LATIN CAPITAL LETTER U WITH DIAERESIS
    0x0087: 0x00e1, # LATIN SMALL LETTER A WITH ACUTE
...
}
```

If you are updating an existing dictionary, use the `make_identity_dict()` function in the `codecs` module. This creates a base dictionary according to the range you supply. For example, to match the standard 256-character 8-bit ASCII map, you would use this:

```
decoding_map = codecs.make_identity_dict(range(256))
```

You can then merge your updated map dictionary using the `update()` method:

```
decoding_map.update({
    0x0080: 0x00c4, # LATIN CAPITAL LETTER A WITH DIAERESIS
    0x0081: 0x00c5, # LATIN CAPITAL LETTER A WITH RING ABOVE
...
})
```

Remember that you'll need two maps: one for the encoding and one for the decoding. Assuming the two translations are opposites of each other (that is, an encode/decode pass on a string should return the original string), then you can create the opposite map using this:

```
encoding_map = {}
for k,v in decoding_map.items():
    encoding_map[v] = k
```

Going back to our `encode()` and `decode()` methods, using the map we've just created, we can define those methods like this:

```
class Codec(codecs.Codec):
    def encode(self,input,errors='strict'):
        return codecs.charmap_encode(input,
                                     errors,
                                     encoding_map)

    def decode(self,input,errors='strict'):
        return codecs.charmap_decode(input,
                                     errors,
                                     decoding_map)
```

Your codec will also need to define the `StreamWriter` and `StreamReader` classes. These are used by the `codecs` module to read and write specific data stream types and convert them into a suitable character format. You probably won't need this for simple Unicode translations, so we can dummy-define them:

```
class StreamWriter(Codec,codecs.StreamWriter):
    pass

class StreamReader(Codec,codecs.StreamReader):
    pass
```

The final step in creating your codec is to register your code with the `codecs` module, which you do by defining a `getregentry()` function. This should return a four-element tuple containing the `encode()` and `decode()` methods from our class, and the `StreamReader` and `StreamWriter` classes. In our case, this produces a definition like this:

```
def getregentry():
    return (Codec().encode,
            Codec().decode,
            StreamReader,
            StreamWriter)
```

After you've created your codec, drop the module into the `encodings` directory. The codec is ready to use.

Here's a complete codec example that performs the relatively useless operation of translating *a* characters into *e* characters and vice versa:

```
import codecs

# Create our Codec class

class Codec(codecs.Codec):
    def encode(self,input,errors='strict'):
        return codecs.charmap_encode(input,
                                     errors,
                                     encoding_map)

    def decode(self,input,errors='strict'):
        return codecs.charmap_decode(input,
                                     errors,
                                     decoding_map)

class StreamWriter(Codec,codecs.StreamWriter):
    pass

class StreamReader(Codec,codecs.StreamReader):
    pass
```

```
# Register ourselves with the codec module:

def getregentry():
    return (Codec().encode,
            Codec().decode,
            StreamReader,
            StreamWriter)

# Create our decode and encoding maps

decoding_map = codecs.make_identity_dict(range(256))
decoding_map.update({
    0x0041: 0x0045,
    0x0061: 0x0065,
    0x0045: 0x0041,
    0x0065: 0x0061,
})

encoding_map = {}
for k,v in decoding_map.items():
    encoding_map[v] = k
```

I've called this codec `'mcb'` and put it into the file `mcb.py` in the `encodings` directory within the standard Python library directory. If I start up Python, I can try it out:

```
>>> unicode('ae','mcb')
u'ea'
>>> u'ae'.encode('mcb')
'ea'
```

Summary

Python's Unicode is largely transparent—we can create, merge, and manipulate Unicode strings natively within Python without the need for any additional modules or functions. Unicode information can be stored within a special Unicode string. This both provides the capability to store Unicode characters and has built-in methods for converting the built-in strings into different Unicode standards such as UTF-8 and UTF-16.

For more in-depth conversion and translation, use the standard `unicodedata` module, which provides named access to individual characters within the Unicode database. For conversions, the built-in `unicode()` function enables you to create strings in different encodings and translate strings to different encodings. You can even create your own conversion modules for translating characters.

## CHAPTER 13

Generating and Parsing XML Documents with Python

- Parsing with SAX

- Using `xmlproc` for Validation

Python supports a number of different systems for parsing and working with XML documents. The entire system is supported under the Python XML package (PyXML for short) and is classed as a separate, but significant, project managed and run by some of the members of the main Python development team.

PyXML includes a validating XML parser, SAX and DOM interfaces, and an interface to the ever-present Expat parser, along with an interface for working with and generating SGML documents and fragments from an XML document base.

However, despite all the different aspects of the PyXML package, it is still considered a work in progress. There's much you can do with the implementation so far, but some aspects don't work correctly and are incredibly unpolished, and much of the system is lacking any real documentation. Work is progressing as this chapter is being written, and the best place to go for information is the PyXML page at SourceForge (`http://pyxml.sourceforge.net`).

In this chapter, we'll take a look at the Python implementation of SAX, with a closer look at the error handling system. We'll also look at the xmlproc parser, which can be used to validate XML documents by ignoring the typical errors that are raised during parsing, and which even includes ready made scripts for just that purpose. For more information and some examples on parsing using DOM, see Chapter 14, "Converting XML Documents Using Python."

Parsing with SAX

The Simple API for XML (SAX) is a standard and consistent interface across all the different implementations. If you can follow the Perl examples given in earlier chapters, beyond the obvious Perl/Python differences, you should be able to easily transfer your software to and from Perl or any other language implementation.

In Python, the SAX handler works through the `xml.sax` package. The package includes a number of modules that handle different aspects of the process. What actually happens is that you first create a generic parser instance by calling `saxexts.make_parser()`.

The parser must then be configured with different handler instances to handle content, DTDs, entities, and errors. For this you'll need to create a class that processes each of the elements that are identified by the parser. Alternatively, you can create one single class, a document handler, that contains the functions for all the different content types.

For convenience, the `saxlib` package includes default classes for the different types made available through the `ContentHandler`, `DTDHandler`, `EntityResolver`, and `ErrorHandler` classes, or through the superclass `DocumentHandler`. You can set the different handlers for an individual parser by using `parser.setContentHandler()` and associated functions for the other handler types, supplying a single argument that should be an instance of the handler type.

To supply XML to the parser, you should call either the `parse()` or `parseString()` method. The `parse()` method accepts a filename or an open file handle from which it will read the entire document. The `parseString()` method accepts a string to be parsed. In each case, the supplied file or string should be self contained—that is, it should be an entire XML document. You cannot "drip" feed the parser, even using the `parseString()` method.

Designing Handlers

The handler or handlers that you create must be self-contained. If you want to record information or use SAX for building another object or nested structure, you must store that information within the handler you create.

NOTE   Actually, you could use global variables to store the information, but as you should already know, global variables are essentially considered to be a bad thing, and there's nothing to make the process of storing the data into the handler class any more difficult.

To put this into practice, Listing 13.1 shows a script that collects information about an XML file (number of tags, individual tag counts, attributes, processing instructions, and characters in character data).

Listing 13.1   **Using SAX for Document Statistics**

```
from xml.sax import saxexts
from xml.sax import saxlib
import sys

class StatHandler(saxlib.DocumentHandler):

    def __init__(self):
        self.tags = {}
        self.elems=0
        self.attrs=0
        self.pis=0
        self.char=0

    def startElement(self,name,attrs):
        if (self.tags.has_key(name) != 1):
            self.tags[name] = 0
```

```
            self.tags[name]=self.tags[name]+1

            self.elems=self.elems+1
            self.attrs=self.attrs+len(attrs)

    def characters(self, data, dummya, dummyb):
        self.char=self.char+len(data)

    def processingInstruction(self,target,data):
        self.pis=self.pis+1

parser = saxexts.make_parser()
statistics = StatHandler()
parser.setDocumentHandler(statistics)

try:
    parser.parse(sys.argv[1])
except IndexError:
    print "You must supply a file name"
    sys.exit(1)
except IOError, msg:
    print "Error opening file:",msg
    sys.exit(1)
except saxlib.SAXException, msg:
    print "Error parsing file:",msg
    sys.exit(1)

for tag in statistics.tags.keys():
    print "%-50s%d" % ('Tag "' + tag + '":',statistics.tags[tag])
print "%-50s%d" % ('Elements:',statistics.elems)
print "%-50s%d" % ('Attributes:',statistics.attrs)
print "%-50s%d" % ('Processing Instructions:',statistics.pis)
print "%-50s%d" % ('Character Data:',statistics.char)
```

If you look at this script in detail, you should be able to see how you collate the information from the XML document. The content handler class knows how to deal with three different types of entities: start tags, character data, and processing instructions (PI).

As the document is parsed, whenever the reader sees these items, the corresponding method is called, just as with the xmllib library you saw in Chapter 11, "XML Solutions in Python." To make your statistics gatherer work, the first job is to set up the properties of a handler instance that will be used to hold the information as the document is parsed.

You do this in the initializer for the class. Then, when you see a start element, character data, or PI, you add up the numbers and update the handler object instance with the information. Then, when the script is run, you know that when the parser has finished, you can pull out the data from your handler instance to get the summary information you were trying to extract.

Running this on the sample client document from the previous chapter, you get this:

```
$ python saxstats.py contact.xml
Tag "empty":                        1
Tag "number":                       7
Tag "type":                         7
Tag "contactmethods":               1
Tag "method":                       7
Tag "name":                         1
Tag "contact":                      1
Elements:                           25
Attributes:                         0
Processing Instructions:            0
Character Data:                     149
```

All SAX-based processing works on the same premise—you have to record the information about what you are processing in order to be able to convert or otherwise translate the information trapped in your XML document into some other format. The reason you have to do this is because of the nature of the SAX parser. It works through and reads each tag, each block of character data, and all the other elements. Then it executes a single function to handle the event.

This can make some processes difficult. For example, to extract the character data stored between two tags, such as this:

```
<message>Come grow old along with me.</message>
```

you have three events triggered. You can't access the child data between the tags directly. Instead, you have to identify the start tag, remember where you are, cache the character data, and then identify when you see the end tag to ensure that you store that cached data in the message property or other structure. In some situations, SAX can be better than DOM, but as you'll see in Chapter 14, DOM can also be better for some solutions than SAX.

Handler Quick Reference

The SAX handler is set in stone as part of the SAX standard, but for a quick reference, I've included the main methods called when processing a document with SAX. By default, all of the methods defined in the base classes (from which you should inherit) do nothing. You'll need to overload the methods with your own versions to actually process information.

Methods within the ContentHandler class are listed in Table 13.1.

TABLE 13.1: Methods for `ContentHandler` Classes

Method	Description
startDocument()	Triggered at the start of a document.
endDocument()	Triggered at the end of a document.
startElement(name, attrs)	Triggered when a start element is identified. `name` is the element name, and `attrs` is a dictionary of the element's attributes.
endElement(name)	Triggered when an end element is identified. `name` is the element name.
startElementNS(name, qname, attrs)	Triggered when a start element is identified when processing in namespace mode. `name` is the name of the element as a tuple, containing the URI and the local name (for example, `mcwords:title` would be returned as `('mcwords', 'title')`). `qname` is the raw element name as identified from the XML, and `attrs` is a dictionary of the attribute.
endElementNS(name, qname)	Triggered when an end element is identified when processing in namespace mode. `name` and `qname` are as for `startElementNS()`.
characters(content)	Triggered when character data is found. Note that this may be triggered multiple times during an apparently single character data block.
processingInstruction(target, data)	Triggered when a processing instruction is identified.
skippedEntity(name)	Triggered when an entity is skipped.

Be aware that single elements (such as `<header/>`) trigger both `startElement()` and `endElement()` methods.

Methods for the `DTDHandler` class are listed in Table 13.2. Currently, the system supports only notation and unparsed entity declarations.

TABLE 13.2: Methods for the `DTDHandler` Class

Method	Description
notationDecl(name, publicId, systemId)	Triggered by a notation declaration.
unparsedEntityDecl(name, publicId, systemId, ndata)	Triggered by an unparsed entity.

The `EntityResolver` class defines only a single method, `resolveEntity()`, which accepts `publicId` and `systemId` arguments and is triggered when an entity is identified.

Error Handling

One of the most important aspects of parsing an XML document is to be able to cope when an error occurs. Errors within SAX are handled during the process of reading the XML document, which is in turn handled by a separate XMLReader class. In order to handle any errors in the XML parsing process, you have to provide an alternative error-handling class to the standard ErrorHandler object used by default.

You can trap and deal with three different types of errors: standard errors, fatal errors, and simple warnings. Each type of error is handled by a different method, as summarized in Table 13.3. In each method, only a single argument is accepted—a SAXParseException instance.

TABLE 13.3: Methods in the ErrorHandler Class

Method	Description
error(exception)	Called when the parser encounters a recoverable error. By default, this method raises an exception (through the SAXException class). If you implement the method but don't raise an exception, then processing can continue.
fatalError(exception)	Called when the parser encounters a fatal error. Parsing should stop when this method is called, and no more information will be supplied to the parser.
warning(exception)	Called when the parser encounters a warning. Parsing will continue after this method returns, and additional data will be supplied to the parser so that the process can continue. If you raise an exception within this method, parsing will cease.

As you can see from the table, you can only deal with standard errors and warnings. The fatalError() method can be overloaded by your own class, but parsing stops when a fatal error occurs.

The SAXParseException exception is a subclass of the main SAXException exception class provided by xml.sax. It conveniently encapsulates the error message and its location and can easily be converted to a useful string form for printing.

The SAXException class is the base class for all errors raised when parsing a document in SAX. The exception passes on a message of the error as standard. Whatever type of processing you are doing, you should be trapping SAXException errors through a try statement when you call the parse() method to parse a particular document.

You might also want to explicitly handle the SAXNotRecognizedException, which is picked up when the XML reader doesn't recognize a given feature or property of the XML document, and SAXNotSupportedException, which is raised when a known unsupported event occurs.

You can use this information to build an alternative parser that will simply bail out and print a suitable message if there is an error during parsing. To do this, you first create a new error handler class that overloads the methods in Table 13.3 and a dummy content handler class that does nothing with any of the information provided to it.

To install the error handler, you need to create instances of your two classes and then set them as the content and error handlers in your parser object. You can see a full script implementing the entire process in Listing 13.2.

Listing 13.2   A Modified SAX Parser Armed for Error Handling

```python
from xml.sax import saxlib, make_parser
import sys

class ValidityHandler(saxlib.ContentHandler):
    def __init__(self):
        pass

class MyErrorHandler(saxlib.ErrorHandler):
    def __init__(self):
        pass
    def error(self, exception):
        print "Error",exception

    def fatalError(self, exception):
        print "Fatal Error", exception

    def warning(self, exception):
        print "Warning",exception

try:
    parser = make_parser()
except saxlib.SAXReaderNotAvailable:
    raise ImportError("No XML Parser")

validity = ValidityHandler()
errors = MyErrorHandler()

parser.setErrorHandler(errors)
parser.setContentHandler(validity)

try:
    parser.parse(sys.argv[1])
except saxlib.SAXException, errmsg:
    print "Error parsing document"+str(errmsg)
```

For example, if you use the script in Listing 13.2 against the following XML document, you get information about the problems dealing with the document:

```
<first>
<second attr=something>First text
<third>Second text</second></third>
</last>
```

The actual errors reported are these:

```
Fatal Error bad.xml:2:13: not well-formed (invalid token)
Fatal Error bad.xml:3:13: not well-formed (invalid token)
```

This highlights the two well-formed errors, the second and third tags not appearing in the right order.

Unfortunately, there's not a lot you can about these errors, and in fact well-formedness errors generally cause problems with most parsing exercises. For example, in the example above, you run the risk of adding the character data in the third element to the data of second and vice versa.

Using xmlproc for Validation

When working with any kind of XML document, there are always issues relating to the validity of the document being parsed. Most of the parsers will check a document for "well-formedness," including SAX, which is used both directly and for building the DOM object model for the Python DOM implementation, and Expat. This involves simply checking that start tags have corresponding end tags and that tags don't overlap each other (start and end tags in different orders).

These basic checks are obviously useful and appreciated when parsing an XML document, but all the parsers we've mentioned raise an exception when such an error occurs. Once raised and reported on, there is no way to tell the parsers to continue working after the error has occurred.

In most instances this is what you want; there's an error in the basic structure of the document that could potentially break the processing and parsing that you are trying to perform. Imagine, for example, trying to parse a document with SAX that doesn't have an end tag or has an end tag in the wrong place. When keying on that end tag to update a structure or dump out an HTML tag, you run into a problem. Cached data will start clogging up, and character data from multiple tags may well end up in the wrong place once you've finished parsing the document.

You can't switch off the exceptions entirely using either SAX or DOM because you can't restart the processing from the point of the error (unless it's a warning or an error that you haven't otherwise ignored). As you saw in Listing 13.2, even in those scripts where you are able to override the exception handlers, you can't get over the issue of fatal errors identified by the parser.

The xmlproc parser was written by Lars Marius Garshol and is an almost complete validating parser. It can be used as a general-purpose parser and provides a similar event-driven interface to the xml.sax package in terms of basic processing.

Its main advantage over both SAX and DOM systems is that, because it validates the XML as it is read by the parser, it can be used to check the document as it is being processed. In addition, unlike SAX, when an error occurs, xmlproc just records the problem and then allows the processing to continue. The parser doesn't apply severities, and therefore the normal exception handling performed by SAX just doesn't apply.

Although you could write your own script for doing this, there's one provided in the PyXML toolkit. If you check the scripts directory, you'll find xmlproc_val, which is a script that operates the front end to the validating portion of the parser.

If you use this to check the XML you used with Listing 13.2, you get a more useful list of errors and problems in the source document:

```
Parsing 'bad.xml'
E:bad.xml:2:14: One of ' or '"' expected
E:bad.xml:2:61: End tag for 'second' seen, but 'third' expected
E:bad.xml:2:69: End tag for 'third' seen, but 'first' expected
E:bad.xml:3:8: End tag for 'last' seen, but 'first' expected
E:bad.xml:3:8: Premature document end, element 'first' not closed
5 error(s), 0 warning(s)
```

Looking more closely at the code that supports this, you can see that the entire process is handled by an Application class defined within the xmlproc system. In fact, ignoring the processing of any command-line arguments, you can actually reduce the script to something like that in Listing 13.3.

Listing 13.3   **The Basis of the Validating Parser in xmlproc**

```
import sys
from xml.parsers.xmlproc import xmlproc, _outputters

application = xmlproc.Application()

parser = xmlproc.XMLProcessor()

errors = _outputters.MyErrorHandler(parser, parser, 1, 0, 0)
parser.set_error_handler(errors)
```

```
parser.set_application(application)

for file in sys.argv[1:]:
    print
    print "Parsing '%s'" % file
    parser.set_data_after_wf_error(0)
    parser.parse_resource(file)
    print "%d error(s), %d warning(s)" % (errors.errors,
                                           errors.warnings)

    errors.reset()
    parser.reset()
```

Unfortunately, we can't go into the details of the system here. Make sure you check out the script; it's one of the best command-line validators I've come across.

If you prefer a visual interface, the wxValidator.py script, also included with the standard distribution, provides the same functionality but with a front end supported by wxPython. You can see a sample in Figure 13.1.

FIGURE 13.1:

Validating a document with wxPython

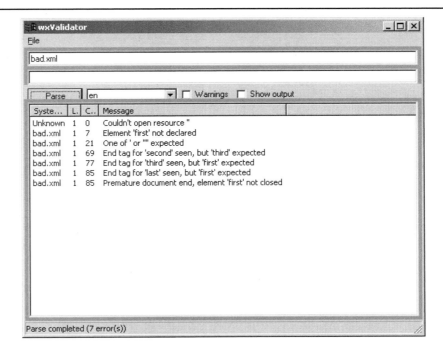

Summary

Python's XML support is provided by a single package called PyXML which encompasses a number of different parsers including those for SAX and DOM-based processing. The SAX parser is the most extensive and it includes facilities for working with most types of XML components. Using SAX is a case of combining a custom-built class that provides methods for the different XML components.

SAX also includes a flexible error-checking system that can be overridden for warnings and non-fatal errors using a special error handling class. If this level of error checking is not enough, the xmlproc parse includes a much more extensive mechanism that can identify errors and report them while continuing to parse the XML source.

CHAPTER 14

Converting XML Documents Using Python

- Converting XML to an Internal Structure

- Converting XML to an Internal Class Representation

You've already had a look at some samples of converting documents from XML using Python, but you haven't covered all the tricks available for making the process easier.

Irrespective of the destination format that you want to convert your documents to, you need to first process your documents using the SAX or DOM parsing system you've already seen. What do you do with the information that you extract?

Ultimately, it depends on what you want to do with the information. Some documents will need to be converted to an internal structure, such as a nested array or dictionary, and others will have more familiar destinations, such as HTML.

In both cases you can use the strict class and object manipulation functions within Python to make the process of representing the information more structured for use within another Python script.

For example, looking back at the simple bank client XML document from Chapter 11, "XML Solutions in Python," included here in Listing 14.1, you can see that you could easily convert the document into a data structure that consists of the client, its name, a list of accounts and their details, and an embedded list of transactions for each account. That structure could be an object instance or just a stand-alone nested structure.

Listing 14.1   The Client Sample

```
<client>
<clientname>Martin Brown</clientname>
<account>
    <accname>Checking</accname>
    <provider>HSBC</provider>
    <balance>$4567.00</balance>
    <transaction>
        <payee>Rent</payee>
        <amount>$280.00</amount>
    </transaction>
    <transaction>
        <payee>Time Subscription</payee>
        <amount>$26.00</amount>
    </transaction>
</account>

<account>
    <accname>VISA</accname>
    <provider>Morgan Dean Stanley Witter</provider>
    <balance>$-3485.00</balance>
    <transaction>
        <payee>Supermarket</payee>
        <amount>$-450.00</amount>
    </transaction>
    <transaction>
```

```
            <payee>Gas Station</payee>
            <amount>$-18.00</amount>
        </transaction>
    </account>
</client>
```

From this internal structure, you could convert the original XML information into just about anything you want, or you could manipulate it before writing the information to a database or even back out to an XML file using the techniques you saw in the previous chapter.

In this chapter, we're going to look at how to use SAX to convert an XML document into a nested structure that you can use and manipulate. We'll also look at using DOM to convert XML to HTML with a special HTML building class that mirrors the DOM node system in its design. Finally, we'll look at a solution using SAX to do the processing while still using the same HTML builder class.

Converting XML to an Internal Structure

Converting any XML document generally requires knowledge of the document structure before you start processing. You need to decide what information you are going to store and what format it needs to be stored in.

In the XML document in Listing 14.1, you can see how the structure of the information is organized. You see the main client, the list of accounts, and a list of transactions. You can easily model that data by using a combination of dictionaries and lists.

When using SAX, you already know that the only way to record information and data about what you are parsing is to use a series of objects within the parser handler. In this instance you need to record information about each transaction, the current list of transactions for the current account, and the information about the current account.

In all other ways, the basic method for implementing the parser is the same as for the examples in Chapter 11 and 13: Before extracting the information, you create a new parser and tell it what content handler to use to process the XML tags.

The full script for this can be seen in Listing 14.2.

Listing 14.2   Using SAX to Create a Nested Structure

```
from xml.sax import saxexts
from xml.sax import saxlib
import copy, string

class SAXToStructureHandler(saxlib.DocumentHandler):
```

```python
    def __init__(self):
        self.structure = {'accounts' : []}
        self.data = ''
        self.transactions = []
        self.transaction = {}
        self.account = {}

    def endElement(self, name):
        if (name == 'clientname'):
            self.structure['clientname'] = self.data

        elif (name == 'accname'):
            self.account['name'] = self.data

        elif (name == 'provider'):
            self.account['provider'] = self.data

        elif (name == 'balance'):
            self.account['balance'] = self.data

        elif (name == 'transaction'):
            self.transactions.append(
                    copy.deepcopy(self.transaction))
            self.transaction = {}

        elif (name == 'payee'):
            self.transaction['payee'] = self.data

        elif (name == 'amount'):
            self.transaction['amount'] = self.data

        elif (name == 'account'):
            self.account['transactions'] = copy.deepcopy(self.transactions)
            self.structure['accounts'].append(copy.deepcopy(self.account))
            self.transactions = []
            self.transaction = {}
            self.account = {}

        self.data = ''


def characters(self, data, dummy, dummyb):
        self.data =+ string.strip(data)

p=saxexts.make_parser()
ch=SAXToStructureHandler()
p.setDocumentHandler(ch)

p.parse('client.xml')
```

There's nothing special in this script—you simply collect any character data using the
`characters()` method, then use the `endElement()` method to corral that data into the nooks
and crannies of the `structure` property of our SAXToStructureHandler object, ch. (The
`structure` property is simply a nested data structure made up of lists and dictionaries.)

At the end of a transaction, you add the transaction to the list of current transactions, and
at the end of an account you add the account information and transaction information to the
dictionary. The most important aspect in this part of the process is that you must use the
`deepcopy()` function from the copy module.

Python doesn't copy references to objects, so you must copy the structure to its final destination. Without this, you put a reference to the structure that you later empty into the final
dictionary; therefore, you'd lose the information about every account except the last one.

You can print out the structure quite easily by adding this:

```
(.+)
```

to the end of the script. The result, formatted slightly to make it easier to read, is shown in
Listing 14.3.

Listing 14.3   **The Parsed XML Document in Its Internal Structure Form**

```
{'clientname': u'Martin Brown',
 'accounts': [
    {'provider': u'HSBC',
     'name': u'Checking',
     'balance': u'$4567.00',
     'transactions': [
          {'amount': u'$280.00',
           'payee': u'Rent'},
          {'amount': u'$26.00',
           'payee': u'Time Subscription'}]},
    {'provider': u'Morgan Dean Stanley Witter',
     'name': u'VISA',
     'balance': u'$-3485.00',
     'transactions': [
          {'amount': u'$-450.00',
           'payee': u'Supermarket'},
          {'amount': u'$-18.00',
           'payee': u'Gas Station'}]
    }]
 }
```

Now you have the information in a more useful internal structure. You could process
the information, write the data to a database or another XML file, or merely work on and
summarize the information for displaying on a web page or Tk, WxPython, or other GUI

application. The key here is that you have the data in a Python, not XML, structure that you can easily use.

Converting XML to an Internal Class Representation

In the previous example we looked at a script that used SAX to convert the client XML data into a standard Python nested structure using lists and dictionaries. The same basic principles could be used to convert an XML document into a class instance, providing your handler had created the instance in the first place as part of the __init__() method and then knew how to add the information to the object.

As an example of this in practice, we'll look at an alternative on the HTML conversion system that uses the HTMLFragment class.

For the actual processing, you'll use a DOM parser. The benefit of DOM in this instance is that you can access the individual components of the document that you want to work on in isolation, without the usual SAX need to keep recording temporary information during the processing just to record the location. For reference, an example of a SAX parser that could be used to produce the same document using the same class is also included.

The HTML Fragment Class

The DOM system uses nodes to represent the structure of the individual components within an XML document. Everything is available as a node, from the tag elements and attributes to the character data.

You can use the same principle for creating HTML documents. You need only two different types for this: the HTML node and any attributes it requires and a text node to hold the character information outside of an HTML tag.

To add to the complexity, you need to deal with HTML tags that work as singles, not pairs, and therefore have a different representation. You also have to hold a list of all the child nodes. For example, the following is the basic layout of an HTML document:

```
<html>
<head><title>Some Title</title></head>
<body>
<h1>Some Header</h1>
<hr>
<p>Some Text.</p>
</body>
(.+)
```

You can see here the typical tag pairs such as `title` and `p` and the individual tags such as `hr`. You also see that the main `html` tag holds child tags of the head and body, which in turn hold their own child tags.

You can see the HTML fragment class in Listing 14.4.

Listing 14.4   **The *HTMLFragment* Class for Building HTML Documents in a DOM Way**

```
import sys, string

htmltagpairs = {'A' : 1,
                'ADDRESS' : 1,
                'B' : 1,
                'BLOCKQUOTE' : 1,
                'BODY' : 1,
                'BQ' : 1,
                'BR' : 0,
                'CENTER' : 1,
                'CITE' : 1,
                'CODE' : 1,
                'DFN' : 1,
                'DIR' : 1,
                'DL' : 1,
                'EM' : 1,
                'FIG' : 1,
                'FONT' : 1,
                'FORM' : 1,
                'H1' : 1,
                'H2' : 1,
                'H3' : 1,
                'H4' : 1,
                'H5' : 1,
                'H6' : 1,
                'HEAD' : 1,
                'HR' : 0,
                'HTML' : 1,
                'I' : 1,
                'KBD' : 1,
                'LISTING' : 1,
                'MATH' : 1,
                'MENU' : 1,
                'OL' : 1,
                'P' : 1,
                'PRE' : 1,
                'S' : 1,
                'SAMP' : 1,
                'SELECT' : 1,
                'STRONG' : 1,
                'STYLE' : 1,
                'TABLE' : 1,
```

```
                    'TEXTAREA' : 1,
                    'TITLE' : 1,
                    'TD' : 1,
                    'TR' : 1,
                    'TT' : 1,
                    'U' : 1,
                    'UL' : 1,
                    'VAR' : 1,
                    'XMP' : 1,
                    'BLOCKQUOTE' : 1,
                    }

class HTMLFragment:
    def __init__(self, tag, data = {}):
        self.type = 'text'
        self.pair = 0

        if htmltagpairs.has_key(string.upper(tag)):
            self.pair = htmltagpairs[string.upper(tag)]
            self.type = 'tag'
            self.tag = tag
            self.attr = data
        else:
            self.data = tag
        self.children = []

    def writeashtml(self):
        if (self.type == 'tag'):
            tagstring = "<" + self.tag
            attrlist = []
            for attr in self.attr.keys():
                attrlist.append('%s="%s"' %
                                    (attr,self.attr[attr]))
            if (len(attrlist)>0):
                tagstring =+ tagstring + " " + string.join(attrlist," ")
            tagstring =+ tagstring + ">"
            sys.stdout.writelines(tagstring)
        else:
            sys.stdout.writelines(self.data)
        for child in self.children:
            child.writeashtml()
        if (self.pair):
            sys.stdout.write("</%s>\n" % self.tag)

    def newtag(self, name, attributes = {}):
        return HTMLFragment(name, attributes)

    def newcontent(self, data):
        return HTMLFragment(data)
```

```
    def appendtag(self, name, attributes = {}, content = ''):
        tagchild = self.newtag(name, attributes).
        self.children.append(tagchild)
        if (len(content)):
            contentchild = tagchild.appendcontent(content)
            return tagchild, contentchild
        else:
            return tagchild

    def appendcontent(self, data):
        child = self.newcontent(data)
        self.children.append(child)
        return child

if __name__ == '__main__':
    root = HTMLFragment('html', {})
    head = root.appendtag('head')
    head. appendtag('title', {}, 'Some Other Title')

    root.writeashtml()
```

To use the `HTMLFragment` class to build a new HTML document, first create your `root` node that will be used to hold all the other nodes. You can do this by just creating an instance of the class and supplying the information for the `root` node. In HTML, when you are writing out a full document, the `root` node should be `html`:

(.+)

When creating a new instance, the `__init__()` method first checks if the first argument is one of the tags in `htmltagpairs`. This is a dictionary that performs two functions. First, it contains a list of all the HTML tags the class recognizes. Also, it tells you whether a particular HTML tag is reproduced individually, as with `hr`, or in pairs, as with most other tags.

Assuming you've identified a valid tag, you create a tag node by setting the properties of the tag to record its type, tag name, whether it's a pair, and the tag's attributes. If it's text, then you just record the raw text. Any children should be added to the `children` property of the object.

For convenience, you can create a tag node from the base object using the `newtag()` method or a new content node using the `newcontent()` method. Note that these don't automatically add the resulting nodes to the parent, they are just simpler interfaces for creating tags. To add a node to its parent, you can either update the node's `children` property directly or use the `appendtag()` or `appendcontent()` method to both create and append the nodes to the current object. For convenience, `appendtag()` will create both tag and content nodes, adding the content node as a child to the tag node and then returning both objects to the caller.

The final method in the class is `writeashtml()` which simply walks through the nodes, dumping the tag and its attributes or the content data as it goes; then it walks through the children. Because the child nodes are other `HTMLFragment` class instances, you can call the `writeashtml()` method recursively to print each node and to build up the final structure. Note that if a tag is identified as a pair, the closing tag is written after the children.

Using the HTML Builder Class with DOM

Working with DOM is a matter of accessing the tags that you want to use, either by referencing them directly or by walking through the structure of nodes and their children to extract the information that you want from the document.

In the case of the client bank accounts XML file, you know that there are four different areas to the XML document. These are the main client name, the list of accounts, the information for each account, and the list of transactions for a given account.

You can extract all of that information by first accessing the `client` tag node in the XML document, then the account node, the account detail nodes, and the transaction nodes.

As you go through and extract the information, you build a structure using the `HTMLFragment` class to create new instances. From that you create new children to build up an HTML document.

You can see the script for this in Listing 14.5.

Listing 14.5   **The DOM Parser for Converting Account Data into HTML**

```
from xml.dom.minidom import parse
from xmltohtml import HTMLFragment

def getdata(nodes):
    rc = ''
    for node in nodes:
        if node.nodeType == node.TEXT_NODE:
            rc = rc + node.data
    return rc

def handleclient(client, html):
    clientname = client.getElementsByTagName("clientname")[0]

    line = html.appendtag('font', {'size' : '+2'})
    line.appendtag('b', {}, getdata(clientname.childNodes))
    html.appendtag('br')

    accounts = client.getElementsByTagName("account")
    handleaccounts(accounts, html)
```

```
def handleaccounts(accounts, html):
    accthdr = html.appendtag('blockquote')
    line = accthdr.appendtag('font', {'size' : '+1'})
    line.appendtag('b', {}, 'Accounts')
    acctlist = accthdr.appendtag('blockquote')
    for account in accounts:
        handleaccount(account, acctlist)
def handleaccount(account, html):
    accname = account.getElementsByTagName("accname")[0]
    provider = account.getElementsByTagName("provider")[0]

    html.appendtag('b',{}, '%s (%s)' % \
        (getdata(accname.childNodes),
         getdata(provider.childNodes)))
    html.appendtag('br')

    table = html.appendtag('table', {'cellspacing' : 5, 'cellpadding' : 5,
'border' : 0 })

    row = table.appendtag('tr')
    cell = row.appendtag('td')
    cell.appendtag('b', {}, 'Transaction')
    cell = row.appendtag('td')
    cell.appendtag('b', {}, 'Amount')

    trans = account.getElementsByTagName("transaction")
    for transaction in trans:
        row = table.appendtag('tr')
        handletransaction(transaction, row)

    balance = account.getElementsByTagName("balance")[0]
    row = table.appendtag('tr')
    row.appendtag('td')
    cell = row.appendtag('td')
    cell.appendtag('b', {}, getdata(balance.childNodes))

def handletransaction(transaction, htmlrow):
    payee = transaction.getElementsByTagName("payee")[0]
    amount = transaction.getElementsByTagName("amount")[0]
    htmlrow.appendtag('td', {}, getdata(payee.childNodes))
    htmlrow.appendtag('td', {}, getdata(amount.childNodes))

client = parse('client.xml')

htmlrepr = HTMLFragment('html')
head = htmlrepr.appendtag('head')
head.appendtag('title', {}, 'Client Record')
body = htmlrepr.appendtag('body', {'bgcolor' : '#ffffff'})
handleclient(client, body)

htmlrepr.writeashtml()
```

The script is divided into three main sections: the DOM parser functions, the single line that parses the XML source document into a DOM structure, and the final section that builds the HTML structure with the `HTMLFragment` class.

The parser is really just a series of functions that work through and process each element. The result of the second section is a DOM structure stored within the `client` object. You pass that off to the `handleclient()` function, which in turn extracts the client data before processing each `account` tag. This in turn passes processing of the all the nodes within a single `account` tag to the `handleaccount()` function.

Once the account data has been extracted and written into the HTML structure, you pass control over to `handletransaction()`, which extracts a list of the individual transactions and translates them to HTML using the `handletransaction()` function.

Through each stage of the process, from the original account to the individual account transactions, you pass along the object referring to the node you are currently working on within the full DOM structure. For example, you start by finding the first `client` tag. Within that tag are nodes that hold information about the two accounts, and it's these subaccount nodes that are handed to `handleaccount()` and so on until you reach the bottom of the structure.

By walking through the document in this way, you can traverse in a logical fashion without losing the structure of the original XML document. You can also process repeated tags in different sections without worrying about how you deal with different locations. For example, you have multiple transactions in the entire XML document, and it's easy to identify that the transaction information is attached to the two accounts.

Had you just accessed a list of all the `transaction` entries in the document, you'd mix up the information between the accounts. In this case, you're extracting only the `transaction` entries that are children of a specific account node.

By the same basic process, you are also walking through the HTML structure and adding appropriate nodes to the structure to build the document. For example, within `handletransactions` you create a node for a `table` tag and from that build individual rows that are children of the `table` node. In `handletransactions`, the new row is the header row, but in `handletransaction` it's a row for each transaction.

Once the HTML structure has been built, all you need to do is dump the HTML node tree as HTML text and you are finished. The resulting HTML can be seen in Listing 14.6; the file as rendered in Internet Explorer is shown in Figure 14.1.

Listing 14.6   The Resulting HTML from the Client XML Document

```
<html><head><title>Client Record</title>
</head>
<body fgcolor="#000000" bgcolor="#ffffff"><font size="+2"><b>Martin Brown</b>
```

```
</font>
<br><font size="+1"></font>
<b>Accounts:</b>
<br><br><b>Checking (HSBC)</b>
<br><table border="0" cellspacing="5" cellpadding="5">
<tr><td><b>Transaction</b></td>
<td><b>Amount</b></td></tr>
<tr><td>Rent</td><td>$280.00</td></tr>
<tr><td>Time Subscription</td><td>$26.00</td></tr>
<tr><td></td><td><b>$4567.00</b></td></tr>
</table>
<b>VISA (Morgan Dean Stanley Witter)</b>
<br><table border="0" cellspacing="5" cellpadding="5">
<tr><td><b>Transaction</b></td>
<td><b>Amount</b></td></tr>
<tr><td>Supermarket</td><td>$-450.00</td></tr>
<tr><td>Gas Station</td><td>$-18.00</td></tr>
<tr><td></td><td><b>$-3485.00</b></td></tr>
</table>
</body>
</html>
```

FIGURE 14.1:

The rendered client record

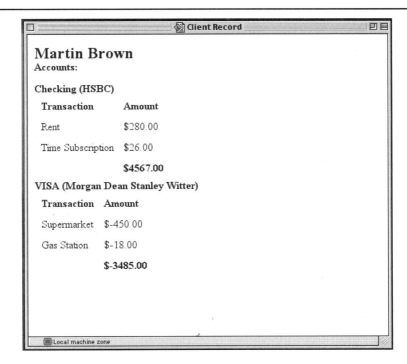

Although you've only created a fairly simple HTML object structure from the source document, you could just as easily have created a `Client` class instance and added the necessary information to that. After all, objects in Python are just combinations of base objects, properties, and complex property types such as lists and dictionaries.

Using the techniques demonstrated in this example, you could have built `Account` and `Transaction` classes directly from the information extracted from the document with the DOM parser, and the accounts and transactions objects could be appended to the base `Client` class.

A SAX Converter

Up to now I've given SAX and DOM parsing methods more or less equal billing when it comes to their usefulness, but there are times when the capabilities and structure of one far outweigh the other.

For example, when converting an XML document to an internal structure, as discussed earlier in this chapter, SAX is the obvious choice because you are parsing an entire document. When converting to an internal node structure, as you did in the last example, DOM makes more sense because you can more easily extract the individual elements such as the account details or a list of transactions for conveniently appending to an existing structure.

Trying the same trick with DOM requires recording lots of information about the structure, the current location, and the character data between each tag until the process becomes essentially unmanageable.

To demonstrate this more fully, Listing 14.7 is an example of a script for converting the same document through SAX using the `HTMLFragment` class.

Listing 14.7   A SAX Version of the XML-to-HTML Converter

```
import string
from xml.sax import saxexts
from xml.sax import saxlib
from xmltohtml import HTMLFragment

class SAXToHTMLHandler(saxlib.DocumentHandler):

    def __init__(self):
        self.data = ''
        self.root = HTMLFragment('')
        self.currenthtml = self.root
        self.htmltagtree = []
```

```
    def startElement(self,name,attrs):
        if (name == 'clientname'):
            self.htmltagtree.append(self.currenthtml)
            line = self.root.appendtag('font',
                                    {'size' : '+2'})
            self.htmltagtree.append(line)
            (rettag,retdata) =
                line.appendtag('b', {}, self.data)
            rettag.appendcontent('Account: ')
            self.currenthtml = rettag

    def endElement(self, name):
        if (name == 'clientname'):
            self.currenthtml.appendcontent(self.data)
            self.currenthtml = self.htmltagtree.pop()
            self.currenthtml = self.htmltagtree.pop()
            self.currenthtml.appendtag('br')
        self.data = ''

    def characters(self, data, dummy, dummyb):
        self.data += data

p=saxexts.make_parser()
ch=SAXToHTMLHandler()
p.setDocumentHandler(ch)

p.parse('client.xml')

ch.root.writeashtml()
```

Aside from the fact that it isn't completed (for reasons that will become apparent shortly), you can already see that you are storing more transient information in the handler class instance than you did in the earlier SAX or previous DOM examples.

Some of this is related to the SAX processing method; because you process each tag in turn, you have to be able to record the current location. With the HTMLFragment class, you also need to record the current HTMLFragment instance, so you know to which object to add the tag or content information. You also have to remember the previous instance, in case there's character data to be added to a tag pair that you haven't finished processing.

You can also see that, unlike the SAX example at the start of the chapter, you now have more to do within the startElement() method, both identifying the element in question and adding HTML tag nodes to the structure to help lay out the document in its ultimate HTML format.

Trying to manage the whole process becomes unmanageable as you try to deal with more and more of the source XML tags and cope with the HTML node structure, in addition to dealing with the existing structure and other transient data.

The result is a perfect example of when using SAX over DOM is a bad idea and vice versa. The same basic rules can be applied to many forms of XML processing.

Summary

In general, converting entire documents to another *serial* format should be done using SAX. That includes conversions to serial structures, as you did in the first script, or to the text and database formats we've covered in other chapters and other languages.

DOM is much better for conversion to more complex structures or to structures, objects, and classes that can't easily be manipulated through a serial format. Examples include objects and other node and tree structures, including some nested structures. DOM is also ideal for when you want to pick out only specific areas of a given document, such as a list of account transactions, without dealing with account data.

## CHAPTER 15

Applying SOAP/XML-RPC in Python

- Using SOAP.py

- Using xmlrpclib

SOAP and XML-RPC are both applications of the XML language that make use of XML's cross-platform and text format to enable us to call remote functions and object methods. You don't need to know how to parse XML, nor do you need to know anything about XML in order to use either SOAP or XML-RPC. However, an understanding of how the mechanism works and how it relates to XML is useful. See Chapter 5, "Data Exchange and XML," for information.

Support in Python is offered by a number of different modules, all of which do their best to hide the complexities of the SOAP or XML-RPC process. You shouldn't ever have to parse any XML to use these technologies, but you should get a good idea of what's possible with XML.

In this chapter we're going to look at two solutions. The SOAP module is one of a number of SOAP solutions available in Python. Written by Cayce Ullman and Brian Matthews, it provides one of the simplest interfaces to the SOAP system. We'll also look at the xmlrpclib module from Fredrik Lundh, the only solution available at the time of writing.

TIP   For other SOAP and XML-RPC solutions in Python, check out the vaults of Parnassus (see Appendix B, "Resource Guide").

Using *SOAP*

If you've read Chapter 10, "Applying SOAP/XML-RPC in Perl," you know how easy it is to create clients within Perl. The SOAP.py module in Python actually follows a very similar format, hiding all the complexity of writing SOAP clients and servers from the programmer.

All SOAP services are based on three elements: the client, the server, and an optional support module that provides the functions you want to support over a remote connection.

The client is straightforward to set up. You supply the location of the remote SOAP request handler using an instance of the SOAPProxy class. Individual functions on the remote server are then accessible as methods to the SOAPProxy instance that you have created. You can see how easy this is in Listing 15.1.

Listing 15.1   A Simple Python SOAP Client

```
import SOAP

server = SOAP.SOAPProxy('http://localhost:8081/')
print server.getmessage()
```

If we look at the server in Listing 15.2, you can see that it's similarly brief. In this case, we're setting up a daemon-based server to run on the `localhost` address on port 8081.

Listing 15.2   **A Simple Python Server**

```
import SOAP

def getmessage():
    return 'Hello world!'

server = SOAP.SOAPServer(('localhost',8081))
server.registerFunction(getmessage)
server.serve_forever()
```

The server actually sets up two elements. First, we set up the configuration of the server itself by supplying the hostname and port on which to serve up your request handler. The SOAP module supports only daemon-based servers at the moment, but more transports are being added all the time.

The next step (and the second element that's required by the server) is to register the functions that we want to provide the client with access to. In this case, we've registered a local `getmessage()` function; we could just as easily have registered a function from an external module.

To actually use the system, first we need to fire up the server so that it can listen for requests from the client. I've deliberately used port 8081, which isn't in use by most machines. Firing up the server is just a case of running the server script:

```
$ pyserver.py
```

If we now run the client, we should get a message back from the server:

```
$ python pyclient.py
Hello world!
```

It works!

You should also have received some output from the server to indicate that a request had been made. For example, the following shows two requests from the same machine as the server is running on:

```
localhost - - [04/Jul/2001 13:11:06] "POST / HTTP/1.0" 200 -
localhost - - [04/Jul/2001 14:30:45] "POST / HTTP/1.0" 200 -
```

Writing SOAP Clients

SOAP clients are surprisingly easy to write when using the SOAP module. You call a function simply by using it as a method to an open server connection. However, there are a few tricks and traps that you should be aware of when passing arguments and accepting return values.

We'll also take a look at how to access objects—since we're working with the Simple Object Access Protocol—and how to access functions registered in an alternative namespace.

Passing Arguments

You can supply arguments to functions just as you would with any normal function. Strings, numbers and multiple objects are passed as normal. Arrays and dictionaries can also be passed as normal to a remote function, but they are given special treatment at the server end. We'll look more closely at the mechanics of this process in the "Return Values" section, later in this chapter.

You are limited in the methods in which you can supply arguments to the remote function. Normal function argument passing, such as

```
server.newaccount('Current', 1000, 'MSDW')
```

work as normal, but if you want to supply arguments using the keyword notation, then the supporting function on the server side must be registered using the `registerKWFunction()` method. See the section "Writing SOAP Servers," later in this chapter, for more information.

Return Values

A remote function can return any type of value to a client, and you can return multiple objects within a single response just as you would with a local function. The string and numeric types are returned as normal, but arrays and dictionaries are handled slightly differently.

Rather than converting the advanced sequence types to one of the core object types supported internally by Python, the SOAP module creates its own object classes. These are based on the core object types, but they have a few little tricks for the unsuspecting programmer.

Handling Lists and Tuples

If there is a server such as the one in Listing 15.3, you can see that we register a function called `getNames()`, which returns a tuple of names. The SOAP standard doesn't include a tuple type, so the tuple is converted to the SOAP array type during serialization into a SOAP envelope.

Listing 15.3   A Server Supporting Multiple Return Values

```python
import SOAP

def getnames():
    return 'Martin', 'Sharon', 'Wendy', 'Rikke'

server = SOAP.SOAPServer(('localhost',8081))
server.registerFunction(getnames)
server.serve_forever()
```

When accessing the information from the client, you must either use `repr()`, because `str()` outputs information about the SOAP module object type, or access the information element by element. You can see the effects of the different access methods by using the client script shown in Listing 15.4.

Listing 15.4   Accessing an Array Returned by a SOAP Server

```
import SOAP

server = SOAP.SOAPProxy('http://localhost:8081/')
result = server.getnames()

print "Direct: ",result
print "Direct: ",str(result)
print "Direct: ",repr(result)
print "Individual: ",
for i in result:
    print i,
```

If you execute the script you get the following output:

```
$ pyclient2.py
Direct:   <SOAP.typedArrayType Result at 135860460>
Direct:   <SOAP.typedArrayType Result at 135860460>
Direct:   ['Martin', 'Sharon', 'Wendy', 'Rikke']
Individual:  Martin Sharon Wendy Rikke
```

Note the output in the third line—the information we returned in the `getnames()` function was returned as a tuple, but there is no tuple type in the SOAP definition, so what is actually returned is a list, not a tuple. This obviously breaks the usefulness of using a tuple in the first place. We've now listed the immutability of a tuple and ended up with a mutable list. There is no way around this (short of changing the SOAP standard), but if you know that you are expecting a tuple back from a function, you might want to embed the call to the function in `tuple()`.

Handling Dictionaries

Dictionaries are exchanged between server and client as the SOAP structure or compound type. They work in a similar fashion to the array type that we've already seen, except that neither `str()` nor `repr()` will print out a usable version of the object. However, you can access the elements within the returned dictionary just as you would with a normal dictionary.

To access a list of keys, though, you must use the _keys() method rather than the normal keys() method (note the underscore prefix). You can see an example of accessing information in this way in the fragment below:

```
for i in dict._keys():
    print i,'=>',dict[i]
```

In all ways, _keys() works in an identical fashion to keys().

Working with Objects

The SOAP module does not enable us to create remote objects directly, but it does enable us to access remote objects that have been suitably registered by the server. For example, Listing 15.5 shows a SOAP server supporting the Account class, which provides three methods: balance(), withdraw(), and deposit().

Listing 15.5   **An Object-Based SOAP Server**

```python
import SOAP

class Account:
    def __init__(self):
        self._account = ''
        self._balance = 0

    def balance(self):
        return self._balance

    def deposit(self, value):
        self._balance += value
        return self._balance

    def withdraw(self, value):
        self._balance -= value
        return self._balance

server = SOAP.SOAPServer(('localhost',8081))
account = Account()
server.registerObject(account)
server.serve_forever()
```

We can now access the methods of the account object that was created in the server, as demonstrated by the script in Listing 15.6.

Listing 15.6   **A SOAP Object Client**

```
import SOAP

server = SOAP.SOAPProxy('http://localhost:8081/')

print server.deposit(100)
print server.withdraw(50)
```

What we can't do is access the object attributes directly—you must always use a method to obtain or set information. Although this may seem like a limitation, it's actually how the SOAP standard was designed to work. The acronym refers to an object access protocol, so you should expect to access instances of an object and not remote classes.

For new classes that you create specifically to support SOAP servers, this shouldn't be a problem. When developing a SOAP interface to an existing module, you might want to consider creating a separate class that inherits from your original class and then provide additional methods that enable you to set and retrieve attribute information remotely using method calls.

Accessing Namespaces

SOAP servers register and support functions in a number of different namespaces. These can be used to enable a single request handler to support a number of different services to a number of different clients and also as a logical way to divide up the services that you offer.

To use a particular namespace, you can either specify the namespace at the time you create your SOAPProxy, as seen in Listing 15.7, or dynamically during a function call, as shown in Listing 15.8. The former is best used when you are calling functions from a single namespace on a remote server. The latter makes more sense when calling functions from multiple namespaces on the same server.

Listing 15.7   **A Client Accessing a Namespace Statically**

```
import SOAP

server = SOAP.SOAPProxy('http://localhost:8081/',
                        namespace='urn:mySOAPmethods')
print server.getmessage()
```

Listing 15.8   **A Client Accessing a Namespace Dynamically**

```
import SOAP

server = SOAP.SOAPProxy('http://localhost:8081/')

print server._ns('urn:mySOAPmethods').getmessage()
```

Note in both cases that we prefix the namespace with a `urn:` prefix definition. This is part of the SOAP standard, but it actually isn't required. If you leave out the `urn` declaration, the string will be used as the prefix.

However, be careful. If your prefix contains a colon, the namespace string will be incorrectly split across the colon. For example, we can access the `SOAP::Demo` namespace created for the Perl server that we created in Listing 10.2 in Chapter 10 using the code in Listing 15.9. Here we *must* include the `urn` prefix because the `SOAP::Demo` namespace, which is a Perl module declaration, contains colons.

Listing 15.9   **Accessing a Perl Namespace from Python**

```
import SOAP

server = SOAP.SOAPProxy('http://test.mchome.pri/SOAP/request.cgi',
                namespace='urn:SOAP::Demo')
print server.getmessage()
```

Note in Listing 10.5 that the address of the proxy points directly to the CGI request handler, since that's how we configured the server in Chapter 10. We can now run the script and get a reply from our Perl-based server:

```
$ python perl.py
Hello, world
```

Writing SOAP Servers

The `SOAP` module currently supports only the daemon form of SOAP server. It inherits from the `socket` and `BaseHTTPServer` modules in order to provide an HTTP interface for serving up object and function requests.

The basic process for creating servers using `SOAP` is first to import the `SOAP` module and then to register each function that you want to expose to a remote client. For example, in our first sample script, you saw how easy it was to set up a simple server to provide remote access to a local function.

We've already covered in this chapter some of the basics regarding the creation of different servers and the methods that you need to employ to provide an interface to modules—SOAP specific and existing. To finish off our look at the SOAP module and SOAP servers, we'll look at how to register functions and objects in specific namespaces and the different methods for registering functions and objects for providing services. We'll also take a brief look at how to access and use arguments supplied from a client in your SOAP server.

Namespaces

The SOAPServer class provides four registration methods: registerFunction(), registerKW-Function(), registerObject(), and registerKWObject(). All the methods support the same basic arguments:

```
register*(FUNCTIONAME|OBJECTNAME [, NAMESPACE])
```

FUNCTIONAME or OBJECTNAME is the name of the function or object that you want to register. In each case, if NAMESPACE is supplied, then it's registered into the supplied namespace. This should be specified as a raw string—you don't have to prefix the namespace with urn as you do with the client, but you do need to specify the namespace.

We have already seen examples of the two primary methods: registerFunction() and registerObject(). These register a single function or a single object and all of its methods so that they can be accessed from a remote client.

The registerKW*() methods register functions (or methods to an object) that use keyword argument passing instead of straight argument passing.

Using External Modules

If you want to export a function from another module, you can import the module and register the individual functions as usual. Note that importing works either into the module's own namespace, as shown in Listing 15.10, or when imported into the server module's namespace, as shown in Listing 15.11.

Listing 15.10   **Exporting a Module's Functions from Its Own Namespace**

```
import SOAP
import pyserver3mod

server = SOAP.SOAPServer(('localhost',8081))
server.registerFunction(pyserver3mod.echo)
server.registerFunction(pyserver3mod.strdict)
server.registerFunction(pyserver3mod.getnames)
server.registerFunction(pyserver3mod.getages)
server.serve_forever()
```

Listing 15.11   **Exporting a Module's Functions from the Server's Namespace**

```
import SOAP
from pyserver3mod import *

server = SOAP.SOAPServer(('localhost',8081))
server.registerFunction(echo)
server.registerFunction(strdict)
server.registerFunction(getnames)
server.registerFunction(getages)
server.serve_forever()
```

Note that the Python namespace has no bearing on or relationship to the SOAP namespace into which the functions are registered.

For objects the process is even easier. Because we are only registering an instance of a class, it makes no difference how we derived the class or instance.

Function/Method Arguments

As we've already covered, server-side functions can accept any form of argument. However, special care needs to be taken when accepting arguments made up of arrays and dictionaries. Just as when we were receiving information back from a server, the way in which you access the contents of the object data supplied as an argument differs from the normal Python object types. In particular, lists need to be accessed individually or output using repr(), and when accessing the individual key/value pairs from a dictionary, you must use _keys(). See "Handling Lists and Tuples" and "Handling Dictionaries," earlier in this chapter for more information and examples of how to extract information from the method/function call.

Debugging

The SOAP module uses the exception system to raise any errors. As you would expect, errors are propagated up from either the socket or HTTP server libraries if there is a problem.

Most problems can be traced either to a transmission fault (a host cannot be found) or to the remote server not responding to connections.

Problems in calling a remote function can be placed into one of two possible categories. Either the remote function does not exist or the call to the function failed because the argument or function implementation didn't work.

In either of these cases, the easiest way to identify any problems is to embed the call in a try statement.

XML-RPC Solutions

If you thought writing SOAP services with Python was easy, then you'll be pleased to hear that supporting XML-RPC is even easier. However, in comparison to the SOAP solutions that are available, the XML-RPC solution written by Python development team member Fredrik Lundh is not quite as mature in its interface.

The xmlrpclib package incorporates three files. The main xmlrpclib module contains all the core elements need to package up request calls into XML-RPC envelopes and unpackage them back into the method and parameters required to make a call on the server. To install the modules, copy them from the TAR package into the site-packages directory in the Python library directory (usually /usr/local/lib/python2.1).

XML-RPC Walkthrough

To use xmlrpclib from the client side, we need only to specify the location of the request handler when creating a new server instance. Once we've created the new instance, just like SOAP, we then access the methods on the remote server by name, as if they were methods to our class instance. You can see this more clearly in Listing 15.12.

Listing 15.12   **A Simple XML-RPC Client**

```
from xmlrpclib import Server

server = Server("http://localhost:8005/")

print server.echo('Hello')
print server.join(['Rod','Jane','Freddy'])
print server.pprint({'Rod'    : 23,
                     'Jane'   : 25,
                     'Freddy' : 26})
```

The module enables us to transfer any of the normal object types, using any of the normal methods for supplying data to the remote procedure. You can see from Listing 15.12 that we've supplied a simple string, a list, and a dictionary to the remote functions.

The server side is equally straightforward. To understand how the server side works, look at the xmlrpcserver.py module that comes with the package, included here in Listing 15.13.

Listing 15.13   **The Sample XML-RPC Server from *xmlrpclib***

```
#
# XML-RPC SERVER
# $Id$
#
# a simple XML-RPC server for Python
#
# History:
# 1999-02-01 fl  added to xmlrpclib distribution
#
# written by Fredrik Lundh, January 1999.
#
# Copyright (c) 1999 by Secret Labs AB.
# Copyright (c) 1999 by Fredrik Lundh.
#
# fredrik@pythonware.com
# http://www.pythonware.com
#
# --------------------------------------------------------
# Permission to use, copy, modify, and distribute this
# software and its associated documentation for any
# purpose and without fee is hereby granted.  This
# software is provided as is.
# --------------------------------------------------------
#

import SocketServer, BaseHTTPServer
import xmlrpclib
import sys

class RequestHandler(BaseHTTPServer.BaseHTTPRequestHandler):

    def do_POST(self):
        try:
            # get arguments
            data = self.rfile.read(int(self.headers["content-length"]))
            params, method = xmlrpclib.loads(data)

            # generate response
            try:
                response = self.call(method, params)
                if type(response) != type(()):
                    response = (response,)
            except:
                # report exception back to server
                response = xmlrpclib.dumps(
                    xmlrpclib.Fault(1, "%s:%s" % (sys.exc_type, sys.exc_value))
                    )
```

```
                else:
                    response = xmlrpclib.dumps(
                        response,
                        methodresponse=1
                        )
            except:
                # internal error, report as HTTP server error
                self.send_response(500)
                self.end_headers()
            else:
                # got a valid XML RPC response
                self.send_response(200)
                self.send_header("Content-type", "text/xml")
                self.send_header("Content-length",
                                 str(len(response)))
                self.end_headers()
                self.wfile.write(response)

                # shut down the connection (from Skip Montanaro)
                self.wfile.flush()
                self.connection.shutdown(1)

    def call(self, method, params):
        # override this method to implement RPC methods
        print "CALL", method, params
        return params

if __name__ == '__main__':
    server = SocketServer.TCPServer(('', 8000), RequestHandler)
    server.serve_forever()
```

As you can see from Listing 15.13, the module creates a new class, `RequestHandler`, which itself inherits from the `BaseHTTPServer` class from the Python standard library. The `do_POST` method then accepts a request from a client, extracts the necessary information, and decodes the XML-RPC envelope to determine the function that has been called. The parameters pass to that function.

The sample also includes a `call` method that prints out the request and echoes back the parameters to the client. We'll be using the `call` method later to set up our own server.

Rather than rewrite this module in its entirety, instead we can inherit from the `Request-Handler` class and override the `call` method to do something more useful.

The `call` method that is invoked by `RequestHandler` must accept two arguments: `method`, which is the text name of the method that has been called, and `params`, which is a tuple of the parameters. We need to convert these two pieces of information into a Python function call that will return information that we can pass on to the client.

In the case of the `method`, we're dealing with a text string, so we'll need to run it through `eval` in order to convert it into a code object that we can execute. We could pass `params` on to any function natively, such as this:

```
realmethod = eval(method)
realmethod(params)
```

We'd have to modify any existing functions to extract a single-element tuple before passing the real arguments supplied to the function. A better solution is to use `apply`, which accepts a tuple of arguments while actually passing them to the function you are calling as normal parameters.

You can see the final solution in Listing 15.14.

Listing 15.14   A Simple XML-RPC Server Using HTTP

```
import xmlrpcserver
import string

def echo(s):
    return 'Echo: %s' % (s)

def join(list):
    return string.join(list,' ')

def pprint(dict):
    str = ''
    for k in dict.keys():
        str += '%s => %s\n' % (k,dict[k])
    return str

class MyRequestHandler(xmlrpcserver.RequestHandler):
    def call(self, method, params):
        realmethod = eval(method)
        return apply(realmethod,params)

import SocketServer
server = SocketServer.TCPServer(('', 8005), MyRequestHandler)
server.serve_forever()
```

Listing 15.14 shows the versatility of allowing us to call virtually any function. Not only are we accepting the different types supplied by the client in the native formats, but we can also format the information and response too. We've even used the information to call an external function (from the `string` module) to handle the request.

The final part to the server process is to create a new socket server on a given port and then supply your request handler class when creating the server instance so that it can handle the requests.

To run the server, just start the script in Listing 15.14. As with all instances of Base-HTTPServer, you'll be given a normal web server–style access log as clients connect, such as this:

```
localhost - - [05/Jul/2001 13:48:27] "POST /RPC2 HTTP/1.0" 200 -
localhost - - [05/Jul/2001 13:48:28] "POST /RPC2 HTTP/1.0" 200 -
localhost - - [05/Jul/2001 13:48:28] "POST /RPC2 HTTP/1.0" 200 -
```

Note that you'll receive one request for each function call from a call—it doesn't batch requests.

From the client end, we get a nicely formatted set of results:

```
$ python xmlrpcc.py
Echo: Hello
Rod Jane Freddy
Jane => 25
Rod => 23
Freddy => 26
```

As you can see from this walkthrough, XML-RPC is incredibly straightforward. In fact, once you've resolved the call method to handle client requests easily, there's not much more to deal with. We can pass arguments and information to remote functions as we would any other function, and we can get the information back from those functions in the same way.

The only limitation of the xmlrpclib is that you cannot handle objects and classes remotely. This is not a limitation of the module at all but a limitation of the XML-RPC standard. If you need object access, use SOAP.

Debugging XML-RPC

As with the SOAP module, the xmlrpclib module raises exceptions when an error occurs. Exceptions are actually raised using the xmlrpclib.Fault exception, and they are propagated across the network connection.

For example, here's the default exception output when trying to call the remote join function with the wrong arguments:

```
Traceback (most recent call last):
  File "xmlrpcc.py", line 7, in ?
    print server.join({'Rod' : 23, 'Jane' : 25, 'Freddy' : 26})
  File "/usr/local/lib/python2.1/site-packages/xmlrpclib.py", line 547, in
➥ __call__return self.__send(self.__name, args)
  File "/usr/local/lib/python2.1/site- packages/xmlrpclib.py", line 630, in
➥ __request request File "/usr/local/lib/python2.1/site packages/xmlrpclib.py",
➥ line 585, in request return self.parse_response(h.getfile())
  File "/usr/local/lib/python2.1/site-➥ packages/xmlrpclib.py", line 601, in
➥parse_response
```

```
    return u.close()
  File "/usr/local/lib/python2.1/site- packages/xmlrpclib.py", line 371, in
➥ close
    raise apply(Fault, (), self._stack[0])
xmlrpclib.Fault: <Fault 1: 'exceptions.TypeError:sequence expected, dictionary
➥found'>
```

Unfortunately, the exception system can make identifying the source of an error difficult, because it's almost impossible to determine the actual location of the fault. To give an example, here's the output from a call to the remote `join` function when calling the function direct, rather than through `apply()`:

```
Traceback (most recent call last):
  File "xmlrpcc.py", line 6, in ?
    print server.join(['Rod','Jane','Freddy'])
  File "/usr/local/lib/python2.1/site-packages/xmlrpclib.py", line 547, in
__call__
    return self.__send(self.__name, args)
  File "/usr/local/lib/python2.1/site- packages/xmlrpclib.py", line 630, in
➥ __request
    request
  File "/usr/local/lib/python2.1/site- packages/xmlrpclib.py", line 585, in
➥ request
    return self.parse_response(h.getfile())
  File "/usr/local/lib/python2.1/site- packages/xmlrpclib.py", line 601, in
➥ parse_response
    return u.close()
  File "/usr/local/lib/python2.1/site- packages/xmlrpclib.py", line 371, in
➥ close
    raise apply(Fault, (), self._stack[0])
xmlrpclib.Fault: <Fault 1: 'exceptions.AttributeError:join'>
```

The best advice I can give is to test your functions thoroughly on the server side by using the client module to import the functions it expects to use, rather than calling them remotely. Make sure that you use the same basic process as used by the `call()` method (see Listing 15.14) in the request handler to invoke the functions.

Summary

Python supports both SOAP and XML-RPC through a number of different modules. The `SOAP.py` is not the only SOAP solution available for Python, but it does provide one of the easiest and simplest interfaces on both the client side and the server side for setting up the remote server and server-side functions and module access.

The entire SOAP system works through the use of a SOAPProxy class—you create a new instance of the class, supplying the location of the remote server that you want to talk to. From that moment, you can call any remote functions by specifying the remote function name as a method of the SOAPProxy class instance.

When communicating information between the server and the client, you need to be careful because the information is transferred using special objects rather than the base object types; although they work in the same fashion, some of the shortcuts you may have used, such as str(), don't work as advertised on the SOAP data types.

For XML-RPC, one of the solutions is xmlrpclib. It works in a similar fashion as our SOAP module: You create a new instance of the Server class, which simply requires the address of the request handler that you want to talk to. Remote functions are called just as methods to that object; then their request and other information is transferred to the remote server.

Both solutions enable you to access and call functions defined within the handler itself and also those imported from an external module.

CHAPTER 16

Zope and XML Documents

- Combining DTML and XML Resources

- Parsing External XML Documents

- Zope and XML-RPC

Zope is a solution for developing web applications. It combines the flexibility of HTML with the programming flexibility and CGI tools of a normal Python CGI script into one simple bundle; it is therefore no stranger to the needs or requirements of working with markup languages. If you don't know Zope already, check out the following sidebar.

Zope Backgrounder

One of the major issues facing most web developers is how to implement an application as a web site. At the simplest level, you use a combination of HTML files and CGI scripts to support your application. This model can lead to problems when you try to marry the two components: how to get the HTML- and CGI-based elements to look the same, for example. The CGI components require you to import and handle CGI and HTTP data and make decisions based on the information before supplying an HTML-formatted document back to the user.

Zope is different. Zope allows you to embed Python objects—or at least the information contained within them—right in the content of an HTML page. You no longer have to worry about marrying static HTML and Dynamic HTML components; HTML documents contain references to the objects and the information you want to display.

Furthermore, Zope provides a very simple way for multiple people to work on the same website at the same time. It uses a special markup language called DTML (Document Template Markup Language), which allows you to create HTML documents based on standard templates. The DTML system also allows you to integrate calls to Python objects and to create links between an HTML page and external data sources such as a SQL database.

The Zope system takes away all of the complexity of CGI programming. Instead, it allows programmers to concentrate on developing interfaces to internal systems, web developers to concentrate on developing suitable document templates, and content managers to concentrate on filling the site with content, without anybody having to cross into anyone else's territory. To help explain this further, let's look at how Zope is organized and how object publishing works.

Zope is made up of four primary components that work together to provide the Zope system. There are the Zope Object Request Broker (ORB), ZPublisher, the DTML markup language, and a Zope Object Data Base (ZODB):

- The Zope ORB is the object request broker in Zope, and it is the heart of the Zope system. The ORB is responsible for turning a client's request into information along the way and converting that into an object and method call on an object instance.

Continued on next page

- ZPublisher is the public interface. It interacts between the web server and the requests, CGI data and ZORB, which is actually a component of ZPublisher, rather than a separate entity. ZPublisher is the frontend to the entire Zope system and works with any number of different web server solutions, including CGI, PCGI, FastCGI, Netscape's Web Application Interface (WAI), COM, Medusa (see the description later in this chapter), and the included ZopeHTTPServer. Most people forget ZPublisher exists and instead refer to it as ZORB—for the most part the two terms are interchangeable.

- DTML provides a simple way of defining HTML templates. The templates are parsed during a request with information from any objects (brokered through ZORB) and external data sources. This allows a web system to be developed by separate Python developers and web programmers without either party worried about how to integrate the Python objects and HTML code.

- Zope's Object Database (ZODB) uses the pickle module (see Chapter 12, "Python and Unicode") to serialize a Python object and store the resulting data stream. Beyond the basics of storing objects, ZODB also includes support for transactions, concurrent access to a single object (similar to the row and table locking mechanisms in an RDBMS), and delayed evaluation of object components, allowing you to access objects without the time overhead of recovering all the information from the database until it's needed. The entire system works through a key, in a similar fashion to pulling information out of a dictionary within Python itself.

In addition to all this, Zope also provides a number of ancillary systems to help you develop Zope solutions. For example, the Zope kit includes an HTTP server module so that Zope can broker all of the requests itself, rather than working through an existing web server. Other components include a management framework for administering your website and a content management system that works with the CVS system to record changes to your website and allow multiple users to update the website content without interfering with another person's work.

Although Zope is familiar with the concept of markup languages—due to its use of DTML, a modified version of HTML—you might be surprised to know that in fact Zope is largely ignorant of XML.

It can export and import its own objects to and from XML format, but there are no built-in controls for processing XML documents. This might appear to be a mistake, but in fact the reason for the omission is far more straightforward. Since Zope enables you to work with external scripts and methods, why not leave the processing of XML information to those external scripts?

In this chapter we're going to look at four main areas in which Zope can be used to integrate with XML. The first is the basic import/export process supported by the core Zope system. Although it's of no use to the end user, it does provide an interesting insight into how you can dump quite complex objects in XML format.

The next section looks at how to produce XML documents from DTML information and how to parse external XML documents within your Zope applications for inclusion in your Zope databases. Finally, we'll look at how Zope exposes itself for use through an XML-RPC client.

The XML Export Format

Despite its heavy web service and integration focus, Zope doesn't actually include the built-in capability to parse and process XML documents. That doesn't mean that it's totally ignorant of XML. Once you have created a folder or collection on Zope, you can export the folder object into an export file. The normal format for this is a binary Zope export format that uses the Python `pickle` and `cPickle` modules to dump Zope objects out to the file.

This export format in Zope is exceedingly useful because it allows you to transport an entire Zope-based web application from one machine to another, incorporating all of the scripts, components, permissions, and other information from one machine to another. This is an excellent and more convenient way of transferring a project from one machine to another without the normal transfer and compatibility problems exhibited by typical HTML/CGI-based solutions.

In addition to the binary Zope export format, you can also export the site in XML format. To do this, go into the main Zope management panel, an example of which is shown in Figure 16.1, and click on the Import/Export button in the button bar at the bottom.

You'll be prompted to provide the name and location of the object that you want to export from the current folder. You can also elect to download to your machine or save onto the server. If you choose the former, then the file will be downloaded as `objectname.ext`. If you elect to save it on the server, it will be written as `objectname.ext` to the `var` directory within the main Zope directory.

To save in XML format, click the XML Format box and then click Export. You can see the window in Figure 16.2.

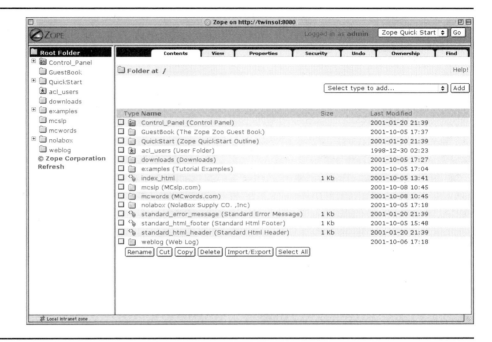

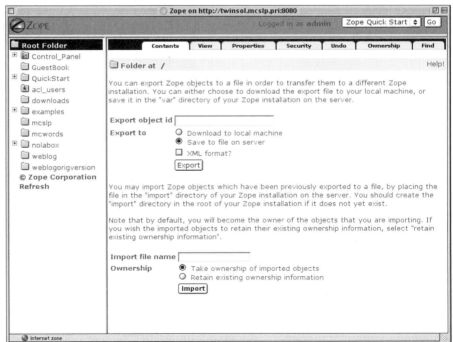

The resulting XML file is at least human readable, which is more than can be said for the Zope export formatted file. You can see a small snapshot of the start, middle, and end of such a file in Listing 16.1.

Listing 16.1   **A Zope Object Export in XML Format**

```xml
<?xml version="1.0"?>
<ZopeData>
  <record id="5065" aka="AAAAAAAAE8k=">
    <pickle>
      <tuple>
        <tuple id="5065.3">
          <string id="5065.1" encoding="repr">OFS.Folder</string>
          <string id="5065.2" encoding="repr">Folder</string>
        </tuple>
        <none/>
      </tuple>
    </pickle>
    <pickle>
...
<item>
        <key> <string id="5822.26" encoding="repr">title</string> </key>
        <value> <string id="5822.27" encoding="repr">Adds an XML
Entry</string> </value>
      </item>
      <item>
        <key> <string id="5822.28" encoding="repr">_function</string> </key>
        <value> <string id="5822.29" encoding="repr">receiveEntry</string>
</value>
      </item>
      <item>
        <key> <string id="5822.30" encoding="repr">func_defaults</string>
</key>
        <value>
          <none/>
        </value>
      </item>
      <item>
        <key> <string id="5822.31" encoding="repr">_module</string> </key>
        <value> <string id="5822.32" encoding="repr">parseXMLEntry</string>
</value>
      </item>
...
      <item>
        <key> <string id="5817.16" encoding="repr">raw</string> </key>
        <value> <string id="5817.17" encoding="cdata"><![CDATA[
```

```
<dtml-var standard_html_header>\n
<h2><dtml-var title_or_id></h2>\n
<p><a href="addEntryForm">Add new entry</a></p>\n
<dtml-in expr="objectValues(\'DTML Document\')"
sort="bobobase_modification_time" reverse>\n
<p><dtml-var bobobase_modification_time fmt="aCommon"><br>\n
<dtml-var sequence-item html_quote newline_to_br>\n
</p>\n
</dtml-in>\n
<dtml-var standard_html_footer>\n


]]></string> </value>
        </item>
...
<item>
          <key> <string id="5069.48" encoding="repr">Python_magic</string>
</key>
          <value> <string id="5069.49" encoding="base64">KusNCg==</string>
</value>
        </item>
      </dictionary>
    </pickle>
  </record>
</ZopeData>
```

If you read through this (great bedtime reading!), you should be able to spot both Zope's Python roots (the use of tuples and dictionaries) and the one situation in which the mapping between Python's attribute system, the Zope/DTML property system, and XML attributes can be seen clearly to complement each other.

You can also find raw DTML documents stored in XML CDATA blocks. You'll also note that individual Zope records are stored within a `<pickle>` XML tag, which relates to the `pickle` module normally used to dump the objects in raw binary format.

Although the XML format is very useful from an overview point of view when looking at a Python service, in essence it's nothing without being imported into a Zope service. Although you could parse and process the contents to determine different pieces of information, it will ultimately only make sense when it's all been reassembled as a Zope project. The DTML is Zope specific, and to extract individual components such as Python scripts and other elements, you'd be better off using the management interface and opening each item.

Currently the only product that understands and can use an XML export from Zope is Zope itself.

Combining DTML and XML Resources

Zope itself doesn't understand XML (except when importing a previous Zope object export in XML format), but that doesn't mean that you can't work with XML and other formats.

For example, you can use the built-in features of DTML and Zope to export a DTML resource in XML format. For this, you first need to have a Zope project to work with; for our examples in this entire chapter, you'll be working with a very simple logging project that allows you to enter a title and message, which is logged with its time in a DTML document.

The Web Log Project

To start with, create a new folder called weblog, into which you'll be creating all of the different elements. Your first job is a simple index page, index_html, which will display your log entries and provide a link to the form for adding new entries (addEntryForm). Log entries are stored within the Zope database as other DTML documents. You can see the script in more detail in Listing 16.2.

Listing 16.2   The *index_html* Main Page (DTML Method)

```
<dtml-var standard_html_header>

<h2><dtml-var title_or_id></h2>

<!-- Add a link at the top of the page so you can add
     new entries
-->

<p>
<a href="addEntryForm">Add new entry</a>
</p>

<!-- Get all the documents and dump their modification
     time, title and comments in a nice way
-->

<dtml-in expr="objectValues('DTML Document')" sort="bobobase_modification_time"
reverse>
<p>
<dtml-var log_title html_quote> at
<dtml-var bobobase_modification_time fmt="aCommon"><br>
<dtml-var sequence-item html_quote newline_to_br>
</p>

</dtml-in>

<dtml-var standard_html_footer>
```

The web form is equally simple; it just provides text boxes for a log entry title and its contents. You don't need to worry about the time because you pick that up from the document properties. The form itself, which is set to hand off processing to the addEntryAction method, is shown in Listing 16.3. You'll need to configure this as a DTML method with the name addEntryForm.

Listing 16.3   **The *addEntryForm* for New Log Entries (DTML Method)**

```
<dtml-var standard_html_header>

<p>Add a new log entry below</p>

<form action="addEntryAction" method="POST">

<p>
Title: <input type="text" name="log_title" value="My Log Entry">
</p>

<p>
Content: <textarea name="logcontent" rows="10" cols="60"></textarea>
</p>

<p>
<input type="submit" value="Add Entry">
</p>

</form>

<dtml-var standard_html_footer>
```

When the user clicks the Submit button, browser will pass the data from the form fields off to the DTML Method addEntryAction, shown here in Listing 16.4. This simply passes the user input off to the addEntry Python script and then displays a thank you message.

Listing 16.4   **Web Log Processing Form (DTML Method)**

```
<dtml-var standard_html_header>

<dtml-call expr="addEntry(log_title, logcontent)">

<h3>Log entry added.</h3>

<p>
<a href="<dtml-var URL1>">Back to Log</a>
</p>

<dtml-var standard_html_footer>
```

The final part of the basic system is our Python script. This determines the next ID number based on the number of objects in the current directory and creates a new object ID. Then it creates a new DTML document object using this ID with the title and content as received from addEntryAction, which in turn pulls the information from addEntryForm.

Finally, you also add the entry title field as an explicit object property to make it easier to obtain and to demonstrate how easy it would be to add more information to your DTML document. You need to create this as a Python script within Zope and configure the parameters passed to the script as log_title and logcontent. You can see the entry window with these options in Figure 16.3; the actual Python script is shown in Listing 16.5.

FIGURE 16.3:

The Python script for handling the request

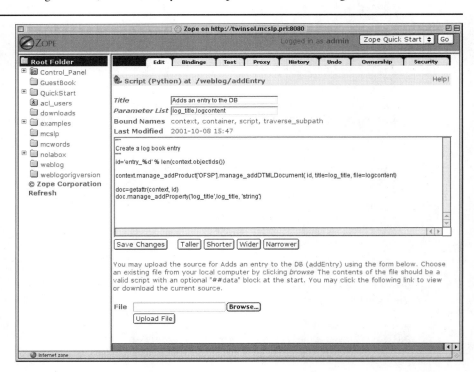

Listing 16.5   **Python Script for Adding the Entry**

```
"""
Creates a log book entry
"""
id='entry_%d' % len(context.objectIds())
```

```
context.manage_addProduct['OFSP'].manage_addDTMLDocument(~CA
 id, title=log_title, file=logcontent)

doc=getattr(context, id)
doc.manage_addProperty('log_title',log_title, 'string')
```

That's it—that's our framework for the log book system. It's simple enough, but it should provide a simple base on which you can demonstrate the real XML facilities of Zope.

You can see the main screen, entry window, and acceptance windows in Figures 16.4, 16.5 and 16.6, respectively.

FIGURE 16.4:

The main index page, showing existing entries

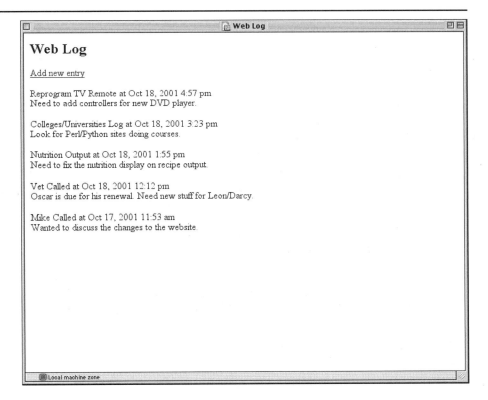

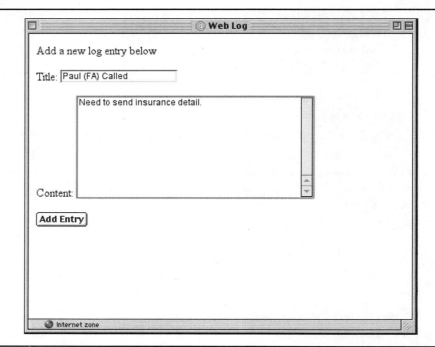

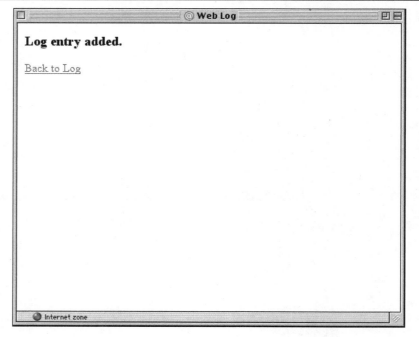

Exporting DTML as XML

Now that you have information in your web logging application, it'd be nice to be able to get it back out again in a more usable—XML—format. You could easily format your log in XML manually using a style such as this:

```
<logbook>
<entry>
<datetime>Oct 8, 2001 1:02 pm</datetime>
<title>Phone call</title>
<comments>From Tom, Lua</comments>
</entry>
<entry>
<datetime>Oct 6, 2001 3:48 pm</datetime>
<title>Email</title>
<comments>From Viki about WWW4Mail</comments>
</entry>
</logbook>
```

We can actually do this ridiculously easily by combining our required XML tags and some DTML instructions into a new DTML Method. The markup and code for this is show in Listing 16.6.

Listing 16.6   XML Export Method (DTML Method)

```
<?xml version="1.0"?>
<logbook>
<dtml-in expr="objectValues('DTML Document')">
<entry>
<datetime><dtml-var bobobase_modification_time fmt="aCommon"></datetime>
<title><dtml-var log_title html_quote></title>
<comments><dtml-var sequence-item html_quote></comments>
</entry>
</dtml-in>
</logbook>
```

To get a better response from this, you might want to get Zope to return the document as XML rather than HTML with unknown tags (which is what's produced otherwise). You can do this by setting the response type in your DTML using this:

```
<dtml-call expr="RESPONSE.setHeader('content-type', 'text/xml')">
```

Exporting in XML format in this way is most useful in applications such as this log book for exporting your document in the RSS format, which we've already looked at in previous chapters. Since we've already looked at the format of an RSS document, you should be able to create a similar DTML method for generating such a file.

Parsing External XML Documents

Zope doesn't have the capability to parse XML documents directly, but it is easy enough to write an external method to process an XML document and then provide an interface within Zope to use the method.

Listing 16.7 is a very simple SAX-based parser that will convert a document of this form:

```
<entry>
<log_title>Some or other title</log_title>
<logentry>Some other message</logentry>
</entry>
```

into an entry posted to the DB. To do this, you have a simple class, EntryHandler, that extracts the information and puts the two values (title and entry) into attributes; then you access those attributes and use the Zope API to create a new DTML document based on this information.

Listing 16.7   **External XML Processor (External Method)**

```python
# Import the SAX libraries/classes you need
from xml.sax import parseString
from xml.sax.handler import ContentHandler

# Create a new class to parse an XML log entry

class EntryHandler(ContentHandler):
    """
    Extracts a log entry from an XML message.
    """

# You need to remember if you are in a particular element
# so you can add the character data to the correct attribute
# These four fields are used to remember where you are and
# hold the information you extract

    log_title=""
    intitle=0
    logentry=""
    inentry=0

# Called when you see a start element, you identify if you are
# in a particular tag and set an attribute accordingly

    def startElement(self, name, attrs):
        if name=="log_title":
            self.intitle=1
        if name=="logentry":
            self.inentry=1

# Called when you see a start element, again you identify the
# element and then reset the current location - this
```

```
# prevents you from processing character data that you
# probably shouldn't be seeing - it doesn't matter in this
# case if the document contains other data, you just ignore
# it.

    def endElement(self, name):
        if name=="log_title":
            self.intitle=0
        if name=="logentry":
            self.inentry=0

# If you're in one of the two tags you are expecting, then you
# need to add the information to the attribute

    def characters(self, content):
        if self.intitle:
            self.log_title=self.log_title+content
        if self.inentry:
            self.logentry=self.logentry+content

# The name of the function that will be called by Zope is
# receiveEntry and accepts a single argument, the actual XML
# text you want to process. Note that you need to insert a
# 'self' argument here, because the external method becomes a
# part of the Zope API - self is in fact the same as the
# context object within an internal Zope Python script.

def receiveEntry(self, message):
    """
    Called by remote client.
    """

# Pass the XML text off to our XML/SAX processor class

    handler=EntryHandler()
    parseString(message, handler)

# Make sure you have the information as string
# representations of the extracted text.

    log_title=str(handler.log_title)
    logcontent=str(handler.logentry)

# Create the next available object ID

    id='entry_%d' % len(self.objectIds())

# Create a new DTML document based on the extracted
# text elements.

    self.manage_addProduct['OFSP'].manage_addDTMLDocument(
                        id, title=log_title, file=logcontent)
```

```
# Set the log_title property

    doc=getattr(self, id)
    doc.manage_addProperty('log_title',log_title, 'string')

# Return a suitable response to the caller.

    return "<h3> Received (%s)</h3>" % (id, logcontent)

# A little test when running it directly.

if __name__ == "__main__":
    content = """
<entry>
<log_title>Some or other title</log_title>
<logentry>Some message</logentry>
</entry>
    """

    print receiveEntry('',content)
```

To use this, create a script called parseXMLEntry.py in the Extensions folder of your Zope installation. To provide access to this external method, you need to add an External method to the Zope directory called addXMLEntry; you can see an example of this in Figure 16.7.

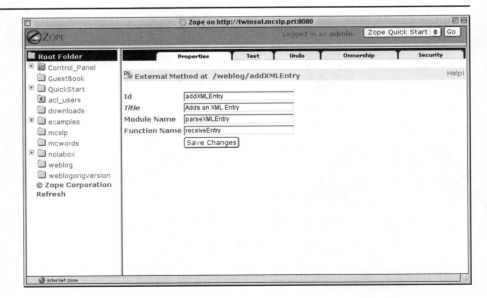

The ID of the external method is the name given to the object within Zope. It's also the name you use to access the method from a web form or DTML method or directly through a URL.

The `Module` name is that of the external module, without the `.py` extension, that you just created in the `Extensions` folder. The `Function` name is the name of the function that you want to call—in this case it's the main `receiveEntry` function in the extension you created.

Once the `External` method connection has been made, you can start to use the XML processor. The easiest way would be to use a web form that accepts a single text area into which you place the XML. The other alternative is to use a URL that accesses and posts the information directly, such as this:

```
http://myzope:8080/weblog/addXMLEntry?message=<entry>
➡ <log_title>Some%20or%20other%20title</log_title>
➡ <logentry>Some%20other%20message</logentry></entry>
```

Like magic, you get a response posted directly into the DB as a DTML document!

You've actually created a pretty clever process here—it converts an XML document (something largely alien to Zope) into a DTML document (something Zope knows very well). Although the example given here is deliberately simplistic, you could use a similar system to process just about any XML document and convert it either into a DTML document or—through the same basic Zope API—straight into a ZODB, Gadfly SQL, or other SQL database.

Note that you could just as easily have submitted your request to the Zope server from a scriptable web client such as Perl or Python—in fact anything that allows you to submit a URL and receive a response. But there is another way.

Zope and XML-RPC

One of the clever things about Zope is that because it hides all that complexity of community with a client from the Zope programmer, there are also other ways in which you can communicate with a Zope service.

Zope exposes objects and scripts over the WWW as well as the powerful Web API for CGI processing. It also provides a built-in parser to convert requests from an XML-RPC client into local function and object calls on the Zope server.

Therefore, you can use XML-RPC to send in a new log entry. The code for that is ridiculously easy, as you can see in Listing 16.8.

Listing 16.8   **XML-RPC Client for Adding an Entry**

```
import xmlrpclib

server = xmlrpclib.Server('http://twinsol.mcslp.pri:8080/')
response=server.weblog.addXMLEntry("""
<entry>
```

```
<log_title>XML-RPC Log</log_title>
<logentry>XML-RPC Entry</logentry>
</entry>
""")

print response
```

The format of the response is important—the location of the server and its port number is straightforward, but the actual remote function you've called is more complex. You've called server.weblog.addXMLEntry(). weblog is the name of the directory on the Zope server where the logging system is located, and addXMLEntry is the name of the External method you created in the previous section for processing an XML document supplied in a web form or other request.

You already know that this takes a single argument—the XML document that you want to parse—and you also know that the result should be a new DTML document within your directory. If you use the script in Listing 16.8 and then check the main page for your web log, you should see something like the image in Figure 16.8.

FIGURE 16.8:

The web log and its XML-RPC–submitted entry

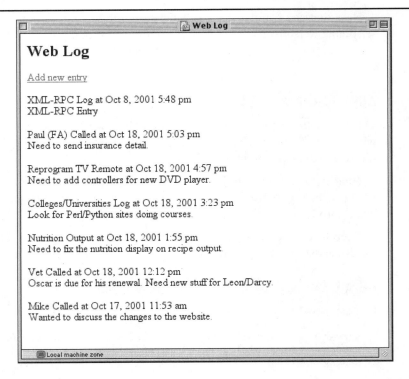

Summary

Zope includes built-in facilities for exporting and importing its own object database in XML format, but is unfortunately limited to this task only. For exporting documents from Zope in XML format all you need to do is embed DTML commands for extracting document object data straight into your XML layout. We can even make use of the multi-record formatter in DTML to output repeating XML elements.

Using an external Python script we can process and format XML within a Zope application. The Python extension script simply acts as an additional method that we can access as though it were a CGI script on your local site. The extension will have access to the same methods and data as a normal Python script within Zope so we can update and create documents within the Zope folder directly from our XML source.

Zope is also capable of servicing requests from XML-RPC clients directly, without the use of an additional extension because of the way in which Zope handles CGI requests. This makes supporting XML-RPC services through your Zope application as easy as writing the CGI script that would normally service your form submissions.

PART IV

XML and PHP

CHAPTER 17

XML and PHP

- Parsing XML with PHP

- XML-RPC with PHP

PHP4 comes with a built-in suite of functions for parsing and working with XML documents. The parser itself is based on the Expat parser, which is an XML 1.0 parser written by James Clark.

Expat is an event-based parser. This means that the parser processes the document in chunks, accepting parts of the XML document (anything from a byte up to the entire document). As each entity within the document is identified, the parser calls a predefined function whose job it is to handle the entity.

Since PHP is an embedded HTML technology, the most obvious use for an XML parser is to turn an XML document into an embedded part of the HTML document you are producing. Other uses include converting a web form into an XML document for storage, either directly or by handing off the XML document to an extension so that it can be translated into a database record.

In this chapter, we'll be looking at the basic mechanics of parsing an XML document within PHP. We'll also look at the basics of translating XML documents into HTML—the typical use of XML within PHP applications. In the next chapter, we'll concentrate on the development of XML-based applications in PHP. XML-RPC will be covered in Chapter 19, "PHP and XML-RPC."

Building a Simple XML Parser

As you already know, the XML parser available within PHP is based on the Expat library. The Expat library uses callback functions that are executed when the different entities in the document are identified.

A number of different entities make up an XML document, but the primary components that all XML parsers are capable of handling are the start tag (such as <data>), the end tag (</data>), and character data (any non-tagged element).

The full process for building an XML parser within PHP can be resolved into five steps:

1. Create the handlers that will deal with the different document entities.
2. Create the XML parser.
3. Register the entity handlers with the XML parser.
4. Feed the XML parser with the XML document, probably read from an external file.
5. Close the parser.

You can see a very simple parser in Listing 17.1.

↪ Listing 17.1   A Simple XML Parser

```php
<?php

// set up the function that will handle any opening
// tags. It must accept the tagname and any
// attributes

function startTagHandler($parser,
                         $tagname,
                         $attributes)
{
    echo("START: $tagname<br>");
}

// set up the function for any end tags
// end tags dont have attributes so we can simply
// accept the tagname for closure

function endTagHandler($parser,
                       $tagname)
{
    echo("END:   $tagname<br>");
}

// set up the function for any character data

function cdataHandler($parser,
                      $data)
{
    echo("DATA:  $data<br>");
}

// create a new XML parser

$parser = xml_parser_create();

// register the tag and data handling functions
// with the parser

xml_set_element_handler($parser,
                        "startTagHandler",
                        "endTagHandler");

xml_set_character_data_handler($parser, "cdataHandler");
```

```
// Open the file, here hardcoded,
//that holds the XML

if (!($xmlfile = fopen("simple.xml", "r")))
{
    die("Could not open the file for reading");
}

// Read data from the file in 2K blocks and send it
// off to the parser. Any error will trigger a call
// to die reporting the line and column number that
// the error occured within the source XML file
// !!!NOT!!! the PHP script

while ($xmldata = fread($xmlfile, 2048))
{
    if (!xml_parse($parser, $xmldata, feof($xmlfile)))
    {
        die(sprintf("XML error at line %d, column %d",
                    xml_get_current_line_number($parser),
                    xml_get_current_column_number($parser)));
    }
}

?>
```

If you feed the parser a simple XML file such as the one shown in Listing 17.2, then you get the HTML output shown in Listing 17.3. The actual output is probably best demonstrated by Figure 17.1, which shows the HTML in its rendered form.

Listing 17.2   **A Simple XML Document to Demonstrate the PHP Parser**

```
<contact>
  <name>Martin Brown</name>
  <address>
    <description>Main Address</description>
    <addressline>The House, The Street, The Town</addressline>
  </address>
  <address>
    <description>Holiday Chalet</description>
    <addressline>The Chalet, The Hillside, The Forest</addressline>
  </address>
</contact>
```

Listing 17.3   **The HTML Generated by the "Simple" XML Parser**

```
START: CONTACT<br>
DATA:
<br>
DATA:      <br>
START: NAME<br>
DATA:  Martin Brown<br>
END:   NAME<br>
DATA:
<br>
DATA:      <br>
START: ADDRESS<br>
DATA:
<br>
DATA:       <br>
START: DESCRIPTION<br>
DATA:  Main Address<br>
END:   DESCRIPTION<br>
DATA:
<br>
DATA:        <br>
START: ADDRESSLINE<br>
DATA:  The House, The Street, The Town<br>
END:   ADDRESSLINE<br>
DATA:
<br>
DATA:      <br>
END:   ADDRESS<br>
DATA:
<br>
DATA:      <br>
START: ADDRESS<br>
DATA:
<br>
DATA:       <br>
START: DESCRIPTION<br>
DATA:  Holiday Chalet<br>
END:   DESCRIPTION<br>
DATA:
<br>
DATA:        <br>
START: ADDRESSLINE<br>
DATA:  The Chalet, The Hillside, The Forest<br>
END:   ADDRESSLINE<br>
DATA:
```

```
<br>
DATA:      <br>
END:       ADDRESS<br>
DATA:
<br>
END:       CONTACT<br>
```

The simple XML document in HTML

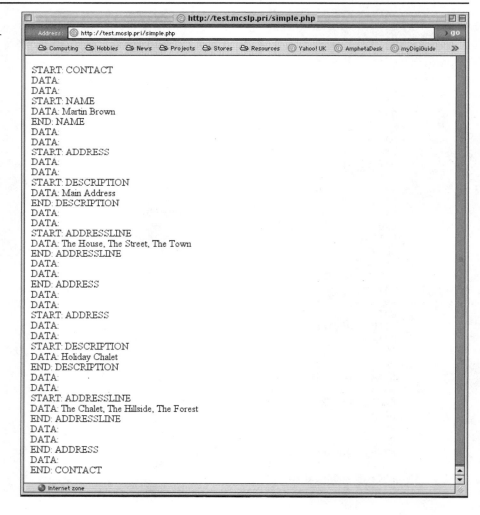

You can see a few important aspects of how the Expat parser works by looking in detail at Listing 17.3. Ignoring the formatting for the moment, you can see how each of the different entities in the source is passed off to handler functions that you created.

You'll also notice that the ASCII output of HTML includes additional spaces and newlines that you might not have expected. These are part of the original source file because of the way Expat (rather than PHP) works.

Expat passes on all characters from the source XML file, including spaces, newline, tab, and other characters. You'll also notice that the blocks of character data as they are processed are not consistent with the source file—even though you know from looking at the XML source that the character data is all in one block, when it's extracted by the Expat parser, it gets split into separate chunks.

Both of these effects are unfortunate side effects of the way Expat parses an XML document. In most instances they are not going to cause a significant problem because these artifacts affect what should be raw data. When converted to HTML, the additional spaces and newlines probably won't seriously affect the output, but you might want to apply a filter to ensure that any blocks of data consisting of any white space are ignored. A simple regular expression will handle this for us; see Listing 17.4 for an updated version of the cdataHandler() function and Listing 17.5 for the somewhat cleaner resulting output from the XML file.

Listing 17.4   **A Version of the Character Data Handler That Filters White Space**

```
function cdataHandler($parser,
                      $data)
{
    if (!ereg("^[ \f\r\t\n]+$",$data))
    {
        echo("DATA:   $data<br>\n");
    }
}
```

Listing 17.5   **A Cleaner Version of the XML File**

```
START: CONTACT<br>
START: NAME<br>
DATA:   Martin Brown<br>
END:    NAME<br>
START: ADDRESS<br>
START: DESCRIPTION<br>
DATA:   Main Address<br>
```

```
END:   DESCRIPTION<br>
START: ADDRESSLINE<br>
DATA:  The House, The Street, The Town<br>
END:   ADDRESSLINE<br>
END:   ADDRESS<br>
START: ADDRESS<br>
START: DESCRIPTION<br>
DATA:  Holiday Chalet<br>
END:   DESCRIPTION<br>
START: ADDRESSLINE<br>
DATA:  The Chalet, The Hillside, The Forest<br>
END:   ADDRESSLINE<br>
END:   ADDRESS<br>
END:   CONTACT<br>
```

As you can see from Listing 17.5, the output is now much cleaner, and the resulting rendered HTML page, although not shown here, doesn't look any different.

Inside the XML Parser

At the risk of repeating myself, the XML parser built into PHP is based on Expat libraries. The standard PHP 4.*x* distributions now include the source for Expat and the extensions for PHP itself to handle the XML processing, and XML should be enabled by default when you configure and build the system.

Information sent to the parser is handled entirely by the parser and the functions that you create to handle the different elements. There's no way to interrupt the flow of parsing and execute another function unless it's been triggered by the existence of an entity within the XML file.

In this section we'll be looking at the specifics of the XML parsing process, the supported XML handlers, and how to debug and trace errors within your XML documents.

Before we get there, two more points should be noted about the PHP XML extensions:

- XML documents are encoded using Unicode; this enables you to write documents that include characters beyond the normal 127 ASCII characters you may be used to. Unicode uses multibyte characters to allow you to include accented Roman characters as well as Kanji (Chinese/Korean and other Far Eastern languages) and all other native forms, including Indian and Middle Eastern characters. Check out the following sidebar, "Unicode Support," for information on how the PHP extensions handle Unicode-encoded XML characters, and remember that the effects are felt by both the character data and entity handlers.

- There is no standard for the case within tags in XML documents; in fact, the XML standard deliberately allows lowercase, uppercase, or mixed-case tags in XML documents. By default, the PHP XML extensions case fold tags so that when supplied as arguments to the entity handlers, they are received as uppercase. You can control this through an option; see the section "Getting/Setting Parser Options," later in this chapter, for more information.

Unicode Support

The PHP XML extensions supports the Unicode character set by using different character encodings for input and output. Input encodings affect how a PHP XML extension interprets incoming characters. The default input encoding is ISO-8859-1, which closely follows the basic Roman character set with extensions as supported by most computer platforms. The ISO-8859-1 set matches the ASCII set for the first 127 characters, so you can parse most ASCII/text–based documents without changing the encoding.

The output encodings are used when transferring information over to the entity handlers that you have configured to parse your XML documents. The output encoding affects all aspects the entities passed on to the entity-handling functions, from tag names to character data.

Any error in handling the input encodings—such as characters that do not match the set input encoding—raises an error. If the input encoding cannot be translated into the desired output encoding, the character is replaced with a question mark.

Initial Setup

The core function in the PHP XML extensions is `xml_parser_create()`. This creates a new instance of the XML parser. You can have many such parsers active in your application at one time, but remember that an XML document is generally executed and parsed from start to finish without any interruption.

If you want to parse multiple XML documents in sequence, it's a good idea to create a new parser each time, even if you place the resulting parser object into the same variable. This is because Expat is not a validating parser—that is, it doesn't verify that the content of the XML document follows a given DTD.

What Expat does is check that the document is structured correctly. Start and end tags must match, and any errors during parsing are raised by immediately falling out of the parser with a false return value. See the section "Error Trapping," later in this chapter, for information on how to identify the location of such errors.

By re-creating a new parser, you reset the information that the parser has built up regarding the structure of the document.

Creating the Parser

The first step to parsing any XML document is to create the parser itself. The format for the `xml_parser_create()` function is this:

```
xml_parser_create([string encoding_format])
```

The optional `encoding_format` is the character source encoding to use when parsing the document. This can only be set once—if you want to parse another document with a different encoding, you'll have to create a new parser. Accepted values for the input encoding format are ISO-8859-1 (the default), US-ASCII, and UTF-8.

The `xml_parser_create()` function returns a true value—actually a parser handle—if the parser could successfully be created or false if there was some kind of error. You need to catch this return value because you'll need the parser handle when you want to supply the parser with some data:

```
$parser = xml_parser_create("US-ASCII");
```

Supplying Data

Once the parser has been created, you can then call the `xml_parse()` function to start the parsing process. Although nothing will happen when the different entities are identified in the XML document or string that you pass to the function, it will cause the XML to be checked for its structure.

If you want to parse the document and perform different operations according to the different entities, you need to register the entity handlers before calling `xml_parse()`.

The format of the `xml_parse()` function is this:

```
xml_parse(int parser, string data [, int isFinal])
```

The parser should be the parser handler that was created when you called `xml_parser_create()`. The `data` argument is the XML data that you want to supply to the parser. You can supply as much or as little of this information as you like. If you're reading the data from an external file, a figure of 1KB or 2KB is enough for most uses. Remember though how Expat deals with character data: If you know that you have large character data elements within your documents, you may want to supply a larger quantity to ensure that the parser identifies the block as one entire unit.

The optional `isFinal` argument defines whether the block of data that you are supplying is the final block or not. The parser needs to know this to ensure that the structure of the document is valid; when you signify the end of XML, it ensures the tags match up and don't overlap. If you're reading from an external file, the easiest way to supply this value is to use the return from the `feof()` function on your file's filehandle.

Freeing the Parser

Once you've finished parsing an XML document, or if you've trapped an error that means you cannot continue processing the document, then you can call the `xml_parser_free()` function. This clears the parser and any resources it was using from memory. Although this is not a vital part of the process—because PHP frees the resources once the script terminates anyway—it is good practice, especially if you expect to be parsing large documents.

Supported Entity Handlers

There are three primary entity handlers: for the start, end, and data elements of your XML document. You've already seen some examples of these, but to recap, the format of each handler function that you need to create is this:

```
startTagHandler(int parser, string tagname, array attributes[]);
endTagHandler(int parser, string tagname);
charDataHandler(int parser, string chardata);
```

The names used here are just examples; a handler function can have any name.

The `parser` argument is just the parser handle that invoked the handler. The `tagname` is the tag text; for example, the tag `<para>` would be supplied simply as the string `para`.

For the start tag handler, the function is also supplied with an associative array of attributes. For example, the tag

```
<ref loc="someotherxml.xml" width=100 height=200>
```

is supplied to the handler function as this:

```
array("loc"    => "someotherxml.xml",
      "width"  => 100,
      "height" => 200);
```

The `chardata` argument is just the text identified by the parser as character data.

In order for these functions to be accepted as the handlers for the different entities, you need to use one of the `xml_set*()` functions. The start and end tag handlers are registered using the `xml_set_element_handler()` function, and the character data handler is registered by the `xml_set_character_data_handler()` function:

```
xml_set_element_handler($parser,
                        "startTagHandler",
                        "endTagHandler");

xml_set_character_data_handler($parser, "cdataHandler");
```

You can see a list of the other handlers for dealing with different entities that are supported by the XML parser in Table 17.1. Note that all entity handlers accept a first argument, the parser handler. Only additional arguments for the handler are listed. Also note that all handler register functions are prefixed by `xml_set_` and have a suffix of `handler`; for example, the `processing_instruction` function listed in the first row of the table should actually be called `xml_set_processing_instruction_handler()`.

TABLE 17.1: Other Entity Handlers Supported by PHP XML

Handler	Register Function	Handler Arguments	Description
Processing Instruction	`processing_instruction`	`target`, `data`	Handles processing instructions, which allow an XML document to execute a particular instruction. The `target` should be the target of the processing instruction (such as php). The `data` is the string to be supplied to the target handler. The usual operation is to supply `data` to the `target` processor.
Notation Declaration	`notation_decl`	`notation`, `base`, `systemid`, `publicid`	The `notation` is the name of the notation, `base` the base for resolving `systemId` (currently always a null string), `systemId` the system identifier, and `publicId` the public identifier.
External Entity Reference	`external_entity_ref`	`entityname`, `base`, `systemid`, `publicid`	The `entityname` is the name of the entity that has been identified, `base` the base for resolving `systemId` (currently always a null string), `systemId` the system identifier (the expansion of the external entity), and `publicId` the public identifier. Most functions should incorporate the contents of `systemId` into the current document.
Unparsed Entity Declaration	`unparsed_entity_decl`	`entityname`, `base`, `systemid`, `publicid`, `notationname`	Handles entities that are unparsed. See previous handlers for descriptions on how to handle the different arguments.
Default Handler	`default_handler`	`data`	The default handler function handles all other entities that do not already have an explicit handler function. The default handler is also called if you have not explicitly registered a handler for a given entity. The `data` contains the entire entity, including angled brackets.

Getting/Setting Parser Options

The PHP XML parser supports two options that change the way the document is parsed and how the information is propagated on to the entity handlers. The two options are discussed in the following.

XML_OPTION_CASE_FOLDING   If this option is set to `true`, tag names are converted to uppercase before they are supplied to the start and end tag handlers. Note that this only affects the tag names; attribute names and other elements within the entities remain unchanged. Case folding is on by default; setting the value to `false` disables case folding.

XML_OPTION_TARGET_ENCODING   This option sets the type of encoding used when data is parsed on to any of the entity handlers. The default type is the same as the input handler, as defined when the parser was created. If the input and output (target) encodings are different, PHP translates the data to the new encoding format. See the sidebar "Unicode Support" earlier in this chapter for more information.

You can obtain the current value of any option use the `xml_parser_get_option()` function. For example, to determine whether case folding is switched on, use this:

```
$casefolding = xml_parser_get_option($parser, XML_OPTION_CASE_FOLDING);
```

To set the value of these options, use the `xml_parser_set_option()` function. For example, to disable case folding, use this:

```
xml_parser_set_option($parser, XML_OPTION_CASE_FOLDING, false);
```

Other options may be added in the future. Check the documentation for PHP for more information.

Error Trapping

The main `xml_parse()` function returns an error code if it sees some problem with the XML document it is parsing. The return code can be matched against one of the predefined XML error codes, listed in Table 17.2. Note that nearly all the error codes refer to problems in the XML document that you are parsing, not a problem in the parser or your PHP code.

TABLE 17.2: XML Error Codes and Descriptions

Error Code Constant	Description
XML_ERROR_NONE	No error.
XML_ERROR_NO_MEMORY	Parser ran out of memory; try supplying the data in smaller chunks.

Continued on next page

TABLE 17.2 CONTINUED: XML Error Codes and Descriptions

Error Code Constant	Description
XML_ERROR_SYNTAX	Syntax error.
XML_ERROR_NO_ELEMENTS	No elements found in the document.
XML_ERROR_INVALID_TOKEN	A tag is not well formed; check for matching <> brackets.
XML_ERROR_UNCLOSED_TOKEN	The tag has not been closed.
XML_ERROR_PARTIAL_CHAR	Unclosed token.
XML_ERROR_TAG_MISMATCH	Start and end tags do not match.
XML_ERROR_DUPLICATE_ATTRIBUTE	Attributes in a tag have been duplicated.
XML_ERROR_JUNK_AFTER_DOC_ELEMENT	There is junk after a document element or end of the XML document.
XML_ERROR_PARAM_ENTITY_REF	The document references an entity that has not been defined.
XML_ERROR_UNDEFINED_ENTITY	The document uses an entity that has not been defined.
XML_ERROR_RECURSIVE_ENTITY_REF	The entity reference refers back to itself or to another reference that points back to itself.
XML_ERROR_ASYNC_ENTITY	Asynchronous entity.
XML_ERROR_BAD_CHAR_REF	Document contains a reference to a bad character number.
XML_ERROR_BINARY_ENTITY_REF	Document refers to a binary entity reference (which cannot be handled).
XML_ERROR_ATTRIBUTE_EXTERNAL_ENTITY_REF	Document refers to an external entity reference within a tag attribute.
XML_ERROR_MISPLACED_XML_PI	An XML processing instruction is not in the right place.
XML_ERROR_UNKNOWN_ENCODING	The XML document uses an unknown encoding format (not UTF-8, US-ASCII, or ISO-8859-1).
XML_ERROR_INCORRECT_ENCODING	The encoding defined in the XML encoding declaration is not supported.
XML_ERROR_UNCLOSED_CDATA_SECTION	A character data portion has not been terminated properly. If reading from a file, check that the entire file was read properly.
XML_ERROR_EXTERNAL_ENTITY_HANDLING	There was an error processing an external entity reference.

You can convert any of these error codes into a more meaningful string by using the `xml_error_string()` function. This accepts the error code number, as returned by `xml_parse()`, and returns a string error message. For example:

```
echo xml_error_string(XML_ERROR_NONE);
```

Once an error has occurred, you can also determine your location within the XML document that you were passing using `xml_get_current_line_number()`, `xml_get_current_column_number()`, and `xml_get_current_byte_index()` to determine the line, column, and byte of the location of the error. Note that these return the location within the XML document or stream you were passing where the parsing error occurred, not the location within your PHP script.

For example, here's a call to the `xml_parse()` function that reports an error detailing the line and column number, taken here from the first PHP XML processing example:

```php
if (!xml_parse($parser, $xmldata, feof($xmlfile)))
    {
        die(sprintf("XML error %d %d",
                    xml_get_current_line_number($parser),
                    xml_get_current_column_number($parser)));
    }
```

Converting XML to HTML

The previous example is unlikely to be the perfect example of what you can do with XML in PHP. Instead, let's have a look at a script, shown in Listing 17.6, which converts an XML document into HTML suitable for display on-screen.

Listing 17.6   **Converting XML to HTML in PHP**

```php
<?php

$file = "alien_r.xml";

// The array which holds the map from XML tag
// to HTML tags and attributes

$xmltohtml = array(
    "TITLE"     => array(array("tag" => "FONT",
                               "attrs" =>
                               array("size" => "+1")),
                         array("tag" => "B"),
                         ),
    "ACTORS"    => array(array("tag" => "FONT",
                               "attrs" =>
                               array("color" => "red")),
                         ),
    "PARA"      => array(array("tag" => "P")),
    "PANEL"     => array(array("tag" => "table",
                               "attrs" =>
                               array("border" => 0,
```

```
                                         "cellspacing" => 0,
                                         "cellpadding" => 0,))),
        "PANELTITLE" => array(array("tag" => "tr",
                                    "attrs" =>
                              array("bgcolor" => "black",
                                    "fgcolor" => "white",)),
                              array("tag" => "td")),

        "PANELBODY" => array(array("tag" => "tr",
                                   "attrs" =>
                             array("bgcolor" => "white",
                                   "fgcolor" => "black",)),
                             array("tag" => "td")),
        "EXTREF"     => array(array("tag" => "A")),


);

// set up the function that will handle any opening
// tags. This function looks up in the xmltohtml
// associative array and matches an XML tag with an
// equivalent HTML entry for displaying the data


function startTagHandler($parser,
                         $tagname,
                         $attributes)
{
    global $xmltohtml;
    if ($html = $xmltohtml[$tagname])
    {
        for($tagindex = 0; $tagindex < count($html); ++$tagindex)
        {
            $mytagdetails = $html[$tagindex];
            echo "<",$mytagdetails["tag"];
            if ($myattrs = $mytagdetails["attrs"])
            {
                while (list($k, $v) = each($myattrs))
                {
                    echo " $k=\"$v\"";
                }
            }

            while (list($k, $v) = each($attributes))
            {
                echo " $k=\"$v\"";
            }

            echo ">";
        }
    }
}
```

```
// set up the function for any end tags

function endTagHandler($parser,
                       $tagname)
{
    global $xmltohtml;
    if ($html = $xmltohtml[$tagname])
    {
        for($tagindex = (count($html)-1); $tagindex >= 0; --$tagindex)
        {
            $mytagdetails = $html[$tagindex];
            echo "</",$mytagdetails["tag"],">";
        }
    }
}

// set up the function for any character data

function cdataHandler($parser,
                      $data)
{
    if (!ereg("^[ \f\r\t\n]+$",$data))
    {
        echo($data);
    }
}

// Create a new XML parser

$parser = xml_parser_create();

// Ensure case folding is switched on

xml_parser_set_option($parser, XML_OPTION_CASE_FOLDING, true);

// register the tag and data handling functions
// with the parser

xml_set_element_handler($parser,
                        "startTagHandler",
                        "endTagHandler");

xml_set_character_data_handler($parser, "cdataHandler");


if (!($fp = fopen($file, "r"))) {
    die("could not open XML input");
}

while ($data = fread($fp, 4096)) {
    if (!xml_parse($parser, $data, feof($fp))) {
```

```
        die(sprintf("XML error: %s at line %d",
                    xml_error_string(xml_get_error_code($parser)),
                    xml_get_current_line_number($parser)));
    }
}
xml_parser_free($parser);

?>
```

The important parts of the script are the $xmltohtml variable and the two start and end tag handlers.

The $xmltohtml variable is a nested structure. The top-level structure is an associative array. The key at this top level is the XML tag that you want to replace, and the corresponding value is an array of HTML tags that you want to use as the replacement text. Note that you use an array of tags, not an associative array. This is because you need to order the HTML tags correctly in the output.

Each HTML tag is made up of the base tag and an associative array of attributes and their values that you want to introduce.

The startTagHandler() function identifies the XML tag in the $xmltohtml array and then works through the resulting tree to output the corresponding HTML tags that you've configured. Once the HTML tags have been output, you also output any XML tags that you've supplied before closing off each HTML tag.

The endTagHandler() function essentially does the same as startTagHandler(), only it processes the HTML tags in reverse so that they nest properly in the resulting HTML. Now you can see why you have an array of these tags—so that you can sequence and desequence in the same order.

We can explain this all better with a sample. In this XML code:

```
<title>Alien Resurrection</title>
```

the tag handlers would generate this:

```
<FONT size="+1"><B>Alien Resurrection</B></FONT><BR>
```

If you supply the script with the whole document, shown in Listing 17.7, you get the HTML output shown in Listing 17.8 (massaged slightly for readability) or the final rendered document shown in Figure 17.2. Note in both cases that I've trimmed the full document (which uses the *Lorem Ipsum* text) for brevity.

TIP   Lorem Ipsum is a standard piece of text that you can incorporate into a document for example purposes in place of regular text.

Listing 17.7   The Sample XML Document

```
<video>
<main>
<para><title>Alien Resurrection</title></para>
<para><actors>Sigourney Weaver, Winona Ryder</actors></para>
<title>Witness the Resurrection</title>
<para>Alien Resurrection is a film...Lorem ipsum dolor sit amet, consectetuer
adipiscing elit, sed diam nonummy nibh euismod tincidunt ut laoreet dolore magna
aliquam erat volutpat.
...
It va esser tam simplic quam Occidental: in fact, it va esser Occidental. A un
Angleso it va semblar un simplificat Angles, quam un skeptic Cambridge amico dit
me que Occidental es.
</para>
</main>
<panel>
<paneltitle>Related Items</paneltitle>
<panelbody>
<para><extref href="vhrefeo/alien.xml">Alien</extref></para>
<para><extref href="vhrefeo/aliens.xml">Aliens</extref></para>
<para><extref href="vhrefeo/alien3.xml">Alien3</extref></para>
<para><extref href="vhrefeo/alien_boxset.xml">Alien Legacy Box
set</extref></para>
<para><extref href="scifi.php">Sci-Fi</extref></para>
<para><extref href="horror.php">Horror</extref></para>
<para><extref href="action.php">Action</extref></para>
</panelbody>
</panel>
</video>
```

Listing 17.8   The Final HTML Document

```
<P><FONT size="+1"><B>Alien Resurrection</B></FONT></P>
<P>
<FONT color="red">Sigourney Weaver, Winona Ryder</FONT>
</P>
<FONT size="+1"><B>Witness the Resurrection</B></FONT>
<P>Alien Resurrection is a film...Lorem ipsum dolor sit
 amet, consectetuer adipiscing elit, sed diam nonummy nibh
 euismod tincidunt ut laoreet dolore magna aliquam erat
 volutpat.
 ...
 It va esser tam simplic quam Occidental: in fact, it va
 esser Occidental. A un Angleso it va semblar un simplificat
Angles, quam un skeptic Cambridge amico dit me que
Occidental es.
</P><table border="0" cellspacing="0" cellpadding="0">
<tr bgcolor="black" fgcolor="white">
<td>Related Items</td>
</tr>
```

```
<tr bgcolor="white" fgcolor="black"><td>
<P><A HREF="vhrefeo/alien.xml">Alien</A></P>
<P><A HREF="vhrefeo/aliens.xml">Aliens</A></P>
<P><A HREF="vhrefeo/alien3.xml">Alien3</A></P>
<P>
<A HREF="vhrefeo/alien_boxset.xml">Alien Legacy Box set</A>
</P>
<P><A HREF="scifi.php">Sci-Fi</A></P>
<P><A HREF="horror.php">Horror</A></P>
<P><A HREF="action.php">Action</A></P>
</td></tr></table>
```

FIGURE 17.2:

The final XML document rendered in HTML

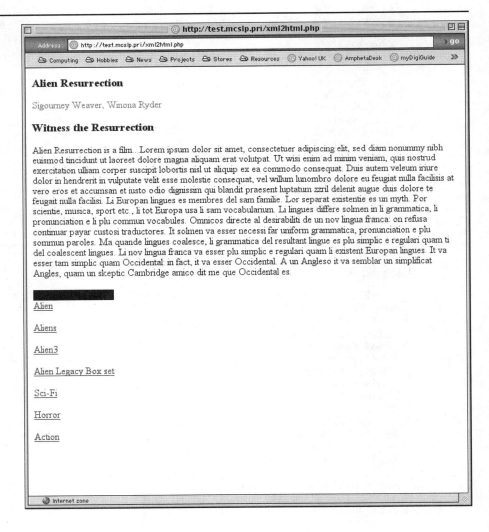

We've really only scratched the surface of what you can do. Once you have the XML document working through the parser, you can more or less translate the information as you like. The important elements are the entity handlers, which treat each individual entity as it is seen.

Summary

The PHP distribution includes XML extensions as standard, and these can easily be used to build parsers for converting XML into HTML or other formats for use within your PHP applications.

As with event-driven XML parsers in other languages, the PHP XML parser works by calling specific functions when the elements, character data, and other elements of an XML document are identified by the parser.

Changing XML to HTML is straightforward because the two are very similar. By creating an associative array structure that maps the XML elements into a series of HTML elements, we can make the translation quite easily. When each XML element is identified, the corresponding HTML elements are generated, character data is translated directly, and each end tag causes the list of HTML tags to be generated in reverse order.

## CHAPTER 18

Developing XML Applications with PHP

- The RSS Format

- Building an RSS Aggregator

Building an application in PHP that makes use of XML is essentially a case of either processing an existing XML document into HTML format for online display or building an XML document from existing information.

We've already looked at simple examples of how to output an XML document as an HTML page by using a static associative array to define the layout and structure of the document you want to display. Although XML can make a suitable format for generating HTML-style documents, it's much more likely that you'll use one or more XML documents from which you extract the information you want to display.

Rich Site Summary (RSS) is a standard for an XML document that enables you to summarize the content of a system. RSS is used on a number of websites to enable them to export a simple summary of news items and other details easily. You can download RSS files from a number of different sites and browse all the news from the different sites on a single page.

If you are like me, you probably regularly visit 5 to 10 or more sites each day in order to pick up the latest information. By downloading each site's RSS file and viewing it through a simple aggregator, I can view all of the news from all of the sites on one page.

In this chapter, we're going to start by taking a look at the RSS format. Then we'll look at the front end to an RSS aggregator that enables you to view the information from a number of different sites and jump directly to either the site's home page or the full expansion of the story you are interested in. You can even search RSS documents for a particular string.

There are sites on the Internet that enable you to view RSS information from a number of other sites. These include `http://mynetscape.com` and O'Reilly's Meerkat service (`http://www.oreillynet.com/meerkat/`).

The last part of this chapter then looks at how you can use the `LibXML` library to build your own RSS files from your own website. `LibXML` is a DOM-based parser that allows you to build XML documents easily through an object interface.

The RSS Format

An RSS document is basically an XML document using the agreed RSS structure. RSS is a standard that comes under the umbrella of the Resource Description Format (RDF), a standard agreed to by W3C for describing metadata—that is, data about data.

An RSS file consists of two main components: the header and the individual news items. The header contains information about the site, its home page, a description of the sort of news that appears on the site, and other metadata such as the editor, the webmaster, and copyright information.

Each news item (stored in an `item` tag) holds the news story title, the link to the page that displays the news item, and a description of the story to help the reader decide if he wants to read it.

Many of these items are essentially optional—for example, the channel needs to hold only the title, link description and image sub-elements; just as news items need to hold only a title and a link to the full story. However, it's customary for sites to include both story summaries and additional detail about the website. Other items can be added, such as details of an image to use as an icon for the site link.

You can see a sample RSS file in Listing 18.1. Obviously you can have as many `item` elements for the different news stories as you like, although in practice most sites limit their RSS file to the last 10 or 20 news items or all the news items for a given day.

Listing 18.1   A Sample RSS News Summary File

```
<rss version '0.91'>
<channel><title>MCwords News</title>
<description>Information about books, articles and sample
scripts from the MCwords writing team.</description>
<link>http://www.mcwords.com</link>
<language>en-us</language>
<copyright>Copyright, 1998-2002, MCslp.</copyright>
<item>
<title>New Scripting XML with Perl, Python and PHP
book released</title>
<link>http://www.mcwords.com/projects/books/sxml</link>
<description>Scripting XML with Perl, Python and PHP
looks at the mechanics of processing and building
XML documents with Perl, Python, PHP, Rebol, Ruby,
Tcl and AppleScript. </description>
</item>
<channel>
</rss>
```

When outputting the information, you obviously first need to output the header information (with or without a description), followed by a list of all the news items. If you are building an aggregator, then you need to repeat the process for a number of different RSS files in order to build a single page with all the information.

Finding your RSS files in the first place is relatively easy. Most sites publicize the fact that you can download their RSS summary files from their sites. Downloading them is left as an exercise for you to try—my preferred method is a very simple script based on Gisle Aas' LWP toolkit under Perl.

Building an RSS Aggregator

The whole point of the RSS forma is that it should make viewing and reading all the websites you normally look through much easier. In general, the majority of news sites that people visit show loads of information, much of which you are not interested in, but often you have to see either a summary or the whole thing.

When I view sites such as /. (http://www.slashdot.org) or even the BBC news site (http://www.bbc.co.uk/news), I spend most of my time looking past the stories I'm not interested in, perhaps clicking on only two or three stories each day.

Although in its basic format RSS doesn't filter out those stories you aren't interested in, it does make it easier to browse over all the stories from all the sites you view each day in order to extract the few stories you do want to read.

For your PHP-based aggregator, you need to cover three main facilities:

- Browse the channel information. This is useful if I want to remind myself what a particular site is about. I have about 200 different sites in my aggregation list, and some of them have somewhat esoteric names that make it difficult to remember what the site is all about.

- Browse the stories. This is just a single-page summary of all the news stories you want to read, incorporating links to allow you to view the full story when you find something you're interested in.

- Search all the sites. Because you have access to the news from a number of different sites, you can search across all the sites for stories that match a particular string. For example, you might want to pull out all the stories relating to PHP from all the different news and scripting sites.

I'm a big fan of the single script for most processes because it often makes the process of updating and managing the script much easier, especially if you're dealing with very similar basic structures and display methods. Your entire PHP RSS aggregator system is therefore held within the single script shown in Listing 18.2.

Listing 18.2   A PHP RSS Aggregator

```php
<?php

$currentTag = '';
$title = '';
$link = '';
$description = '';
$channels = array();
```

```
$items = array();
$pubdate = '';

function startTagHandler($parser,
             $tagname,
             $attributes)
{
  global $currentTag;
  $currentTag = $tagname;
}

function endTagHandler($parser,
             $tagname)
{
  global $currentTag, $items, $title, $link,
       $description, $channels,
$pubdate, $search;

  if (strcmp($tagname,"CHANNEL") == 0)
  {
    $channels[] = array("title" => $title,
                        "link" => $link,
                        "description" => $description,
                        "pubdate" => $pubdate);

    $title = '';
    $link = '';
    $pubdate = '';
    $description = '';
  }
  elseif(strcmp($tagname,"ITEM") == 0)
  {
    if (ereg("^[a-zA-Z0-9].*",$search))
    {
      if (eregi($search, $title) ||
        eregi($search, $description))
      {
        $items[] = array("title" => $title,
                         "link" => $link,
                         "description" => $description,
                  );
      }
    }
    else
    {
      $items[] = array("title" => $title,
                       "link" => $link,
                       "description" => $description,
                  );
    }
```

```php
    $title = '';
    $link = '';
    $description = '';
  }
}

function cdataHandler($parser,
            $data)
{
  global $currentTag, $title, $link, $description, $channels;

  if (strcmp($currentTag, "TITLE") == 0)
  {
    $title .= $data;
  }
  elseif (strcmp($currentTag, "LINK") == 0)
  {
    $link .= $data;
  }
  elseif (strcmp($currentTag, "DESCRIPTION") == 0)
  {
    $description .= $data;
  }
  elseif (strcmp($currentTag, "PUBDATE") == 0)
  {
    $pubdate .= $data;
  }
}

function getchannelinfo($channelfile)
{
  global $channels;

  $parser = xml_parser_create();

  xml_parser_set_option($parser, XML_OPTION_CASE_FOLDING, true);

  xml_set_element_handler($parser,
            "startTagHandler",
            "endTagHandler");
  xml_set_character_data_handler($parser, "cdataHandler");

  if (!($fp = fopen($channelfile, "r"))) {
    die("could not open XML input");
  }

  while ($data = fread($fp, 4096))
  {
    if (!xml_parse($parser, $data, feof($fp)))
```

```
      {
        die(sprintf("XML error: %s at line %d in %s",
              xml_error_string(xml_get_error_code($parser)),
              xml_get_current_line_number($parser),
              $channelfile));
      }
    }
  }

  xml_parser_free($parser);
}

function getallchannels($showsub)
{
  global $channels, $items;
  $handle=opendir("rss/");
  while (($file = readdir($handle))!==false)
  {
    if (ereg("^[a-zA-Z0-9].*\.xml$",$file))
    {
      getchannelinfo("rss/" . $file);
      if (count($items) > 0)
      {
        print "<b>" . $channels[$i]["title"] . "</b>";
        print "<font size=\"-1\"><a href=\"" .
            $channels[$i]["link"] .
            "\">Jump to Homepage</a></font>";

        if (ereg("[a-zA-Z0-9]+",
            $channels[$i]["pubdate"]))
        {
          print " (" . $channels[$i]["pubdate"] . ") ";
        }
        print "<br>";

        if ($showsub == 0)
        {
          print $channels[$i]["description"];
        }
        else
        {
          print "<br>";
          for($j=0;$j<count($items);$j++)
          {
            print "<a href=\"" . $items[$j]["link"] .
                "\">" . $items[$j]["title"] . "</a><br>";

            if (ereg("[a-zA-Z0-9]+",
                $items[$j]["description"]))
            {
```

```php
                    print $items[$j]["description"] .
                            "<br><br>";
                }
            }
        }
        print "<br><br>";
    }

    $channels = array();
    $items = array();

    }
  }
  closedir($handle);
}

?>

<html>
<head>
<title>News Channel List</title>
</head>
<body>
<font size="+2"><b>News Feed</b></font><br>
<form action="sitelist.php" METHOD=GET>
<input type="hidden" name="expandStories" value="1">
<font size="-1">
<a href="sitelist.php?expandStories=0">View Channel Information</a>
 | 
<a href="sitelist.php?expandStories=1">Show All News</a>
</font>
 | 
<input type="text" size="40" name="search">
<input type="submit" value="Search"></form><br>
<?php
  if (ereg("^[a-zA-Z0-9].*",$search))
  {
    print "Search results for $search<br><br>";
  }
  getallchannels($expandStories);
?>
</body>
</html>
```

You should be able to follow the structure and comments in the code to see what's going on, but there are special notes on the different components of the system in the next section.

The RSS Parser

The RSS parser is actually just a standard XML parser with functions defined for start, end, and character data tags. You could have used a DOM system to extract the information, but since you need to parse the whole document when producing the story list or searching, you may as well use an event-based parser to work through the entire document and just ignore what you don't need.

The three handlers do all the main work, and we'll look at each one individually.

The *startTagHandler* Function

The startTagHandler records the current tag name:

```
function startTagHandler($parser,
            $tagname,
            $attributes)
{
  global $currentTag;
  $currentTag = $tagname;
}
```

You'll need to know this in order to know where you need to record the information about the title, link, description, or other data. You use global variables to hold the information until you're ready to process it when you reach an end element.

The *cdataHandler* Function

The cdataHandler function adds whatever character data has been extracted from the XML file into one of the appropriate global variables that will hold the title, description, link, or publication date information. You know which variable to store the information in because startHandler has been recording this information.

For example, here's the fragment for adding text to your global $description variable:

```
function cdataHandler($parser,
            $data)
{
  global $currentTag, $title, $link, $description, $channels;
...
  elseif (strcmp($currentTag, "DESCRIPTION") == 0)
  {
    $description .= $data;
  }
...
}
```

Note that you don't actually make a distinction between the title, link, or description within the channel section or a news item. This is not an oversight—by the time you've finished working with the channel data, these variables will be empty. The reason for this is that the endHandler function deals with these global variables, adding them to suitable structures so that the information can be easily displayed later.

The *endTagHandler* Function

Once you've collected the character data within the different elements that you know make up a particular component, you can then build a summary of the information and store it. In the case of the channel section within an RSS document, you know when you see the channel end tag that the data in your global $title, $link, $description, and $pubdate variables contains the channel data. You put the information into an associative array, $channel, as you can see from this fragment from the main script:

```
if (strcmp($tagname,"CHANNEL") == 0)
{
   $channels[] = array("title" => $title,
                       "link" => $link,
                       "description" => $description,
                       "pubdate" => $pubdate);

   $title = '';
   $link = '';
   $pubdate = '';
   $description = '';
}
```

If the end element is item, then you know that $title, $link, and $description refer to the information within an individual news item. This information is placed into an associative array, but there's one more check needed before you add the associative array of information to the global list of news stories for this site.

Searches occur at this point. If a search item has been defined (which you check by looking for a repeating alphanumeric sequence in a regular expression), then you search for a match between a search string and either the news item's title or its description. If it's found in either element, you add the item to the global $items array; otherwise you just forget the information.

If there is no valid search string, then you place the associative array into the global $items list, thereby building a list of all the stores in the RSS file. It's important to remember to zero out the global variables used to hold the temporary character data. Otherwise, you start adding information to news items you've already identified.

The *getchannelinfo* Function

The getchannelinfo function opens the file that is passed to it, creates a parser instance, sets up the handlers (start, end, and character data) in order to parse the XML file, and then provides the parser with the contents of the RSS file itself.

The *getallchannels* Function

The final part of the process is to open each file within your list of RSS documents and send that to getchannelinfo() to parse the document and extract the channel information and news items. I've put the RSS files I've downloaded into a subdirectory called rss, which is searched by using opendir() with each file being matched by a regular expression to ensure I only load files ending in .xml:

```
$handle=opendir("rss/");
  while (($file = readdir($handle))!== false)
  {
    if (ereg("^[a-zA-Z0-9].*\.xml$",$file))
```

getallchannels() is also responsible for displaying the information. There are two parts to the process. First you need to decide whether to display news items (which is handled by the value of the supplied $showsub function argument). Second, you need to account for the layout when the information from the RSS files doesn't match what you could generate.

For example, there's no point in adding an extra <br> tag to the output if there is a description for a channel or news item. Another such example would be to ignore those channels that don't contain any items matched in a search.

The Aggregator in Action

All the pages include three links at the top to show the channel summary and the news stories and perform a search across all the RSS channels.

Displaying the Channel Summary

The channel summary is just a dump of the title, link, and description tags from the channel portion of each RSS file in your directory. You can see a sample of the output in Figure 18.1. In addition to the basic information, you also provide a link to take the user straight to each channel's website.

FIGURE 18.1:

Your news channel
summary

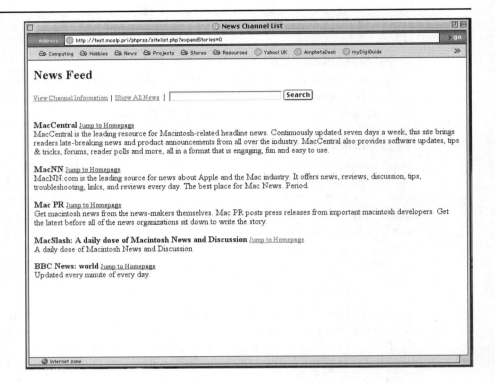

Displaying the News Stories

When displaying the news stories, you output only the channel name and jump link, followed by a list of each story title, which is itself a link to the real story on the full website. Therefore, clicking on a story title will take you to the site so that you can read the full story.

If there is a story description, you print that below each story as well. Figure 18.2 shows a sample of this in action.

Performing a Search

The final example is the search result screen. Every page has a search box into which you can type a word or words to search for from the titles and story summaries in the RSS feeds. Figure 18.3 shows the result when searching for "DVD" in your story list.

Note that, because you've used a free-form regular expression search, the system already supports the capability to do complex regular expression–based searches without making any changes to the script.

Full news feeds and
stories

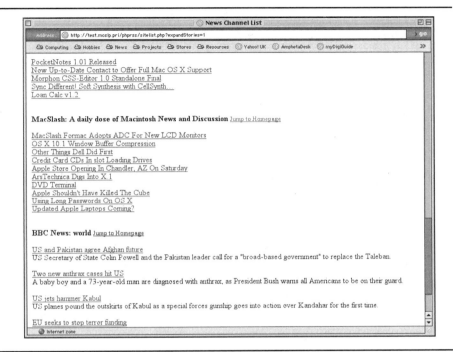

Search results

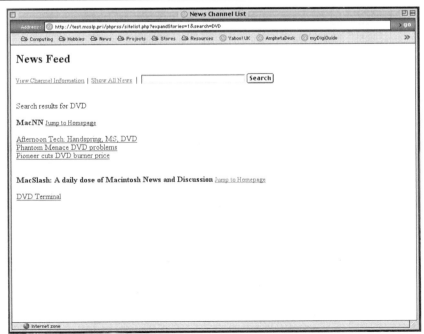

Writing RSS Documents

If you've developed a site that has a "news" feel to it, you want to be able to write your own RSS document from your website. Although you could do this manually by outputting the tags, a much easier way is to use a DOM parser to build up the document in a structured fashion, tag by tag.

As you already know if you've looked at Chapter 5, "Data Exchange and XML," an XML document that is parsed by a DOM parser produces a tree structure that is based on a number of different nodes. As well as parsing an existing XML document into a DOM structure, you can create an XML document by creating the different nodes that make up the document.

PHP, through the GNOME XML library, supports a DOM parser in the form of LibXML. We'll ignore the process of parsing a document in this form for the moment and instead concentrate on how to build an RSS document using the LibXML DOM node system.

NOTE   PHP4 includes the necessary functions for working with the DOM parser, but the implementation is subject to change because the new features are added to the PHP system. For example, function names have already changed a number of times since the original release. Those used here were correct at the time of writing, but check http://www .php.net/manual/en/ref.domxml.php to get the latest information.

Creating a DOM Document

The entire system works by creating a nested structure of objects. The base object of any DOM structure is a document object. You create a "blank" document object by using the domxml_new_xmldoc() function. The result is a document into which you can start building the XML content. The function accepts a single optional argument, the version of the XML being produced:

```
$doc = domxml_new_xmldoc("1.0")
```

There are four base methods to your new document object:

- root() returns a node object containing the root element of the document.

- add_root() adds a new root node to your document.

- dtd() adds a DTD object.

- dumpmem() returns a string of the DOM structure as XML.

add_root() is the most important element because it starts the root element of your XML document. The function accepts a single argument, the name of the root element itself. We're dealing with RSS, so we'll use rss:

```
$root = $doc->add_root("rss");
```

The return value is a node object. The next stage is to start adding nodes to your `root` object to build the document.

Adding Nodes

Nodes account for all the different components within an XML document, from the XML tags to the tag attributes down to the character data contained between tags.

You can navigate around nodes in a document by using the `parent()` and `children()` methods to a node object. The `children()` method returns an array of all child nodes belonging to the current object. The `parent()` method returns a reference to the parent node of the current object. For example, from an attribute node, this returns the parent tag node.

You can add new nodes to an existing node by using the `new_child()` method. This accepts two arguments: the name of the XML element you want to create and the data that you want to add to the current node. For example, you can add your `channel` node to your `root` `rss` node using:

```
$root->new_child("channel","");
```

The result in each case is a new node object, although you can ignore the result if you do not want to add any children to the node.

The last part of the puzzle is the capability to add attributes to an existing element node. You do this with the `setattr()` method, which accepts the attribute name and its value.

In Listing 18.3 you can see the code required to build an RSS document that mirrors the example RSS file in Listing 18.1.

Listing 18.3   **Generating an RSS File**

```
$doc = domxml_new_xmldoc("1.0");

$root = $doc->add_root("rss");
$root->setattr("version", "0.91");

$channel = $root->new_child("channel","");
$channel->new_child("title","MCwords News");
$channel->new_child("description","Information about books, articles and sample
scripts from the MCwords writing team.");
$channel->new_child("link","http://www.mcwords.com");
$channel->new_child("language","en-us");
$channel->new_child("copyright","Copyright, 1998-2002, MCslp.");

$item = $channel->new_child("item","");
$item->new_child("title","New Scripting XML with Perl, Python and PHP book
released");
```

```
$item->new_child("link","http://www.mcwords.com/projects/books/sxml");
$item->new_child("description", "Scripting XML with Perl, Python and PHP looks
at the mechanics of processing and building XML documents with Perl, Python,
PHP, Rebol, Ruby, Tcl and AppleScript.");
```

Writing the XML

Once you've produced your DOM structure for your XML document, the final stage is to output the structure as XML. You can do that easily with the dumpmem() method to the original document object you created with domxml_new_xmldoc().

In fact, just adding this:

```
print($doc->dumpmem());
```

is enough to generate the XML. If you want to display the XML within a browser, then use the htmlspecialchars() filter function:

```
print(htmlspecialchars($doc->dumpmem()));
```

The resulting document looks like Listing 8.4, which is almost identical to Listing 18.1. Note, by the way, that I've cleaned up the output in Listing 18.4 to make it easier to read. The dumpmem() method doesn't pretty-print the output.

Listing 18.4   PHP-Generated RSS in XML Form from a DOM Structure

```
<?xml version="1.0"?>
<rss version="0.91">
<channel><title>MCwords News</title>
<description>Information about books, articles and sample
scripts from the MCwords writing team.</description>
<link>http://www.mcwords.com</link>
<language>en-us</language>
<copyright>Copyright, 1998-2002, MCslp.</copyright>
<item>
<title>New Scripting XML with Perl, Python and PHP
book released</title>
<link>http://www.mcwords.com/projects/books/sxml</link>
<description>Scripting XML with Perl, Python and PHP looks
at the mechanics of processing and building XMLdocuments
with Perl, Python, PHP, Rebol, Ruby, Tcl and AppleScript.</description>
</item>
</channel>
</rss>
```

Summary

The RSS format is an XML structure that allows us to summarize the information from a website or other information source into a convenient document. By collecting together a number of RSS files from different sites we can aggregate the information into a single page.

Many different news sites create their own RSS summary files and we can use the abilities of PHP to read and summarize the stories—including links to the full story on the home site—into a single page. This allows you to scan through the stories and different pieces of information from a variety of sites only choosing the stories that interest you.

In addition to summarizing RSS documents from other sites, PHP can also be used to create an RSS file from the news and information on your own site. All we need to do is generate the XML document structure based on the information from your site. This could be done manually or if you are using a database to hold your news and other stories, it could be created automatically from your database.

## CHAPTER 19

PHP and XML-RPC

- Writing an XML-RPC Server

- Writing an XML-RPC Client

- Inside XML-RPC for PHP

XML-RPC is a technology that uses an XML document transferred over a transport (usually HTTP) that requests a remote function on a machine to be executed. The function called can be any supported function and you can supply arguments to it just as you would a local function. Also, just like a local function, the results of the function call are sent back over the transport link back to the caller.

XML-RPC is useful in those situations when you want to execute a piece of code on a remote machine without resorting to designing your own network protocol and without the need to parcel up information in a CGI request and get it back in HTML format from the server.

It's particularly useful in distributed applications where you may have a number of individual web servers providing information and services to your clients, but with only one or two back-end servers actually processing information and exchanging data on a secure network.

Using XML-RPC, the user requests a document from the server, the sever finds that it needs some information from one of the data servers, send the request by XML-RPC to the data server, receives the response back and then displays that information to the user.

The critical point here is that the remote server is doing much more than simply supplying the data back; after all, we can do this already using MySQL, PostgreSQL or many other database solutions. The remote server is executing a function written in PHP (or any other language, since XML-RPC is language- and platform-independent).

The server side function could access data from the database and put it into a structure suitable for returning from the XML-RPC function call. It might be a summary function that not only accesses the data from the database but also summarizes it before returning the summary data to the XML-RPC client. All the processing occurs on the database server, allowing the XML-RPC client (the web server) to concentrate on processing web requests from the end user.

The XML-RPC solution available with PHP is not quite as easy to use and straightforward as those we've seen for some other languages. Requests and responses still have to be manually packaged and unpackaged when exchanging data for example. Although this adds extra complexity to the process the whole system is still straightforward enough.

As has been explained elsewhere, XML-RPC doesn't require any XML parsing abilities in order to use the system. XML-RPC is just a technology that uses XML to exchange information about functions, arguments and return values between a server and a client.

The XML-RPC implementation under PHP works using the HTTP/CGI protocol, so the server acts just like any other CGI script on your web server, and the client communicates with the server by sending a normal POST request. The information is then sent back as if we were dealing with any normal HTTP request, except that the information returned is an XML-RPC envelope which we decode into the response.

We'll be looking at both a client and server implementation using PHP. In addition, since XML-RPC is platform- and language-independent, we'll also be looking at a client that accesses a Perl or Python server.

In order to use XML-RPC you will need to install the XML-RPC package on your machine which can be found at `http://xmlrpc.usefulinc.com/php.html`.

Writing an XML-RPC Client

The XML-RPC client communicates from one machine to another, sending a request to execute a specific function, along with the arguments you want to supply to the function, and then extracting and printing or using the returned values in some other calculation or operation.

The basic sequence for creating an XML-RPC client in PHP is:

1. Create a request object. This is the object which is "serialized" into XML and sent to the server.

2. Create a client object. This holds the information about the remote handler, its host and the port on which to communicate.

3. Send the request to the server, using the information we've just built into client and request object that we've just created.

4. Decode the response, extracting the elements returned by the remote function into local variables that we can print or use accordingly.

We can see all of this put into a full script in Listing 19.1.

Listing 19.1   **A simple XML-RPC Client in PHP**

```
<html>
<head><title>XML-RPC Client Demo</title></head>
<body>
<?php

// Include the necessary XML-RPC code we need
include("xmlrpc.inc");

// Create a new request, based on the name of the remote
// function, and an array of the arguments that you want
// to supply to the remote function
$request = new xmlrpcmsg('remote_echo',
```

```
                              array(new xmlrpcval("Hello")));

  // Create a new XML-RPC client instance using the
  // location of the handler that will deal with the request,
  // the address of the machine and its port number
  $server = new xmlrpc_client("/xmlrpcs.php",
                              "test.mchome.pri", 80);

  // Switch debugging on
  $server->setDebug(1);

  // Execute the remote function, retrieving the reponse
  // from the remote function
  $response = $server->send($request);

  // Check that the reponse was received
  if (!$response) { die("Couldn't send request"); }

  // Make sure that we got a reasonable reponse from
  // the server
  if (!$response->faultCode())
  {
  // Extract the value of the response
      $value = $response->value();

  // Print out the value
      print "Remote response: " .
             $value->scalarval() . "<br>\n";
  }
  else
  {
  // If we had a fault at the remote end, decode the
  // fault response packet and print out the errors
      print "Fault: (" . $response->faultCode() .
          ") " . $response->faultString() . "<BR>";
  }

  ?>
  </body>
  </html>
```

The vital parts are building the request object, which is actually an instance of the xmlr-pcmsg class. The arguments to the object's creation are the name of the remote function that we want to call, in this case remote_echo, and the second argument is an array which contains a list of the values we want to supply to the remote function.

The remote function name should actually be composed of the namespace and the function name. We'll see a Python compatible version later in this chapter.

You build each argument by using the xmlrpcval class which accepts the value you want to encode and an optional argument defining how you want it interpreted—for example we've used a string here which is automatically identified as a string, but you might want to supply a number as an integer or floating point value. The encoding affects how the information is serialized into the XML-RPC packet sent to the server.

The other vital part is the creation of the client object. The object holds information about the remote host, its address and port number, and the name of the handler (usually the URL of a CGI script) that will process your request. In this example we've used the name of our PHP server which we'll be looking at shortly. You could leave it blank, which assumes a direct HTTP connection to a server running in Daemon mode.

If you execute this script, assuming you've modified it to reflect your environment and installed the server sample shown later in this chapter correctly, then you should see something similar to the output shown in Listing 19.2.

Listing 19.2   **Sample Output from an XML-RPC Client**

```
---GOT---
HTTP/1.1 200 OK
Date: Fri, 06 Jul 2001 14:14:57 GMT
Server: Apache/1.3.20 (Unix) PHP/4.0.6 mod_perl/1.25
X-Powered-By: PHP/4.0.6
Connection: close
Content-Type: text/xml
Content-length: 204

<?xml version="1.0"?>
<!-- DEBUG INFO:

0 - new xmlrpcval("Hello", 'string')


-->
<methodResponse>
<params>
<param>
<value><string>Echo: Hello Hello</string></value>
</param>
</params>
</methodResponse>
---END---

---EVALING---[44 chars]---
new xmlrpcval("Echo: Hello Hello", 'string');
---END---
Remote response: Echo: Hello Hello
```

The bulk of the output shown here is actually debugging information—if debugging were switched off we'd only see the final line, but you get the idea.

Now let's have a look at a PHP XML-RPC application that talks to a Python XML-RPC server. In this example we're going to call the `join` function on the Python server which accepts a list of words and returns a string containing the words joined together by spaces. Listing 19.3 shows the client.

Listing 19.3   Accessing a Python Daemon-based XML-RPC Server

```
<html>
<head><title>XML-RPC Client Demo (Python)</title></head>
<body>
<?php

include("xmlrpc.inc");

$myxmlargs=new xmlrpcval(array(
            new xmlrpcval("Tom"),
            new xmlrpcval("Dick"),
            new xmlrpcval("Harry")), "array");

$request = new xmlrpcmsg('join',array($myxmlargs));

$server = new xmlrpc_client("/RPC2", "localhost", 8000);

$response = $server->send($request);

if (!$response) { die("Couldn't send request"); }

if (!$response->faultCode())
{
    $value = $response->value();
    print "Remote response: " . $value->scalarval() . "<br>\n";
}
else
{
    print "Fault: (" . $response->faultCode() .
        ") " . $response->faultString() . "<BR>";
}

?>
</body>
</html>
```

There are two critical elements from this script. The first is the arguments that we supply. We need to supply an array as a single argument, so we first build an `xmlrpcval` array which in turn contains a list of XML-RPC value objects which contain the words we want joined together. We then supply that in the array of arguments that we define when building the request.

Second, because the Python server is daemon based (rather than CGI based) we need to access the server through a different port, in this case 8000 and we specify the host name rather than a URL to the CGI script that will handle the request.

The request handler is the /RPC2 specification—this is defined according to the XML-RPC standards but it's hidden under Perl, Python and other languages which automatically append the information when they realize they are communicating directly with an HTTP daemon and not through a CGI service.

Needless to say, the output we get is what we expect:

```
Remote response: Tom Dick Harry<br>
```

Writing an XML-RPC Server

The XML-RPC server is equally straightforward once you understand how to extract the information from the client and then repackage the response up to send back to the client. The basic sequence for creating a PHP based XML-RPC server is:

Define the functions that you want to support on your server.

Each function needs to extract the data from the request manually, then build the response, and then return the response back to the client.

Create a new server instance during which you register the functions that you want to support remotely.

You can see the server that supports the function we used in the client in Listing 19.4.

Listing 19.4   A Simple XML-RPC Server in PHP

```php
<?php

// Include the necessary XML-RPC code

include("xmlrpc.inc");
include("xmlrpcs.inc");

// Setup a function to echo back a string

function remote_echo($params)
{
```

```
// Get the XML client information
   global $xmlrpcerruser;

// Extract the first parameter from those supplied
   $param = $params->getParam(0);

// Check the parameter is the right type
   if ((isset($param)) && ($param->scalartyp()=="string"))
   {
// Extract the actual value from the parameter
      $mesg = $param->scalarval();
// Build our response string
      $retval = "Echo: $mesg $mesg";
// Create a new response object and return it
// the contents of the response will be sent back
// to the client
      return new xmlrpcresp(new xmlrpcval($retval));
   }
   else
   {
// We didn't get the type of argument we were expecting
// So build an error respinse to be returned to the client
      return new xmlrpcresp(0, $xmlrpcerruser,
                            "Invalid argument");
   }
}

// Create a new instance of an XML-RPC server
// and register our remote_echo function
$s=new xmlrpc_server( array("remote_echo" =>
                            array("function" =>
                                  "remote_echo")));

?>
```

The important elements here are the way we get the information from the arguments, how we package the response and how we register the function(s) that we want to support.

To extract the arguments sent to the remote function from the client we use the `getParam()` method which accepts one argument, the index of the argument that we want to retrieve. In our case there is only one argument, the string we want to echo back. We then test that the variable and value that we received is the correct type for the rest of the function.

To create a response, whether the return value or an error packet, we create an instance of the `xmlrpcresp` class. In the case of the return value, we supply a single `xmlrpcval` object—identical to the one we created when sending the request in the client. If you want to return more than one argument then use the technique we used for the Python XML-RPC client to build an array based `xmlrpcval` object.

For an error we build the response from a false value, the XML user information and the error message we want to use.

The final part of the process is to register the function within a new instance of the `xmlrpc_server` class. The class handles all of the communication and extraction for us.

The first argument should be an associative array where each key is the name of the function as it is exposed to the client. In our case we've used a value of `remote_echo` which exists within the standard namespace. You could also prefix the name with the namespace you want to support, for example `example.remote_echo`.

The value of that element of the associative array is then an embedded array—the `function` key defines the name of the actual function that will respond to the request. By using this two-tier system we can expose the real `remote_echo` function as `example.echo` for example.

That's really all there is to it. Obviously you could add more functions to the list, assuming you have definitions. All you need to do to enable the server is to copy it over into your web server directory.

XML-RPC Data Conversion

Unlike the Perl and Python examples which we have already seen, XML-RPC under PHP requires a lot more work when dealing with complex data types. The Perl and Python implementations we looked at in earlier convert nearly all of the built-in data types of those languages, including nested structures for you automatically.

In the PHP implementation the only types which are directly mapped to the equivalent types within the XML-RPC standard are the `int`, `string` and `double`. To preserve other types the type data must be encapsulated into an object. This is especially true with the array types which in PHP can be used for normal serial and associative arrays. These obviously required different handling, but there is no way to distinguish between the two.

XML-RPC for PHP actually creates its own typing system which you must use explicitly for everything but the base types and when supplying multiple arguments (i.e., arrays). We've actually already seen examples of the process within the examples in this chapter, but the process warrants some closer inspection.

PHP to XML-RPC

The `xmlrpcval` class provides the necessary wrapper to convert any value into a format suitable for transmission over XML-RPC. For example, we can convert a string into a suitable XML-RPC compatible value using:

```
$xmlstr = new xmlrpcval("Hello World!");
```

This assumes that we are dealing with a string. For a more explicit conversion you need to supply a second argument which a string constant which defines the type of value that you want to encode. For example, we can more explicitly convert integer, floating point (double) and string values into XML-RPC values using:

```
$xmlint = new xmlrpcval(34, "int");
$xmldbl = new xmlrpcval(3.141, "double");
$xmlstr = new xmlrpcval("Hello World!", "string");
```

The full list of types supported by the system are listed in Table 19.1—note that they are backed up by a number of predefined variables which you should in preference to the raw strings to prevent typographical errors tripping up your programs.

TABLE 19.1: XML-RPC for PHP Data Types

Type string	Variable
i4	$xmlrpcI4
int	$xmlrpcInt
boolean	$xmlrpcBoolean
double	$xmlrpcDouble
string	$xmlrpcString
dateTime.iso8601	$xmlrpcDateTime
base64	$xmlrpcBase64
array	$xmlrpcArray
struct	$xmlrpcStruct

The `$xmlrpcDateTime` value can be used to encode dates and times either from a raw string, as in:

```
$xmldatetime = new xmlrpcval("2001-10-02T16:49:06",
                             $xmlrpcDateTime);
```

Or, when used in conjunction with the `iso801_encode()` function with a raw epoch value as returned by the PHP function `time()`:

```
$xmldatetime = new xmlrpcval(is801_encode(time()),
                             $xmlrpcDateTime);
```

Binary objects such as graphics, sounds or even applications can be encoded using the `base64` type—the XML-RPC code will automatically encode the binary string into base64 for you during the conversion process.

The array and struct types are slightly more complex. For an array type, you must create an array using array() and mark that array as the XML-RPC array type, while simultaneously embedding the new types for the individual elements you want in the array. For example, to create an array containing an integer, double, and float, you would use:

```
$xmlarray = new xmlrpcval(array(
    new xmlrpcval(12374);
    new xmlrpcval(19.99);
    new xmlrpcval("Widget with a handle")), $xmlrpcArray);
```

For a struct you supply an associative array instead of a linear one, with the keys as the struct member names:

```
$xmlarray = new xmlrpcval(array(
    'productcode' => new xmlrpcval(12374),
    'price'       => new xmlrpcval(19.99),
    'description' => new xmlrpcval("Widget with a handle")),
    $xmlrpcStruct);
```

XML-RPC to PHP

For converting information back from its XML-RPC encoded format you first need to identify the variables data type. If you know what type is and the return value is a scalar then you can obtain the data directly using scalarval() on the returned value. For example:

```
$response = $server->send($request);
$value = $response->value();
print "Remote response: " . $value->scalarval() . "\n";
```

If you need to know the scalars type, use the scalartyp() method.

If you don't know what the return value's type is, you can use the kindOf() method on the value to return the data type (scalar, array, struct) as a string.

To extract the values from a XML-RPC array you need to use the arraymem() method to extract a single element from the array. The method accepts a single argument, an index into the array. Combined with the arraysize() method we can use this to extract elements from the array directly—but note that these will encoded as XML values so you'll also need to use scalarval() to extract their values. For example, you could iterate over a simple, single dimension array like this:

```
for($i=0; $i < $value->arraysize(); $i++)
{
    $v = $value->arraymem($i);
    print "Got " . $v->scalarval() . "\n";
}
```

For `struct` types it depends on whether you know the member names or not. If you do know the member names, then you can use the `arraymem()` method to access the values. For example, to extract the description of the product from our earlier example you would use:

```
$descval = $value->arraymem("description");
$description = $descval->scalarval();
```

If you don't know the type, then you need to use the `structeach()` method which works in the same way as the PHP `each()` function to iterate over the value. The `structreset()` method also works in the same way as the `reset()` function, setting up and resetting the iterator for the `structeach()` method.

The example below also includes an example of the use of the `kindOf()` method:

```
$value->structreset();
while(list($key, $structval)=$value->structeach())
{
   switch($structval->kindOf()) {
     case "scalar":
       print "$key is " . $structval->scalarval() . "\n";
       break;
     default:
       print "$key is type " . $structval->kindOf() . "\n";
       break;
   }
}
```

Quicker Conversions

The techniques we've already seen are very awkward, especially when working with both very simple scalar values, and also with more complex scalar and array values. They certainly break the flow, and make it very difficult for anybody else reading the code to understand exactly what is going on.

There are quicker ways of encoding and decoding the information to and from the internal PHP variables. The `xmlrpc_encode()` function and its companion `xmlrpc_decode()` function will convert information between the PHP and XML-RPC formats. For example, we can shorten our earlier example, which used:

```
$xmlint = new xmlrpcval(34, "int");
$xmldbl = new xmlrpcval(3.141, "double");
$xmlstr = new xmlrpcval("Hello World!", "string");
```

to:

```
$xmlint = xmlrpc_encode(34);
$xmldbl = xmlrpc_encode(3.141);
$xmlstr = xmlrpc_encode("Hello World!");
```

Unfortunately, we can't use this method to convert to the date, boolean or binary formats supported by XML-RPC as there is no direct equivalent in PHP that can be identified and therefore converted. Frustratingly we can't convert arrays either, because PHP cannot distinguish between a serial and an associative array.

However, we can make conversion of a `struct` easier using `xmlrpc_encode()`, so the sample

```
$xmlarray = new xmlrpcval(array(
    'productcode' => new xmlrpcval(12374),
    'price'       => new xmlrpcval(19.99),
    'description' => new xmlrpcval("Widget with a handle")),
    $xmlrpcStruct);
```

Becomes:

```
$xmlarray = xmlrpc_encode(array(
    'productcode' => 12374,
    'price'       => 19.99,
    'description' => "Widget with a handle"));
```

Which is just a little easier to handle!

Decoding works in a similar fashion, converting an XML-RPC value directly into a PHP equivalent:

```
$phpint = xmlrpc_decode($xmlint);
$phpdbl = xmlrpc_decode($xmldbl);
$phpstr = xmlrpc_decode($xmlstr);
```

For `struct` types the process becomes even easier, since the value that is returned by `xmlrpc_decode()` is in fact just an associative that we can iterate over:

```
$phparray = xmlrpc_decode($xmlstructvalue);
reset($phparray);
while(list($key, $value)=each($phparray))
{
    print "$key is $value\n";
}
```

Benefits of XML-RPC in PHP

Armed with the basic information on how to write and use a PHP based XML-RPC service, let's have a look at a few solutions that actually use the facilities of XML-RPC to provide a service.

The benefit of XML-RPC is that it allows us to execute a procedure on a remote machine, and that means we can use in all those situations where we would otherwise need some special tool or interface to communicate with another machine.

PHP is a web-based publishing environment and so we already have all sorts of tools and interfaces available to us that allow us to pull in information on to our web pages from a number of sources. For example, in a single PHP generated web page we can already pull information from a number of different databases through PHP itself from either local or remote database systems.

We can also add and introduce graphics, text elements and JavaScript components from a wide variety of different servers into that single page. If we're using frames, we can easily mix and match whole generated pages for a number of different machines.

So, why use XML-RPC in the first place, if we've already got access to this array of different and distributed data sources?

The first and foremost reason is that XML-RPC is an easy way to get a simple answer to a query from a remote machine that may not actually be either capable or configured to handle a full web-based request.

We can also use XML-RPC on both a local and remote basis to communicate with a piece of software or service that is normally supported by a different language. For example, we've already seen a solution here that allows us to communicate with a Python-based server using a PHP client.

Finally, we can use XML-RPC in those situations where we want to combine the abilities and functionality of two or more websites into a single page. For example, you could combine a news site and a discussion service together to allow people to comment on web stories from two different sites into one amalgamated site.

Summary

One of the limitations of PHP is that it's difficult to combine information and resources from a number of computers simultaneously. Although we can embed information from other servers, there are limits to the ways in which we can combine this information.

Using XML-RPC we can execute procedures on remote machines and include the information directly within our page, without relying on HTML generated by another service. This makes integration of data from different sources much easier, and we can control the method in which the data is formatted to the user from the PHP service generating the page.

Using XML-RPC is a simple case of creating a server connection and then submitting a request. Most standard data types and arguments are supported and for types not supported by PHP and/or XML-RPC directly we can build the structures manually.

We can also use PHP to service XML-RPC requests and to act as a service to other sites which can be useful if you want to exchange information between multiple machines.

PART V

XML and Other Languages

## CHAPTER 20

XML and REBOL

- Parsing XML Information in REBOL

- XML-RPC with REBOL

REBOL (pronounced "rebel") has a slightly different approach to programming and developing applications than most other languages, even scripting languages. In most other languages, the data and variables you use are tools that you use to store information as you are processing data. In REBOL, everything is data. REBOL knows that an e-mail address is an e-mail address and that a URL is a URL.

Unsurprisingly, this also stretches to files that have been created using a markup format such as HTML or XML. When loading a document or URL, you can automatically mark it as a markup document, which has the effect of converting your document into a set of blocks. REBOL even knows when it's working with a tag through the use of a tag! data type.

The only downside to this approach is that it matches neither the event-based processing nor the DOM model. Technically, the system supports serial parsing because you can work through each element of the XML document. There are a few tricks you can use to at least simulate DOM parsing—with some limits—and serial parsing is at least similar in principle to the whole-document parsing used in typical event parsers.

In this chapter, we're going to look at some basic parsing techniques with REBOL and at RXR, a solution for communicating with servers using XML-RPC.

Parsing XML Information in REBOL

The simplest way of extracting information from an XML document with REBOL is to load the file and then use the parse function to parse the document and extract the text between a given set of tags. For example, you could extract the character data between two tags like this:

```
xmlsource: read %simple.xml
```

```
parse xmlsource [ thru <title> copy text to </title> ]
print text
```

This copies the text between the <title> and </title> tags. The only problem with this method is that it's fairly limited in the simple form shown here. You can't pick out specific tag element data, and you certainly can't traverse through to pick out a particular tag within a nested structure.

Processing XML as Markup

The easiest way around this limitation is to tell REBOL to load the XML document in markup mode, using an option to the load function to tell it to parse the XML tags and character data into separate blocks. You can demonstrate this quite easily using the following script:

```
xmlsource: load/markup %simple.xml
probe xmlsource
```

When used on the following XML file:

```
<simple>
<title>Some Other Title</title>
<paragraphs>
<paragraph refid="p1">Some text</paragraph>
<paragraph refid="p2">Some more text</paragraph>
</paragraphs>
</simple>
```

you get the following output:

```
[<simple> "^/" <title> "Some Other Title" </title> "^/"
<paragraphs> "^/" <paragraph refid="p1"> "Some text"
</paragraph> "^/" <paragraph refid="p2"> "Some more text"
</paragraph> "^/" </simple>]
```

You can see from this that you now have a list of the different elements—character data and tags—in a single block. To extract some information from the XML file, all you need to do is process this list of elements.

Note from the list that elements are not quoted; this is because among all the different types that REBOL is aware of, one of them is the tag! data type.

You can use this differentiation between XML tags and character data to process the information within a more complex XML document by using many of the same techniques that you used when dealing with event-driven—and especially SAX-based—parsers within other languages. After all, you are working through the document in a similar fashion.

For example, you can print out the titles and link test from an RDF/RSS file. Listing 20.1 gives an example of such a script, and Listing 20.2 shows the eventual output.

Listing 20.1   An RDF/RSS-to-HTML Converter

```
REBOL [
        Title: "RSS Parser"
        File: %xml.r
        Purpose: {Print out Title/Links for stories from RDF/RSS}
]

xmlsource: load/markup %freemarket.xml
```

```
current: ""
linktext: ""
titletext: ""
foreach item xmlsource [
    either tag? item [
        if item == <title> [ current: item ]
        if item == </title> [
            print join "<B>" [:titletext "</b><br>" ]
                                current: ""]
        if item == <link> [ current: item ]
        if item == </link> [
            print join {<A href="} [:linktext
                                    {">Read Story</a><br>}]
                        current: ""
                        linktext: ""]
    ]
    [
            if current == <link> [ linktext: :item ]
            if current == <title> [ titletext: :item ]
    ]
]
```

Listing 20.2   Output from the RSS-to-HTML Converter

```
<B>FreeMarket</b><br>
<A href="http://freemarket-project.org/">Read Story</a><br>
<B>FreeMarket</b><br>
<A href="http://freemarket-project.org/">Read Story</a><br>
<B>3/18/2001 IRC Session</b><br>
<A href="http://freemarket-project.org//article.php?sid=14">Read Story</a><br>
<B>You need your input</b><br>
<A href="http://freemarket-project.org//article.php?sid=13">Read Story</a><br>
<B>IRC Session, 3/11/2001</b><br>
<A href="http://freemarket-project.org//article.php?sid=12">Read Story</a><br>
<B>Idea Scratchpad</b><br>
<A href="http://freemarket-project.org//article.php?sid=11">Read Story</a><br>
<B>Prototype Work</b><br>
<A href="http://freemarket-project.org//article.php?sid=10">Read Story</a><br>
<B>Repository of Tradestation/Metastock articles/scripts</b><br>
<A href="http://freemarket-project.org//article.php?sid=9">Read Story</a><br>
<B>List of Requirements Started</b><br>
<A href="http://freemarket-project.org//article.php?sid=8">Read Story</a><br>
<B>Need Help?  Got a problem?</b><br>
<A href="http://freemarket-project.org//article.php?sid=7">Read Story</a><br>
<B>Technical analysis script repository</b><br>
<A href="http://freemarket-project.org//article.php?sid=6">Read Story</a><br>
<B>Comments on the FreeMarket Project</b><br>
<A href="http://freemarket-project.org//article.php?sid=5">Read Story</a><br>
```

The script works very simply. First you load the XML document in markup mode to end up with a list of elements and character data. Then you use a `foreach` loop to work through each element of the list. The `either` test identifies whether each item within the list is an element or character data.

If it's an element tag, you first identify what type of element tag it is. You are interested only in either `<title>` or `<link>` elements from the RSS file. If it's an opening tag of one of these types, then you have a record of that fact so that you can record the information when processing character data. If it's an end tag, then you build suitable HTML output to produce the story title and a link to go with it.

The major difference between the event-driven parsers you've seen for other languages and the solution used in REBOL is that you identify the link type while accessing the XML fragments directly. There is no function called when you identify the different fragments (elements, character data, and so on). You should also note that you don't have to jump through the normal hoops when working with character data. In markup mode, each element of the resulting list is either a single block of character data or a single XML element.

Manipulating Tags

Because REBOL knows what a tag is, it also knows how to manipulate tags. For example, if you have a tag object, you can add attributes to it using `append`:

```
imgtag: <img src="logo.jpg">
append imgtag { alt="Company Logo"}
```

The resulting tag includes both attributes:

```
<img src="logo.jpg" alt="Company Logo">
```

You can also build a new tag very easily using `build-tag`:

```
probe build-tag [a href http://www.mcwords.com/]
<a href="http://www.mcwords.com/">
```

The `tag!` type in REBOL is a serial type, so you can access the information from a tag in the same way as any other serial object within REBOL. Unfortunately, accessing attribute information is not easy. The only way to extract an attribute and its value is to search for the information using `parse`.

For example, from the XML file you used earlier:

```
<simple>
<title>Some Other Title</title>
<paragraphs>
<paragraph refid="p1">Some text</paragraph>
<paragraph refid="p2">Some more text</paragraph>
</paragraphs>
</simple>
```

You can extract the `refid` data from a tag using the fragment demonstrated in Listing 20.3.

Listing 20.3   **Extracting Attribute Data**

```
REBOL []

tag: <paragraph refid="p1">

if parse tag [
        "paragraph" thru "refid="
        [{"} copy attr to {"} | copy attr to ">"]
        to end
        ]
        [
                print join "Attr: " attr
        ]
```

The script does two things: First you ignore the text from the tag name (`paragraph`) until the attribute definition (`refid=`), then you copy the text between double quotes into the `attr` variable. It shouldn't happen in an XML file, but just in case quotes are not used, you also have the option to copy all the text from the end of `refid=` until the closing >. The whole process is trapped up within an `if` statement so that if it doesn't exist you don't raise an error.

Building Your Own Event Parser

Although it's not always needed, you could easily build your own event-driven parser using REBOL and the techniques you've seen here. In essence you have the start of an event-driven parser; you can load the file and determine the difference between a tag and character data as you proceed through the block list that is returned when you load the XML document in markup mode.

All you have to do is create functions that accept the fragment types, as you would in a SAX parser, and a wrapper function that is capable of parsing the contents of a tag to identify the difference between XML declarations, processing instructions, and start and end tags.

For example, you can quickly identify a start or end tag using this:

```
foreach item xmlsource [
    if tag? item [
        either find item "/" [
            print ["End tag: " item] ]
                               [
            print ["Start Tag: " item ]]
    ]
]
```

Other elements can be extracted in much the same way.

XML-RPC with REBOL

XML-RPC support within REBOL is still relatively new, despite REBOL's heavy data focus. There are two solutions currently available: one from Thomas Jensen and the other, RXR, from Chris Langreiter. We'll be looking at the RXR solution.

The RXR solution is still in its early stages and, although the client side of the process appears to be relatively stable, the server side is still particularly prone to problems. Because of these limitations, we'll be having a quick look at the client side of the process. Watch for an update on the website (http://www.mcwords.com) for information on how the client and server sides can be used.

The client side is very easy to use. You load the XML-RPC library, create a new object based on the xmlrpc-server class, and use this class to call remote procedures.

For example, you can create a connection to the XML-RPC demo server at UserLand using this:

```
stateserver: make xmlrpc-server [ host: "betty.userland.com"
                                  port: 80 uri: "/RPC2"]
```

The host and port arguments should be self explanatory: These are the hostname and port number of the XML-RPC server you want to communicate with. The final argument, uri, is the name of the service on the host/port combination you want to use to service requests. With XML-RPC, this value is always /RPC2.

The procedure call is handled by the xmlrpc-call function:

```
print xmlrpc-call stateserver "examples.getStateName" [21]
```

The function accepts three arguments, the xmlrpc-server object that you want to use for communication, the name of the remote function that you want to call, and a block of arguments that you want to supply to the remote procedure.

The entire script is shown in Listing 20.4.

Listing 20.4   **Calling a Remote Procedure with XML-RPC**

```
REBOL []

do load %xmlrpc-lib.r

stateserver: make xmlrpc-server [ host: "betty.userland.com"
                                  port: 80 uri: "/RPC2"]

print xmlrpc-call stateserver "examples.getStateName" [21]
```

Just to verify that it works, the result is shown here:

```
Massachusetts
```

You can interface to any XML-RPC server using the same process. For example, to talk to the Python XML-RPC server you saw demonstrated in Chapter 15, "Applying SOAP/XML-RPC in Python," you might use a script like the one in Listing 20.5.

Listing 20.5　　**Communicating with the Python XML-RPC Server**

```
REBOL []

do load %xmlrpc-lib.r

localserver: make xmlrpc-server [ host: "twinsol.mcslp.pri"
                                  port: 8009 uri: "/RPC2"]

print xmlrpc-call localserver "echo" ["Martin"]

arglist: make xmlrpc-object [ type: 'array data: [
                              "Martin" "Charles" "Brown"] ]

print xmlrpc-call localserver "join" [arglist]
```

Note that you have to build the argument for the join remote procedure beforehand. This is because you cannot mutate a REBOL list into an XML-RPC list directly. Instead, you must construct an XML-RPC array using the xmlrpc-object function. This translates a given data block into an array of the required type, which in turn you use as the single array argument to the join function.

Summary

REBOL provides a number of different methods for processing XML documents. If you only want to extract information from an XML document then we can use the parse method within REBOL to extract information between two tags within a document.

For a more interactive form of processing we can use the built-in facilities of REBOL to load an XML document in "markup" format—this translates the structure of XML elements and character data into a sequence of elements and strings that we can process and identify using methods similar to those we employed when processing XML documents using SAX in other languages.

The RXR tool is a REBOL XML-RPC solution that allows us to communicate easily with remote servers and execute procedures.

## CHAPTER 21

XML and Ruby

- Parsing XML

- Ruby and XML-RPC

R uby is a relatively new language developed by Yukihiro Matsumoto in 1995. It offers the flexibility of an object-oriented interface along some of the systems we've come to expect in all scripting languages, such as easy access to a regular expression engine, some handy data types—including hashes—and big integers.

There is no XML parser that comes standard with Ruby, but there are plenty of packages out there. We'll be looking at my favorite, REXML, which offers an incredibly simple method for accessing and modifying XML documents through Ruby. Ruby is a general-purpose scripting language, so there's no specific job I would recommend it for when working with XML. Even so, once you've used Ruby and REXML to parse and manipulate your documents, you may wonder why it's so difficult to perform the manipulation in other languages.

Parsing XML

There are a number of different solutions for working with XML in Ruby, all of which are available through the Ruby Application Archive (RAA) at `http://www.ruby-lang.org/en/r1aa.h1tml`. You can find the more traditional event-driven and DOM-based parsers as well as tools for dealing and working with specific XML formats such as RSS and for processing documents with XSLT.

Of all the solutions available, my favorite is REXML by Sean Russell. It combines the easy access and control of an XML document through a DOM-like interface while merging the API with XPath to allow easy searching of elements. You can even use REXML to process the individual elements of an XML document, just as you would if processing it through an event-based parser.

In its simplest form, it turns your source XML document into an `REXML::Document` object. For example, to open an existing document and process it into an XML document object, you'd use this:

```
require "rexml/document"
file = File.open("document.xml")
xmldoc = REXML::Document.new file
```

Once you've opened the document it's simply a case of accessing the different elements in the document to determine it's structure and extracting the information. Most of the information is stored in a series of subobjects (many of which have their own classes). For example, the `REXML::Element` class includes all of the information in order to store a single element, with the `text` property holding the character data within a given tag, and the `attributes` property unsurprisingly holding a list of the attributes for a given element.

For example, working from this XML:

```
<products>
<item code="1001"><name>Thingy</name></item>
<item code="1003"><name>Whatsit</name></item>
<item code="1002"><name>Doohickey</name></item>
</products>
```

you can access the root element (products) using this:

```
doc.root = xmldoc.root
```

The root element properties contain the information about the element itself. As we've already mentioned, text holds the character data in an element, and attributes are the attributes defined in the tag. A list of subelements can be found in the elements property, which is actually an array. You can access the first subelement within the root element using this:

```
el1 = docroot.elements[1]
```

Incidentally, an interesting artifact of this approach to XML parsing is that printing out a particular element will dump the element as XML source. For example, if you print out the first subelement from the root tag, you get this:

```
<item code='1001'>
   <name>Thingy</name>
</item>
```

This makes REXML one of the best tools for manipulating XML documents, especially if you are trying to bond together the XML source of a number of elements into a single XML document.

The XPath Access Mechanism

The XPath part of the solution makes accessing the elements within the XML document much easier than a traditional event-driven or even DOM-based parser. To use the XPath interface is simplicity itself. For example, to get a list of all the subelements, you need to do is access the elements property of the parent element. The each() method accepts an XPath definition that in turn returns a list of all the subelements that it finds.

For example, you can work through all the items using this:

```
xmldoc.elements.each("*/item") { |element| print element }
```

which in turn generates this:

```
<item code='1001'>
   <name>Thingy</name>
</item>
<item code='1003'>
```

```
    <name>Whatsit</name>
  </item>
  <item code='1002'>
    <name>Doohickey</name>
  </item>
```

You can also use XPath to access a specific element. For example, to extract the element with a code attribute matching 1001, you would use this:

```
doc.root.elements["[@code='1001']"]
```

A list of the fully supported XPath constructs is shown in Table 21.1.

TABLE 21.1: XPath Constructs Supported by REXML

Construct	Description
/	root element.
.	Self.
..	Parent element.
*	All child elements.
//	All document elements.
//child	All child elements in document matching child.
parent//child	All child elements of the element parent.
parent/child	All child elements of parent.
[...]	All predicates (attribute, index, or text) matching supplied text. You can prefix a specific element with @; for instance, to search for an attribute match use @attribute.
[...][...]	Compound predicates.
element	Child element element.

Building a To-Do List

To demonstrate how easy it is, let's look at a simple to-do list manager that uses XML to store a list of the to-do items and their status. The basic format of the XML document is this:

```
<todo>
  <idseq>5</idseq>
  <item id='1'>
    <description>Call Mike</description>
    <status>Done</status>
  </item>
</todo>
```

The idseq tag holds the sequence number of the ID attribute of each individual to-do list item, and obviously it needs to be updated each time you add a new entry. The description and status tags should be self explanatory.

Showing the To-Do List

Actually dumping a list of all the to-do list items in the XML document is simply a case of iterating over all the item elements and extracting the description, to get the information about the item itself, and an ID number, which you'll need when you want to mark a to-do item as completed. The script for doing this is shown in Listing 21.1.

Listing 21.1   Getting the List of Things to Do

```
require "rexml/document"
file = File.open("todo.xml","r")
doc = REXML::Document.new file
doc.elements.each("todo/item") { |item|
    if item.elements["status"].text == "Open" then
        printf("%03d -> %s\n",
                item.attributes["id"],
                item.elements["description"].text)
    end
}
```

The script works very simply: You call each on the document elements with an XPath specification to get a list of all the items. For each item, you check the status element text and display the information only if the item is marked Open. Then you use printf to print out the id attribute and the description element text.

The following is the result of running this on a previously built XML file:

```
$ ruby todo.rb
001 -> Call Mike
002 -> Call Sharon
003 -> Complete XML chapter
004 -> Check Ruby XML-RPC
005 -> Write Ruby XML Adding Script
```

Conveniently, the last item leads us on to the next task—building a script that allows us to add information to the to-do list.

Adding to the To-Do List

Because the REXML system turns a document into a series of objects, you can also produce an XML document by creating a series of objects, which can then be dumped as XML. You already know that when you print an REXML::Element object, you get a textual version of the object in XML.

To create a brand new element:

```
todoitem = REXML::Element.new "item"
```

To set any character data, just assign a value to the `text` property:

```
todoitem.text = "Some other item text"
```

You can add attributes to the element by setting the `attributes` property:

```
todoitem.attributes["id"] = 4
```

To add a subelement, you can use the `add_element()` method:

```
tododesc = todoitem.add_element "description"
```

The following adds a subelement with attributes:

```
product = products.add_element "product", {"code" => "1001"}
```

Alternatively, you can create the subelements and then append them to the element list for the parent:

```
todoitem = REXML::Element.new "item"
tododesc = REXML::Element.new "desc"
todostat = REXML::Element.new "stat"
todoitem << tododesc
todoitem << todostat
```

For the to-do list manager, there are six steps to the process:

1. Read the existing document.

2. Create the new to-do element and its children.

3. Add the new to-do element to the parent element.

4. Rename the old file.

5. Write the new XML document to a new file.

6. Delete the old file.

The script for doing this in Ruby is shown in Listing 21.2.

Listing 21.2   Giving Ourselves More to Do

```
require "rexml/document"
include REXML
require "ftools"

file = File.open("todo.xml","r")
doc = REXML::Document.new file
file.close
```

```
description = Element.new "description"
description.text = ARGV.join(" ")
status = Element.new "status"
status.text = "Open"

seqid = doc.elements["todo/idseq"].text
doc.elements["todo/idseq"].text = (seqid.to_i+1).to_s

todoitem = Element.new "item"
todoitem.attributes["id"] = seqid
todoitem.elements << description
todoitem.elements << status

doc.root.elements << todoitem

File.move("todo.xml","todo.xml.bak")
outfile = File.new("todo.xml","w")
doc.write outfile
outfile.close
File.unlink("todo.xml.bak")

print "Todo list:\n"
doc.elements.each("todo/item") { |item|
    if item.elements["status"].text == "Open" then
        printf("%03d -> %s\n",
               item.attributes["id"],
               item.elements["description"].text)
        end
}
```

The process of the script is quite straightforward. You read in the existing document and then take the entire content of the command line as the words to make up the new to-do item.

The new item needs a new ID number, and you use the value from the idseq XML tag. This value should always contain the *next* value to be used so that you can use its current value when you create the new to-do item. You can access that directly using this:

```
seqid = doc.elements["todo/idseq"].text
```

You also need to update the seqid item, which means converting it to an integer and writing back the new number into the idseq tag. All string objects in Ruby can be converted to an integer using the to_i() method, and the result of the calculation, which is a numeric object, needs to be converted back to a string so that it can be written into the idseq tag. As with the string, you use a method, to_s(), to create a string version of the number:

```
doc.elements["todo/idseq"].text = (seqid.to_i+1).to_s
```

The final aspects of the script are simply to create the elements, create the compound item element, and then add that to the list of subelements of the root todo element.

Then you just dump the contents of the document back out as XML to a new file; rename and then delete the old one. The final stage is to output the new to-do list.

For example, you can add a new item using this:

```
$ ruby todoadd.rb Write Ruby XML completion script
Todo list:
001 -> Call Mike
002 -> Call Sharon
003 -> Complete XML chapter
004 -> Check Ruby XML-RPC
005 -> Write Ruby XML Adding Script
006 -> Write Ruby XML completion script
```

Marking an Item Completed

To mark an item as completed, you need to update the status tag character data with Done instead of the default Open. The basics are identical to adding a new item; you find the entry you are looking for (with the item id attribute) and set its text, then you repeat the XML dumping as text procedure to write the new document before printing the to-do list summary again. The full script is shown in Listing 21.3.

Listing 21.3   **Crossing an Item Off the List**

```
require "rexml/document"
require "ftools"
file = File.open("todo.xml","r")
doc = REXML::Document.new file

for id in ARGV
    idstr = sprintf("todo/item[@id='%s']",id)
    doc.elements.each(idstr) { |item|
        item.elements["status"].text = "Done" }
end

File.move("todo.xml","todo.xml.bak")
outfile = File.new("todo.xml","w")
doc.write outfile
outfile.close
File.unlink("todo.xml.bak")

print "Todo list:\n"
doc.elements.each("todo/item") { |item|
    if item.elements["status"].text == "Open" then
        printf("%03d -> %s\n",
                item.attributes["id"],
                item.elements["description"].text)
    end
}
```

The script allows you to mark multiple items in the to-do list as completed just by supplying multiple IDs on the command line. For example, you now know that items 5 and 6 from the list are completed, so you can mark them as such using this:

```
$ ruby todocomp.rb 5 6
Todo list:
001 -> Call Mike
002 -> Call Sharon
003 -> Complete XML chapter
004 -> Check Ruby XML-RPC
```

Ruby and XML-RPC

The XML-RPC solution for Ruby is written by Michael Neumann and is called `xmlrpc4r`. Like the other XML-RPC solutions that you've seen in this book, the actual interface is about as simple as it can be, providing a transparent and natural interface for communicating with a remote server.

> **NOTE**   You'll need Ruby 1.6.5 (from `http://www.ruby-lang.com`), NQXML (from `http://www.io.com/~jimm/downloads/nqxml/index.html`) and the latest `xmlrpc4r` distributions (from `http://www.fantasy-coders.de/ruby/xmlrpc4r/`). Trying to install earlier versions if either doesn't work because of the installation script used in `xmlrpc4r`.

We'll have a quick look at the processes behind creating a client to access both CGI and stand-alone services. We'll also look at the mechanics of building a stand-alone server to service requests.

XML-RPC Client

The client side of the process with `xmlrpc4r` is quite straightforward. You create a new client instance, supplying the server name, directory, and port number (if applicable) of the server you want to talk to. For example, to connect to the XML-RPC server at UserLand from the URL `http://betty.userland.com:80/RPC2`, you'd use this:

```
require "xmlrpc/client"
server = server = XMLRPC::Client.new( "betty.userland.com",
                                      '/RPC2')
```

Then you use the `call` method on the new object to call a particular procedure, using the first argument as the name of the procedure that you want to call and separating a procedure and namespace with a period. Additional arguments to `call` are then used as the arguments to the remote procedure. You can see an example of the UserLand U.S. state name client in Listing 21.4.

Listing 21.4 **Getting U.S. States by Number from UserLand**

```
require "xmlrpc/client"

server = XMLRPC::Client.new( "betty.userland.com", '/RPC2')

result = server.call("examples.getStateList",
                    [1, 12, 34, 50])
print "States: ", result, "\n"
```

You can see from this that you've supplied a single array as the first argument. The `result` that you get back is a string in this case, but `xmlrpc4r` supports string, array, hash, and object types in return values. The result of the script can be seen here:

```
$ ruby xmlrpcstate.rb
States: Alabama,Idaho,North Dakota,Wyoming
```

XML-RPC Server

The XML-RPC server implementation is also very straightforward. In fact, all you have to do is create the server either as a stand-alone or CGI service and then add the functions you want supported to the new server class.

With this method, you can add support for procedures supported by inline (block) definitions. You can also import methods from a Ruby object instance into a server namespace. You can see this more clearly from the stand-alone server example in Listing 21.5, which is itself a modified and slightly tidier version of an example server provided with the source code.

Listing 21.5 **An Example Stand-Alone Server in Ruby**

```
require "xmlrpc/server"

class MyMathClass
  def subtract(a,b)
    a-b
  end
  def square(a)
    a ** 2
  end
end

s = XMLRPC::Server.new(8001, "127.0.0.1", 4,
                      nil, true, true)

s.add_handler("pubmath.add") {|a,b| a+b }
s.add_handler("pubmath.div") {|a,b|
```

```
if b == 0
    raise XMLRPC::FaultException.new 1, "division by zero"
  else
    a / b
  end
}

s.add_handler(XMLRPC::iPIMethods("pubmath"), MyMathClass.new)

s.serve
```

The main components are the initial call to create the new server, which accepts the port number and hostname or IP address. The remaining options set the default options (debugging and logging) and are passed directly on to the underlying HTTP server class, which accepts and services the requests.

The add_handler() method adds a new remote procedure using code blocks to hold the actual code that will be executed. The argument you pass is the name of the remote procedure, including its namespace. In this case, both pubmath.add and pubmath.div are added in this way. The XMLRPC::iPIMethods() will import a series of methods from an object instance into the supplied namespace, making the methods available to the outside world. Note that this doesn't make objects available, but there is nothing to stop you from supporting the capability to publish the new method and its response to the client.

Finally, you just need to call the serve() method to start the server so that you can process requests. The client call to access the server is shown in Listing 21.6.

Listing 21.6   Calling the Server

```
require "xmlrpc/client"

server = XMLRPC::Client.new( "localhost", '/RPC2', 8001)

addresult = server.call("pubmath.add", 5, 3)
subresult = server.call("pubmath.subtract", 13.1, 4.5)
divresult = server.call("pubmath.div", 22, 7)

print "Add: ",addresult,"\n"
print "Sub: ",subresult,"\n"
print "Div: ",divresult,"\n"
```

Error Handling

As you can probably tell from Listing 21.7, you can raise any errors in the requests by returning an instance of the XMLRPC::FaultException class, which accepts two arguments: the error number and an error message.

In the client, this is treated as an exception, and you'll need to identify any problems by using a normal `begin/end` block and the `rescue` statement to pick up the error.

For example, you should change the client example to the one in Listing 21.7.

Listing 21.7   **Error Handling with *xmlrpc4r***

```
require "xmlrpc/client"

server = XMLRPC::Client.new( "localhost", '/RPC2', 8001)

begin
  result = server.call("pubmath.div", 17, 0)
  print "17/0 is ", result, "\n"
rescue XMLRPC::FaultException => e
  puts "Error:"
  puts e.faultCode
  puts e.faultString
end
```

Summary

The Ruby XML parser REXML supports a simplified system for accessing information and data from an XML document. In essence it is a DOM-based solution that also includes an XPATH system for extracting information from specific elements and locations within the document.

As well as allowing easy access to the elements and data within an XML document REXML also allows us to update and add information to an XML structure and then dump the new XML structure out to a new file. Using this we can use an XML document as a storage container for information adding new records and making modifications to existing records easily.

The XML-RPC solution, `xmlrpc4r`, provides a simplified interface both for creating clients and for servicing requests on the server side.

CHAPTER 22

XML and Tcl

- The TclXML Parser

- Viewing XML with Tk

- XML-RPC with Tcl

Tcl has one of the longest histories of dealing with XML of any of the scripting languages, largely because it was one of the first scripting languages to introduce Unicode support as an integral part of the language. John Ousterhout and the rest of the Tcl development team produced one of the best Unicode-handling systems of any language. Even now, Tcl still provides an excellent base for supporting multiple languages and integrating internationalization into your scripts; it is an ideal base for translating between the different encoding formats supported by Unicode.

Tcl's other advantage is that it provides excellent integration with the Tk GUI development system, making it an ideal language for creating cross-platform–compatible scripts with a consistent GUI whether you are working on Unix, Windows, or Mac OS.

For XML, Tcl provides a single solution called TclXML developed by Zveno Pty Ltd. TclXML is comparable in functionality to Simple API for XML (SAX) in terms of its speed and capability.

TclXML is essentially just a suite of tools that provides you with the information you need to parse XML documents. TclXML supports two different parsers: a parser called TclExpat that is based on the now-familiar Expat parser (see Chapter 5, "Data Exchange and XML") and a native XML parser written entirely in Tcl that is supported directly in the TclXML extension.

Also available is a layer called TclDOM that sits on top of TclXML. It supports the access to and modification of XML documents using the Document Object Model (DOM) API within Tcl. DOM can be a useful way of viewing and manipulating information, especially if you integrate with the capabilities of the Tk interface-building toolkit, which uses an object-like interface.

The TclXML Parser

The TclXML parser is based on Expat, which is an event-based parser. In event parsers, different procedures are registered with the parser class when it is created. Then, each time a different entity is identified within the XML file, the command is called and operates on the entity information.

For example, if you register procedures for the start and end tags, then when parsing the XML file

```
<name backref="00120">Martin C Brown</name>
```

the parser would call the registered start command once, supplying the tagname and the attribute list as arguments, and the end procedure once, again supplying the tagname as an argument.

For example, here you can see a simple handler for a start tag:

```
proc Start {name attlist args} {
    puts "Start: $name"
}
```

You create a new instance of the XML parser and register the procedures that you want to use for the different entities using something like the following fragment:

```
set p [xml::parser -elementstartcommand Start \
                   -elementendcommand End \
                   -characterdatacommand CData]
```

You can configure a number of different XML entities to be identified and handled by setting up different commands to handle them and configuring the parser accordingly. See the section "Configuring the Parser," later in this chapter, for more information.

Creating the parser is only part of the story, however. You also need to supply the parser with some XML for it to process. You do this by using the parse method on the newly created parser object. For example

```
$p parse "<mytag>mydata</mytag>"
```

You can call this method as many times as necessary in order to supply an entire XML document to the parser. The parser will handle—and if necessary bond together—all of the text in order to build and identify entire entities. Typically, of course, you'll be reading data from an external file as we do in our sample scripts by opening the file and embedding an evaluation of the read command on the file.

You can see an example of an XML parser that generates a very simple annotated list of the start, end, and data portions of the XML document in Listing 22.1.

Listing 22.1   A Simple XML Parser

```
#!/bin/sh
# \
exec tclsh8.3 "$0" "$@"

# Import the xml package

package require xml

# set up the handler for opening (start)
# tags. Must accept the tag name, list
# of attributes and a list of additional
# arguments

proc Start {name attlist args} {
    puts "Start: $name"
}
```

```
# set up the handler for the closing (end)
# tags. Must accept the tag name and any
# additional arguments

proc End {tag args} {
    puts "End: $tag"
}

# set up the handler for character data
# we ignore data entirely composed of
# whitespace characters

proc CData {data args} {
    if {![regexp {^[ \t\r\n]+$} $data ]} {
        puts "Data: $data"
    }
}

# Open each file in the argument list

foreach in $argv {
    if {[catch {open $in} ch]} {
        puts stderr "unable to open file \"$in\""
        exit 1
    }

# create a new instance of the XML parser

    set p [xml::parser -elementstartcommand Start \
                       -elementendcommand End \
                       -characterdatacommand CData]

# supply the parser with the test we read from
# the file, catching (and reporting) any errors

    if {[catch {$p parse [read $ch]} err]} {
        puts stderr $err
        exit 1
    }
    catch {close $ch}
}

exit 0
```

The core elements of the script are the procedures that handle the entities as the XML parser actually sees them. The Start and End procedures are straightforward enough: They get passed the name of the tag that has just been identified (as well as other information). All we do is print out the tag with a suitable prefix.

The character data procedure is slightly special. One of the problems with the way the Expat parser works is that it parses on all information to the procedures. In the case of tags, the information passed on is what you would expect. For the character data, this means that the handler may be called a number of times for what appears to you to be a single data block within the XML file.

Furthermore, because it can be called a number of times, on occasion it will be composed merely of white space (spaces, tabs, newline/carriage return). So that we don't end up outputting useless data, we check the supplied data first by running it past a regular expression. Of course, this is an issue only when using Expat; the TclXML parser doesn't exhibit this problem.

TIP   You can ask the parser to ignore white space by setting the −ignorewhitespace option on the parser.

If we run the script on a simple XML file, we get the following:

```
Start: contact
Start: name
Data: Martin Brown
End: name
Start: address
Start: description
Data: Main Address
End: description
Start: addressline
Data: The House, The Street, The Town
End: addressline
End: address
Start: address
Start: description
Data: Holiday Chalet
End: description
Start: addressline
Data: The Chalet, The Hillside, The Forest
End: addressline
End: address
End: contact
```

Configuring the Parser

You can configure the parser when you create the parser instance, such as the following:

```
set p [xml::parser -characterdatacommand CData]
```

You also can configure it after the parser has been created by using the `configure` method, such as this:

```
$p configure -elementstartcommand Start
```

You can see a full list of the configurable options supported by the parser in Table 22.1. The option is the name of the option that you can configure. The Command Arguments are the arguments supplied to the command that is evaluated when a particular entity is identified.

TABLE 22.1: Configurable Options for the TclXML Parser

Option	Command Arguments	Description
-attlistdeclcommand script	name attrname type default value	Defines the command prefix to be evaluated whenever an attribute list declaration is encountered within an XML document's DTD.
-baseurl URI		The base URI to use when resolving any relative URIs in the document.
-characterdatacommand script	data	The command prefix evaluated when any character data is encountered.
-commentcommand script	data	The command prefix to be evaluated when a comment is encountered.
-defaultcommand script	data	The command prefix to be evaluated when an entity not otherwise covered by another configured option.
-defaultexpandinternalentities Boolean		If True, resolves entities declared in the DTD with the expanded version.
-doctypecommand script	name publicid system id dtd	The command prefix to be evaluated when a document type declaration is identified.
-elementdeclcommand script	name model	The command prefix evaluated when an element markup declaration is encountered.
-elementendcommand script	name args	The command prefix evaluated when an end tag is identified.
-elementstartcommand script	name attributes args	The command prefix evaluated when a start tag is identified.
-endcdatasectioncommand script		The command prefix evaluated when the end of a data section is identified.
-enddoctypedeclcommand script		The command prefix evaluated when the end of the document type declaration is identified.
-entitydeclcommand script	name args	The command prefix evaluated when the entity declaration is encountered.

Continued on next page

TABLE 22.1 CONTINUED: Configurable Options for the TclXML Parser

Option	Command Arguments	Description
-entityreferencecommand script	name	The command prefix evaluated when an entity reference is identified.
-errorcommand script	errorcode errormessage	The command prefix evaluated when a fatal error is detected. See the "Error Handling" section, later in this chapter.
-externalentitycommand script	name baseuri uri publicid	The command prefix evaluated when an external entity reference is identified. If the parser is validating the document (see the **-validate** option), then a default script is supplied that recursively parses the entity's data.
-final Boolean		When data is being supplied to the parser in multiple chunks, this should be set to **False** while there is additional data to be parsed. When you run out of data, set it to **True** to indicate that the final chunk has been supplied.
-ignorewhitespace Boolean		If set to **True**, then the parser automatically ignores character data segments in the document that are composed entirely of white space.
-notationdeclcommand script	name uri	The command prefix evaluated when a notation declaration is encountered.
-notstandalonecommand script		The command prefix evaluated when the parser determines that the XML document requires and/or uses other documents.
-paramentityparsing Boolean		If set to **True**, then external parameter entities are parsed.
-parameterentitydeclcommand script	name args	The command prefix evaluated when a parameter entity declaration is identified.
-parser name		The name of the parser class to use for this parser object. Only valid when the parser is created.
-processinginstructioncommand script	target data	The command prefix evaluated when a processing instruction is encountered.
-reportempty Boolean		If **True**, then additional arguments are appended to the element start and end callbacks to indicate that the element was empty. Empty elements are ignored otherwise.

Continued on next page

TABLE 22.1 CONTINUED: Configurable Options for the TclXML Parser

Option	Command Arguments	Description
-startcdatasectioncommand script		The command prefix evaluated when the start of the character data section is identified.
-startdoctypedeclcommand script		The command prefix evaluated when a document type declaration is identified.
-unknownencodingcommand script		The command prefix evaluated when a character using an unknown encoding format is identified.
-unparsedentitydeclcommand script	systemid publicid notation	The command prefix evaluated when a declaration is identified for an unparsed entity.
-validate Boolean		If set to True, forces the parser to validate the structure of the XML document.
-warningcommand script	warningcode warningmessage	The command prefix to be evaluated when a warning condition is raised by the parser (see the "Error Handling" section, later in this chapter, for more information).
-xmldeclcommand script	version encoding standalone	The command prefix evaluated when an XML declaration is encountered.

NOTE   Character data can be handled in two ways. If you want only to output the character data string, then use the -characterdatacommand option. If you want to identify the start and end of any character data sections—useful when converting XML to another format—use the -startcdatasectioncommand and -endcdatasectioncommand options. Note that, when using the latter option, you still need to use -characterdatacommand to obtain the character data.

Error Handling

The simplest way to handle errors is to catch any errors generated during the parsing process using a catch statement. However, you may want to handle the errors a bit more exclusively. The best way of handling errors is to set up a callback to be triggered when an error occurs. To use this method you'll need to set call-back either as part of the options supplied when the parser is created or afterwards using the configure command.

The parser handles two different error conditions:

- *Warnings* occur when an XML document has not been created properly, such as when an empty element is used but not declared. The default command for the `-warningcommand` option silently ignores any problems.

- *Errors* are raised when the document is not well-formed; that is, when tags do not match (or there is no closing tag) or the nesting is bad. Errors can be trapped by creating a command and setting the `-errorcommand` option to the parser. The default command set for errors hands back an error response to the caller.

To define a command for either of these options, you must create a command that accepts two arguments, the `errorcode` (numerical) and the error message (a textual description). How you handle this information is up to you.

If you want your commands to raise an error with the parser, then you can return an error from your handlers. For example, when translating your XML documents into HTML, you may want to raise an error if a tag is identified in the XML document without a matching conversion. The supported return codes and their effects are listed in Table 22.2.

TABLE 22.2: Command Statements for Handlers

Code	Description
break	Terminates parsing of the XML document, suppressing the invocation of any further entity-handler commands. The parse method returns the TCL_OK return code.
continue	Stops invocation of callback handlers until the current element has finished.
error	Terminates the XML processing immediately. The parse method also returns the TCL_ERROR return code.
default	Any other return code suppresses invocation of all further callback scripts. The parse method returns the same return code.

Tcl and Unicode

The TclXML parser will read Unicode encoded documents directly, so you need to identify or display either entities or character data. Then you will need to be able to translate between Unicode formats.

Tcl 8.1 and after includes the `encoding` command, which will convert strings between the different encoding formats for you. See the following sidebar for information on determining which encodings are supported by your system.

Supported Encodings

To determine which encodings are supported by your Tcl installation, use the following:

```
lsort [encoding names]
```

This will produce a list of the available encodings. See Appendix A, "Unicode Quick Reference," for information on what each of these encodings means. For example, on my Solaris system running Tcl 8.3, the list is as follows:

```
ascii big5 cp1250 cp1251 cp1252 cp1253 cp1254 cp1255 cp1256 cp1257 cp1258
➥ cp437cp737 cp775 cp850 cp852 cp855 cp857 cp860 cp861 cp862 cp863 cp864
➥ cp865 cp866 cp869 cp874 cp932 cp936 cp949 cp950 dingbats euc-cn euc-jp
➥ euc-kr gb12345 gb1988 gb2312 identity iso2022 iso2022-jp iso2022-kr iso8859-1
➥ iso8859-2 iso8859-3 iso8859-4 iso8859-5 iso8859-6 iso8859-7 iso8859-8
➥ iso8859-9 jis0201 jis0208 jis0212 koi8-r ksc5601 macCentEuro macCroatian
➥ macCyrillic macDingbats macGreek macIceland macJapan macRoman macRomania
➥ macThai macTurkish macUkraine shiftjis symbol unicode utf-8
```

The `encoding` function supports a number of different options:

```
encoding convertfrom ?encoding? data
```

This converts data to Unicode format from the specified encoding. For example, the following would convert the ASCII string into Unicode format:

```
set s [encoding convertfrom ascii "Hello World"]
```

The `convertto` option translates a bytestring from Unicode format into the specified encoding.

```
encoding convertto ?encoding? string
```

In both cases, the system encoding is used if the encoding format is not specified. You can set the system encoding using this command:

```
encoding system ?encoding?
```

Note that modifying the system encoding may affect the names of commands you evaluate, because the system encoding is used for command names. Using a non-ASCII–compatible system encoding is not recommended.

Viewing XML with Tk

An obvious use of Tcl (in combination with the Tk GUI builder) is to develop an application that enables us to view an XML document marked up so that we can identify start and end tags in the document more easily. We don't really need to do anything clever here—we're not checking the validity of the document in any way. We just need an easier way to view the contents.

You can see a sample of the script in action in Figure 22.1. Start tags are identified by coloring them red; end tags are blue. Character data is left untouched, but all the elements are indented according to the structure, so you can also identify the nesting and document structure.

FIGURE 22.1:

Viewing an XML document with Tcl/Tk

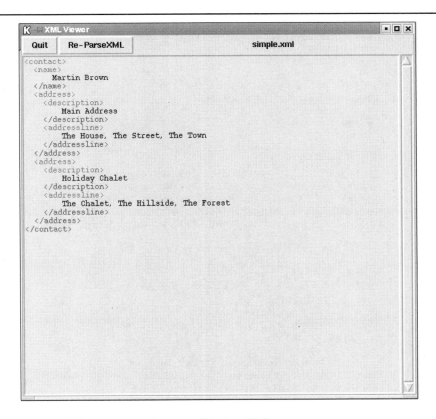

The code that generated the viewer is shown in Listing 22.2.

Listing 22.2   **The Tcl/Tk XML Viewer**

```
#!/bin/sh
# \
exec wish8.3 "$0" "$@"

# set up our main Tk window

wm title . "XML Viewer"

# Set up our global variables
# indent holds the indentation value
# tagnumber keeps track of the text paragraphs
# input contains the name of the XML file

set indent 0
set tagnumber 0
set input [lindex $argv 0]

# Set up the button bar at the top
# Contains a Quit button and
# a Reparse button to re-read the XML
# and the name of the file

set bf [ frame .menubar ]
pack $bf -fill x
button $bf.quit -text Quit -command exit
button $bf.parse -text Re-ParseXML -command ParseXML
label $bf.label -textvariable input
pack $bf.quit $bf.parse -side left
pack $bf.label -side right -fill x -expand true

# Set up the main textbox to hold our XML

set tf [ frame .text]
pack $tf -side top -fill both -expand true
set t [text $tf.t \
        -setgrid true \
        -wrap word \
        -width 80 \
        -height 40 \
        -yscrollcommand "$tf.sy set"]
scrollbar $tf.sy -orient vert -command "$tf.t yview"
pack $tf.sy -side right -fill y
pack $tf.t -side left -fill both -expand true

# Create two tags to markup the start and end
# enetities without our XML file
```

```
$t tag configure opentag -foreground #ff0000
$t tag configure closetag -foreground #0000ff

# Import the XML parser

package require xml

# The start handler accepts the XML tag name
# and outputs the tag, formatted, to the text box

proc Start {name attlist args} {
    global t indent tagnumber
# Increment the paragraph number so we can set the tag
    incr tagnumber
# Add the XML tag to the text box, using the current
# indentation
    $t insert end [format "%*s%s\n" $indent "" "<$name>"]
# Set the style of the paragraph that we just added
    $t tag add opentag \
            [eval format "%0.1f" $tagnumber] \
            [eval format "%d.end" $tagnumber]
# Now increase the indent so that any nested tag or
# character data appears to be within this tag
    incr indent 2
}

# The end handler accepts the XML tag name
# and outputs the results to the text box
# But we mark it with a different text color
# and decrement the indentation so that
# tags line up

proc End {name args} {
    global t indent tagnumber
# Decrment the indent, to bring the end tag into
# line with the opening tag
    incr indent -2
# Increment the paragraph number
    incr tagnumber
# Add the tag to the text box
    $t insert end [format "%*s%s\n" $indent "" "</$name>"]
# Set the style of the previous paragraph
    $t tag add closetag \
            [eval format "%0.1f" $tagnumber] \
            [eval format "%d.end" $tagnumber]
}

# The character data handler adds the data (except
# whitespace) to the text box
```

```
proc CData {data args} {
    global t indent tagnumber
# Check were dealing with a valid text block
    if {![regexp {^[ \t\r\n]+$} $data ]} {
# Increment the indentation
        incr indent 2
# Increment the paragraph number to keep the
# paragraph numbers in check
        incr tagnumber
# Add the text to the text box, using the indent
        $t insert end [format "%*s%s\n" $indent "" $data]
# Decrement the indent
        incr indent -2
    }
}

# Set up the parser. Since this is the same procedure
# called when we click on the Re-ParseXML button
# we also reset the indentation, paragraph numbers
# and the contents of the text box

proc ParseXML {} {
    global input t tagnumber indent
    set tagnumber 0
    set indent 0
    $t delete 0.0 end
    if {[catch {open $input} ch]} {
        puts stderr "unable to open file \"$input\""
        exit 1
    }
    set p [xml::parser -elementstartcommand Start \
                       -elementendcommand End \
                       -characterdatacommand CData]
    if {[catch {$p parse [read $ch]} err]} {
        puts stderr $err
        exit 1
    }
    catch {close $ch}
}

# Call the ParseXML procedure and start processing the file
# supplied on the command line

ParseXML
```

The script actually builds on our simple parser example earlier in this chapter. Before we get to the actual parsing of the XML we set up a simple window with a few buttons and a main text box to hold the XML.

We then use the text tags feature in a Tk text box to mark up the start and end tags as we see them in the XML document. To ensure that we mark up the right element, we have to keep a count of the paragraphs that we write to the text widget (in the *tagnumber* variable). To aid display, we also indent the structure like a tree (using the *indent* variable). The application was designed as an active viewer for XML documents while editing the XML document in another application. You can reparse the document and redisplay XML by clicking on the Re-ParseXML button. It's not perfect—supply an XML document that has multiple linefeeds/paragraphs in a character data block and the numbering goes awry, but it's a great way to view a basic XML document.

Using XML-RPC

Back in Chapter 5, we looked at XML-RPC, a solution for executing functions, procedures, and commands on a remote machine using a standard interface. The system is cross-platform and cross-language compatible, and it's all made possible because the request to the remote machine and its response to the client are handled entirely using XML.

When you submit a request, it's packaged into an XML document, which is then sent over your desired transport (TCP/IP and usually HTTP). The whole process is then reversed when sending back the response. Because the request and response are in XML, we can use any XML-capable language.

There are a few XML-RPC solutions available for Tcl, but the one with the easiest interface is the XML-RPC Tcl toolkit written by Eric Yeh.

Writing an XML-RPC Client

The client interface for calling a remote procedure is not that different from evaluating a local procedure. In fact, we can dissect the line that performs the call very simply, as in the following line, extracted from our full client sample:

```
[xmlrpc::call "http://localhost:5557" "bond" {{string Cats} {int 101}}]
```

The first part is just the command xmlrpc::call, which submits the request to the remote server. The first argument to the call is the URL we want to use to answer queries. In this instance, we're using a server running on port 5557 on the local machine.

The next argument, bond, is the name of the remote function that we want to call. The last argument is a list of the arguments that we want to supply to the remote procedure as part of the call. In this example, we've supplied a string and an integer. Note that you must type these values explicitly so that the XML-RPC package knows how to mark up the values when it builds the request envelope sent to the server.

You can see the full server, which includes error checking and the reporting of the response, in Listing 22.3.

Listing 22.3   **A Simple XML-RPC Client in Tcl**

```
package require xmlrpc
if {[catch {set res [xmlrpc::call "http://localhost:5557" "bond"
➥ {{string Cats} {int 101}}]}]} {
        puts "xmlrpc call failed"
} else {
        puts "Join: $res."
}

if {[catch {set res [xmlrpc::call "http://localhost:5557" "circlearea"
➥ {{int 2}}]}]} {
        puts "xmlrpc call failed"
} else {
        puts "Area of circle: $res."
}
```

If you execute this script while running the server—which we'll see shortly—you get the following output:

```
Join: {} Cats101.
Area of circle: {} 12.566370616.
```

Although these seem like fairly simple examples (and they are), the flexibility of XML-RPC cannot be underestimated. We've run a couple of commands on a local machine, but the server could just as easily have been on the other side of the world. In fact, we could have been calling the remote procedures on an embedded system inside a soft drink machine.

Writing an XML-RPC Server

The XML-RPC server handles requests from a given client. The server needs to set up only two pieces of information: the port on which it will accept requests from a client and the one or more functions that you want to support remotely. The XML-RPC toolkit handles the rest of the process; you don't have to register the commands separately that you want to support, as you do with some toolkits.

For example, Listing 22.4 shows a very simple client that supports two commands: bond, which bonds two arguments into a single string, and circlearea, which calculates the area of a circle if given the radius.

> **Listing 22.4   A Simple XML-RPC Server in Tcl**

```
package require xmlrpc

xmlrpc::serve 5557

proc circlearea {r} {
    return [list string [expr 3.141592654 * ($r * $r)]]
}

proc bond {a b} {
        return [list string $a$b]
}

vwait forever
```

The primary line sets up a daemon-based XML-RPC server on TCP/IP port 5557. Then we define two commands, which will be those supported and accessible by any remote clients.

Arguments to commands are supplied and accessible as normal. However, when returning information, you must ensure that you return a list of items. Each item within the returned list should also be typed explicitly (through `int()`, `double()`, or `string()`) before being returned. For example, you can see in Listing 22.4 that the result of the area calculation is converted explicitly into a double during its calculation and return.

Finally, we set the server to wait for incoming connections forever. The server will handle all connections until either a fatal error or you terminate the process. During execution, the server will display diagnostic information, including the client host and port and the XML-RPC–encoded envelope returned to the client.

For example, the abbreviated snippet that follows is produced when running our client script.

```
in serveOnce: addr: 127.0.0.1
in serveOnce: port: 41179
in doRequest: response:
HTTP/1.1 200 OK
Content-Type: text/xml
Content-length: 142

<?xml version="1.0"?>
<methodResponse>
        <params>
                <param>
                        <value><string>Cats101</string></value>
                </param>
        </params>
</methodResponse>
...
```

As you can see, both the client and the server are very easy to write. In fact, this is one of the easiest implementations of the XML-RPC system of any of the languages covered in this book.

See Chapter 5 for more information on how XML-RPC works and how to debug the information shown in the above output.

Summary

Although Tcl is a very useful language in its own right, it really comes into its own when you combine the language with the Tk user interface builder.

The Tcl system supports two main XML parsers: TclXML, which parses documents using an XML parser written entirely in Tcl, and TclExpat, which uses the popular Expat parser system to process the XML document.

In both cases, the system works by passing off the individual elements to a Tcl command. It's up to these commands to process the information, whether it's simply printing out the information or formatting it in a more structured form, such as the Tk XML viewer.

Tcl also supports the XML-RPC system for executing remote procedures. By supporting an HTTP service, a Tcl server script can service requests from a Tcl client, enabling the client to execute commands directly on the server and obtain responsses.

CHAPTER 23

AppleScript and XML

- XML Parsing with AppleScript

- XML-RPC with AppleScript

- XML and MacOS X

AppleScript is the scripting system built into MacOS. Although it's not most people's first choice for parsing XML documents, it's actually remarkably capable at processing and working with XML documents.

Also, because it's the standard scripting language for communicating with many of the various systems and applications under MacOS, we can use it to integrate the applications and XML documents that they would otherwise not understand.

XML support for AppleScript is available only through a third-party extension available from Late Night Software (`http://www.latenightsw.com/freeware/XMLTools2/index.html`). They also provide an XML-RPC extension (`http://www.latenightsw.com/freeware/XMLTools2/xml-rpc.html`) that we'll be looking at in this chapter.

When using MacOS X, we still need to use the Late Night Software solution for AppleScript when parsing XML, but support for both XML-RPC and SOAP solutions is actually built into the operating system. MacOS X will automatically encode a request into the desired XML format for you and send it to a destination, decoding the result.

In this chapter, we'll be looking at the basic mechanics for parsing XML using AppleScript and how to generate XML documents from within AppleScript. We'll also be looking at XML-RPC in MacOS before moving on to look at how MacOS X uses XML and how to use XML-RPC and SOAP within MacOS X to access remote servers.

XML Parsing with AppleScript

Once you've downloaded XML Tools from Late Night Software's website, you need to install the tools by copying the `XML Tools` AppleScript extension in the `ScriptingAdditions` folder in your `System` folder. This is seen with some other extensions in Figure 23.1.

To actually parse some XML, you use this expression:

```
parse XML XMLSOURCE
```

`XMLSOURCE` is a text object containing the source of the document you want to parse. The return value from the call is an `XML Document` class structure. Normally you'd use this information with `set` to put the class structure into a variable that you can conveniently use and process later.

FIGURE 23.1:

The Scripting-
Additions folder

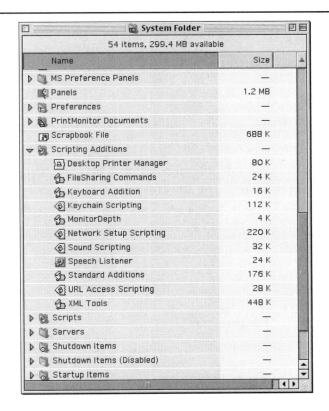

For example, to parse this simple XML:

```
<simple>
Wrapper text
<paragraph book='Fox' chapter='16'>
The Quick Brown Fox
</paragraph>
</simple>
```

you might use this:

```
set theXML to parse XML "
<simple>
Wrapper text
<paragraph book='Fox' chapter='16'>

The Quick Brown Fox
</paragraph>
</simple>
```

You can also parse text strings:

```
set theXMLSource to "
<simple>
Wrapper text
<paragraph book='Fox' chapter='16'>
The Quick Brown Fox
</paragraph>
</simple>"

set theXML to parse XML theXMLSource
```

You can parse information read from a file using this:

```
set theXML to parse XML (read file ("sample.xml"))
```

Note that AppleScript will try to load this from the AppleScript folder on your machine. If you want to load from a specific location you'll need to specify the location explicitly.

The result is an AppleScript structure containing our XML as a series of objects and properties:

```
{
    class: XML document,
    XML tag: "simple",
    XML contents:{
        "Wrapper text",
        {
            class: XML element,
            XML tag: "paragraph",
            XML attributes: {
                book: "Fox",
                chapter: "16"
            }
            XML contents: {
                "The Quick Brown Fox"
            }
        }
    }
}
```

We can access this information using the standard record access techniques. Note that the information here is stored by name, so you must access the XML tag by its name. Notice also that attributes are stored as properties within the XML attributes entity.

It's also important to note that you must process nested structures directly—unlike the other serial XML parsers such as SAX and those built on most Expat bases that we've seen elsewhere in this book. Instead, we've basically created a DOM tree from an XML document that we can access directly within AppleScript.

Also note that we've create a new structure based on our XML that, unlike the other solutions we've seen in this book, we can't identify when we reach the end of a particular XML tag. Although initially this looks like a problem, it actually makes the processing sequence easier. Instead of having to identify the end of an XML tag using a separate function, we can identify it when we finish processing that tag's content. We also get to access the entire content of an XML tag without jumping through the hoops we've used in other solutions using SAX or even DOM processing—we don't have to process the entire document to extract a single piece of information.

Parsing Quick Reference

The XML Tools parser, you may not be surprised to discover, is based on the Expat parser that is the basis of so many other parsing interfaces we've covered in this book. Because of this, the parser is completely Unicode compliant and should process Unicode text in most of the standard forms without any problems.

The parse XML statement accepts a number of different parameters that control the parsing process. A list of these parameters is shown in Table 23.1. All the parameters are optional, and the table includes data types and default values for each of the supported parameters. Most of these correspond to similar parameters supported in other Expat interfaces.

TABLE 23.1: parse XML Parameters

Parameter	Data type	Default	Description
strict standalone	boolean	false	Raises an error, trappable through the try statement, if the XML that is being parsed is not entirely standalone.
expanding external entities	boolean	false	When true, it triggers the XML Tools to use the URL Access Scripting extensions to download and parse any external entities referenced in the document.
including comments	boolean	false	When true, includes any comments from the XML file within an XML comment record. See the example in the main text.
including processing instructions	boolean	false	When true, it causes XML processing instructions to be incorporated into the resulting XML document record within an XML processing instruction record. See the example in the main text.
serializing	boolean	default	When enabled, it automatically adds an id property to the XML attributes record of each XML tag within the resulting record. See the main text for an example.
base path	Unicode text	none	If supplied, it's used as the base URL for all the external entity IDs. For example, specifying http://www.mcwords.com/dtds/ would cause this URL to be used as the prefix for any implied entity requests.
preserving whitespace	boolean	false	When true, it causes any white space (carriage returns, newlines, and tabs) to be included in the character data. The default is for this information to be trimmed from the data when the XML is parsed.

For example, with `including comments`, the code in Listing 23.1 would produce the record in Listing 23.2. You can see how the comments become part of the XML document record.

Listing 23.1   **Simple XML with Comments**

```
parse XML "
<theory>
    Here is my theory:
    <!-- Here is the theory which is mine and that I have written -->
    My theory is:
</theory>" with including comments
```

Listing 23.2   **An *XML document* Record with Comments**

```
{
    class:XML document,
    XML tag:"theory",
    XML contents:{
        " Here is my theory:",
        {
            class:XML comment,
            XML comment:" Here is the theory which is mine and that I have
written "
        },
        "My theory is:"
    }
}
```

You might notice that the comment actually includes any white space between the `<!--` and `-->` sequences.

When we include processing instructions, the information is placed into a special XML processing instruction class within the tag in which the processing instruction was created. For example, when executing the script in Listing 23.3, we get a record with the structure shown in Listing 23.4.

Listing 23.3   **Simple XML with a Processing Instruction**

```
parse XML "
<theory>
    My theory is:
    <?linebreak  'with horizontal'?>
    Brontosaurses are very thin at one end, thicker in
    the middle, and thin at the other end.
</theory>" with including processing instructions
```

Listing 23.4   **An *XML document* Record with *processing instruction***

```
{
    class:XML document,
    XML tag:"theory",
    XML contents:{
        "My theory is:",
        {
            class:XML processing instruction,
            XML target: "linebreak",
            XML target data: "with horizontal"
        },
        "Brontosaurses are very thin at one end, thicker ➡
        in the middle, and thin at the other end.",
    }
}
```

You can see from Listing 23.4 how the XML processing instruction class includes separate properties for the processing instruction's target and target data.

When using the serializing function, we get a more useful unique ID number for each tag in the output, as demonstrated from the XML in Listing 23.5 and the resulting record in Listing 23.6.

Listing 23.5   **Simple XML with Serialization**

```
parse XML "
<simple>
Wrapper text
<paragraph book='Fox' chapter='16'>
The Quick Brown Fox
</paragraph>
</simple>" with serializing
```

Listing 23.6   **An *XML document* Record with a Serialized ID**

```
{
    class: XML document,
    XML element id: 1

,
    XML tag: "simple",
    XML attributes: {
        id: 2
    },
```

```
XML contents:{
    "Wrapper text",
    {
        class: XML element,
        XML element id: 1,
        XML tag: "paragraph",
        XML attributes: {
            book: "Fox",
            chapter: "16",
            id: 1
        }
        XML contents: {
            "The Quick Brown Fox"
        }
    }
}
}
```

The resulting output in Listing 23.6 shows the ID number in place within the record. We can use this information if we decide to restructure the document but still need to refer to earlier elements. All we need to do is search for an element by a given ID number, rather than by its name, to update the contents.

Processing an RSS Feed to HTML

We can use the XML parser in combination with the URL Access Scripting extension (a standard part of the OS) to download and parse RDF/RSS news summary files from websites into an HTML document. We can use that document in Internet Explorer or Netscape Navigator to browse and link to the stories.

For our example, we'll use the Macintosh News Network site (http://macnn.com), which publishes an RSS feed at http://www.macnn.com/macnn.rdf. A fragment of the resulting RSS feed can be seen in Listing 23.7.

Listing 23.7   **The MacNN RDF File**

```
<?xml version="1.0" encoding="ISO-8859-1" ?>
    <rdf:RDF xmlns:rdf="http://www.w3.org/1999/02/22➡
    -rdf-syntax-ns#" xmlns="http://my.netscape.com/rdf/simple/0.9/">
...
    <image>
    <title>MacNN</title>
    <url>http://www4.macnn.com/media/logo-macin-90.gif</url>
    <link>http://www.macnn.com/</link>
```

```
    </image><item>
<title>Apple to introduce new iBooks, PowerBooks</title>
<link>http://www.macnn.com/news.php?id=9900</link>
</item>

<item>
<title>Media 100 completes $16M sale to Discreet</title>
<link>http://www.macnn.com/news.php?id=9904</link>
</item>

<item>
<title>Adobe reaffirms earnings, despite 9-11 attack</title>
<link>http://www.macnn.com/news.php?id=9903</link>
</item>

    </rdf:RDF>
```

We've already looked at the structure of an RSS or RDF feed when we looked at a PHP script for formatting RSS/RDF data within a PHP application. To recap, the header includes information about the site itself (trimmed from Listing 23.7) and links to the site from which the RSS/RDF feed was downloaded. Then individual stories are contained within `item` tags with the story title and corresponding URL in `title` and `link` tags, respectively.

Using this information, we can quickly produce an AppleScript that downloads the RDF file and then processes the output to produce an HTML file (after prompting you for the location and filename). The RSS file is then processed, the required elements extracted, and the HTML written to the HTML file of your choice. You can see the AppleScript source in Listing 23.8.

Listing 23.8   **Downloading and Converting an RSS to HTML**

```applescript
on loadxml()
  local infile, fileRef, theXMLSource, theXML

  tell application "Finder"
    set theFolder to temporary items folder as string
    if exists file "macnn.xml" of temporary items folder then ¬
      delete file "macnn.xml" of temporary items folder
  end tell
  tell application "URL Access Scripting"
    activate
    download "http://www.macnn.com/macnn.rdf" to file (theFolder & "macnn.xml")
with progress
    quit
  end tell
```

```applescript
    set theXML to parse XML (read file (theFolder & "macnn.xml"))

    return theXML
end loadxml

on writeFile(outFileRef, theData)
  write theData to outFileRef
end writeFile

on openDestFile(outFile)
  local outFileRef

  set outFileRef to open for access outFile with write permission
  try
    set eof outFileRef to 0
    write "<html>
    <head><title>Latest News</title></head>
    <body bgcolor=\"#ffffff\" fgcolor=\"#000000\">
    <h1>Latest News</h1>" to outFileRef
  on error errMsg number errNumber
    close access outFileRef
    error errMsg number errNumber
  end try
  return outFileRef

end openDestFile

local theXML, theOutFile

set outFile to choose file name
set theXML to loadxml()
set theOutFile to openDestFile(outFile)

repeat with anElement in XML contents of theXML
  set theText to XML tag of anElement
  if XML tag of anElement is "item" then
    repeat with itemElement in XML contents of anElement
      if XML tag of itemElement is "title" then
        set theText to XML contents of itemElement as string
        writeFile(theOutFile, "<b>" & theText & "</b>")
      else if XML tag of itemElement is "link" then
        set theText to XML contents of itemElement as string
        writeFile(theOutFile, "  <a href=\"" & theText & "\">Read
Story</a><br>")
      end if
    end repeat
  end if
end repeat

write "</body></html>" to theOutFile
close access theOutFile
```

The major parts of the script are in the line that gets the RSS feed:

```
download "http://www.macnn.com/macnn.rdf" to file (theFolder & "macnn.xml") with
progress
```

This uses the URL Access Scripting extension to allow you to download an RSS file to your machine. The other is the `repeat` loop at the bottom of the script. The outer loop iterates through the outer RSS `item` tags, and the inner `repeat` loop iterates through the tags within an `item` tag. You then write a suitable line when you find the `link` and `title` tags.

If you save this script and execute it, you'll be prompted for a file into which to save the HTML, as shown in Figure 23.2. Once the processing has finished, the script will exit, and you'll need to open the file in Internet Explorer, Netscape, or another browser to view the output. You can see the resulting news item page in Figure 23.3.

FIGURE 23.2:

The prompt for a file-name and location

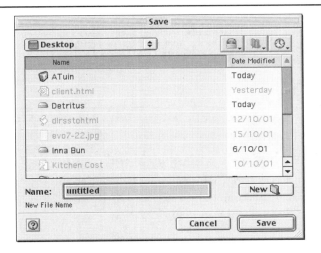

You could easily extend the code in Listing 23.8 to download other pages. In the past, I have used the system to download RSS feeds to an AppleShare IP server to build a series of HTML pages of news for a client. Combined with something like CronTask or MacAT (both available from `http://www.macupdate.com`), the news pages can be updated at regular intervals.

The resulting
news page

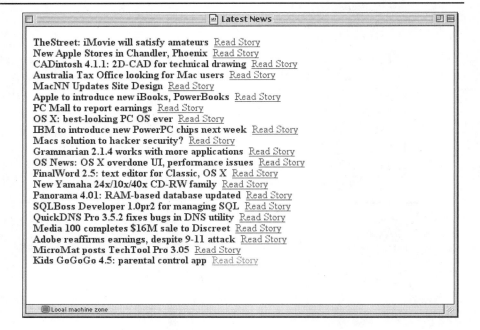

Generating XML with AppleScript

You can build an XML document by creating the record and then using the generate XML command to dump the record as an XML string. You can see a simple example of an Apple-Script script for this in Listing 23.9.

Listing 23.9   **Generating XML from an XML Record**

```
set theXML to ¬
    { class:XML element, ¬
     XML tag:"chapter", ¬
     XML attributes: ¬
         { title:"XML and AppleScript", ¬
           chapnumber: "03"}, ¬
         XML contents:¬
             { class:XML element, ¬
               XML tag:"paragraph", ¬
               XML contents:{¬
                   "The Quick Brown Fox"} ¬
             } ¬
     }

generate XML theXML
```

The output of the script is shown in Listing 23.10.

Listing 23.10   **XML Generated by XML Tools**

```
"<?xml version=\"1.0\"?>
<chapter
    title=\"XML and AppleScript\"
    chapnumber=\"03\">
    <paragraph>
        The Quick Brown Fox
    </paragraph>
</chapter>
"
```

You can change certain aspects of the generated XML through a number of parameters to the generate XML command, as listed in Table 23.2. Most of these enable dumping of different XML entities back to text format, in the same way as the parsing parameters enable conversion from XML to AppleScript record format. Unlike the parsing command, most of these are enabled by default.

TABLE 23.2: Parameters for Generating XML

Parameter	Data type	Default	Description
including XML declaration	boolean	true	Includes the XML declaration in the output.
including DOCTYPE declaration	boolean	true	Generates a DOCTYPE declaration in the XML string if one exists in the source record.
including processing instructions	boolean	true	Includes processing instruction declarations.
including comments	boolean	true	Includes XML comments.
generating unicode	boolean	false	When false, outputs a standard Apple-Script string. When true, generates Unicode text.
pretty printing	boolean	true	When true, formats the XML with indentation and line breaks to make the XML easier to read. When false, XML tags and character data are printed raw, with no indentation or groupings.

The XML Tools Dictionary

As with most AppleScript extensions, you can get more information and examples about the XML Tools by opening the XML Tools dictionary in your AppleScript editor. For example, using the standard Script Editor application (in the AppleScript directory of the Apple Extras directory on your hard disk), select File ≻ Open Dictionary and find the XML Tools extension. You should get a window like the one shown in Figure 23.4.

FIGURE 23.4:

Viewing an AppleScript dictionary

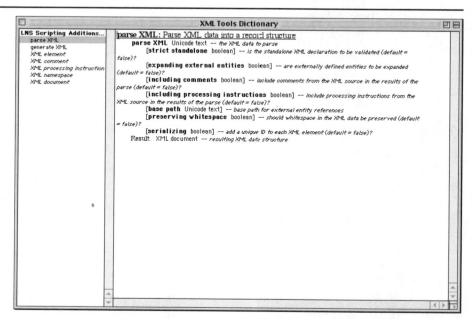

XML-RPC with AppleScript

Late Night Software also provides an XML-RPC extension that enables you to access XML-RPC services from AppleScript easily.

You need to place the extension, which is actually an AppleScript library, in a location that is found easily. Ideally, this should be somewhere in the System folder. On my system, I created a Libraries folder in System Folder:Scripts and then copied the XML-RPC Lib library into that folder.

Once there, you first need to load the library in your script. For example, if you've copied the library into the location I suggested, you can do so with this:

```
property XMLRPC : XMLRPC of (load script alias ((path to scripts folder as
    string) & "Libraries:XML-RPC Lib"))
```

To connect to a remote machine, you call the newly created XML-RPC object's `invoke-Method`. For example, to access the UserLand XML-RPC example server, you'd use this:

```
set stateName to XMLRPC's
invokeMethod("http://betty.userland.com:80/RPC2",
"examples.getStateName", 13)
```

This sets the value of `stateName` to the result of calling the `getStateName()` function in the `examples` directory on the XML-RPC server. Note that we've supplied only a single argument here. To supply multiple arguments, you must embed an AppleScript list. To supply a list as a single argument, use a list in a list, as in this example that gets the first and last U.S. state names from the server:

```
set stateNames to XMLRPC's invokeMethod("http://betty.userland.com:80/RPC2",
"examples.getStateList", {{1,50}})
```

Unfortunately, AppleScript is not the ideal solution to able to handle XML-RPC requests on the server side. We can't use it to service requests from remote machines, even when combined with a suitable web server such as Webstar or Apple's AppleShare IP web service. If you want to support XML-RPC services on your machine, use Python or Perl.

XML and MacOS X

Apple has embraced XML to a significant extent in MacOS X. XML is used by many parts of the operating system to store configuration and other information in a convenient format for parsing and processing by the OS services and applications. For example, the information about the current version of MacOS X can be found in the `System/Library/CoreServices/SystemVersion.plist` file. The file from MacOS X 10.1 build 5G27 is shown in Listing 23.11.

Listing 23.11   **System Information in MacOS X in XML Format**

```
<?xml version="1.0" encoding="UTF-8"?>
<!DOCTYPE plist SYSTEM
"file://localhost/System/Library/DTDs/PropertyList.dtd">
<plist version="0.9">
<dict>
    <key>ProductBuildVersion</key>
    <string>5G27</string>
    <key>ProductName</key>
    <string>Mac OS X</string>
    <key>ProductVersion</key>
    <string>10.1</string>
</dict>
</plist>
```

From this you can see the build number, version strings, and other information about the operating system. Further investigation will show you just how much of the operating system relies on XML to store information.

Many of the built-in applications that come with MacOS X use XML. For example, Mail, the MacOS X e-mail application, uses XML for everything from your e-mail account settings to the cache of mail message recipients, senders, and subjects that have been downloaded from your mail server.

You can see plenty of examples of the different preference files by looking in `~/Library/Preferences`. All of the files ending in `.plist` are actually XML files, and in keeping with the uniqueness of the XML files and DTD system, they are stored using their unique Internet addresses as filenames. For example, the preferences for Mail are stored in `com.apple.mail.plist`, and Finder preferences are in `com.apple.finder.plist`. Even Dock uses XML to store information about its contents, icons, and layout.

Basic XML Parsing

For XML processing you'll need to use the Late Night Software XML Tools with the MacOS X version of the tools you installed for MacOS 9.

To install the tools in MacOS X:

1. Install XML Tools under MacOS 9. You can do this through a Classic install or by booting into MacOS X.

2. Create a folder named `ScriptingAdditions` in the `root` level `Library` folder of your MacOS X startup disk. This will make the extensions available to all users on your system. To restrict access to a specific user, create a folder of the same name in the `Library` folder of that user's home directory.

3. Copy `XML Tools.osax` into the `ScriptingAdditions` folder using the MacOS X Finder.

Once installed, the system works the same as the examples in this chapter. In fact, the only changes you might need to make relate to the methods when talking to the Finder and selecting locations to store specific files, due to the changes in the underlying file system structure.

Using XML-RPC and SOAP

Although not supported in the earlier versions, in MacOS X version 10.1 (which was released on September 28, 2001), Apple incorporated the capability to communicate with external XML-RPC and SOAP services within the operating system. AppleScript support on the new OS automatically encapsulates a request in XML and then sends it off to the remote server.

This negates the need for Late Night Software's extension and allows you to use these services on any MacOS X installation without additional software.

To call an XML-RPC server, you use `call xmlrpc` and then supply the method `name` and `parameter` properties with the remote function name and arguments.

For example, we can rewrite the earlier MacOS 9.x XML-RPC example under MacOS X in this way:

```
tell application "http://betty.userland.com:80/RPC2"
    set returnValue to call xmlrpc { method ¬
        name:"examples.getStateName",¬
        parameters: { 13 }}
end tell
```

That's even easier than the Late Night Software solution!

The SOAP interface works in much the same way, except that we use the `call soap` command. The connection and method names and arguments are supplied in the same way. For example, we can communicate with the BabelFish service to convert a string from English to French on the `xmethods.com` server using this:

```
tell application ¬
    "http://services.xmethods.net:80/perl/soaplite.cgi"
    set returnValue to call soap {
        method name:"BabelFish",¬
        method namespace uri:"urn:xmethodsBabelFish", ¬
        parameters: { translationmode: "en_fr", ¬
        sourcedata: "Hello World" }, ¬
        SOAPAction: "urn:xmethodsBabelFish#BabelFish"}
end tell
```

Again, the whole process is incredibly easy.

At the time this is being written, I've been unable to test the capabilities completely. As an Apple developer in the UK, I'm still waiting for my full version of the 10.1 update, and beta versions have proven to be unstable. Check my website at `http://www.mcwords.com` for some further examples.

Apple has a "book" in its developer documentation that contains more examples and detailed information at `http://developer.apple.com/techpubs/macosx/Carbon/ interapplicationcomm/soapXMLRPC/`.

Summary

AppleScript can make use of a simple XML processing toolkit that converts any XML document into an internal AppleScript record structure which we can access and process using the same methods as we would in any other AppleScript that uses records for storing information.

With an XML document in its record form we can easily convert to other formats, such as converting an RSS document into an HTML document. We can also couple AppleScript's existing URL Access Scripting extension to first download an RSS feed before conversion.

Mac OS X uses XML documents within the OS to store all sorts of information from preferences right through to system information and layouts. However, we still need to use a third-party XML scripting extension to be able to parse these files.

In Mac OS, a third party extension is also required when accessing servers using XML-RPC, but in Mac OS X the facilities for XML-RPC and SOAP access are supported natively by the AppleScript implementation. Using both services in Mac OS X is as easy as using `tell` to control an application.

Appendix A

Unicode Quick Reference

- Base Character Sets

- XML Character Set Names

ne of the parts of the XML standard was a way of storing different characters for different languages in a platform-independent fashion. This appendix contains a list of the base character sets (and associated tables) and a list of the different character sets and encoding standards supported by the XML standard.

Base Character Sets

Although there are several different character sets supported by XML, Unicode, and the different platforms, many are actually based on a few standard sets. The oldest standard is ASCII, which is the basis of most of the character sets supported by XML.

In addition, most computers use the ISO-8859-1 (or Latin-1) character set to provide extended characters for more Western European languages. Nearly all the ISO-8859 character sets are modifications of the ISO-8859-1 standard. All the ISO-8859 standards modify the characters specified within a single byte (8-bits) as an extension of ASCII.

Unicode, on the other hand, has separate character planes, with each plane containing the characters for a different language or dialect. Unlike the ISO standards, each character in Unicode has its own unique character number, up to 65,535.

ASCII

The basic ASCII character is made up of 127 characters, 33 of which (0 through 31 and 127) are officially known as the C0 control characters. The Unicode standard does not allow for the inclusion of these control characters, except for the linefeed, carriage return, and tab characters.

You can insert these characters either directly or through the use of character/entity references. If you need to include a particular character in an XML document, you should use a specific tag and then handle that tag within your parser. For characters that would otherwise be classed as instructions (vertical tab, form feed, or bell), consider using a processing instruction.

The full character table for the ASCII set can be seen in Table A.1.

TABLE A.1: ASCII Character Set

Decimal	Hexadecimal	Character	XML Entity
0	0	\0	N/A
1	1	[SOH]	N/A
2	2	[STX]	N/A
3	3	[ETX]	N/A
4	4	[EOT]	N/A

Continued on next page

TABLE A.1 CONTINUED: ASCII Character Set

Decimal	Hexadecimal	Character	XML Entity
5	5	[ENQ]	N/A
6	6	[ACK]	N/A
7	7	\a	N/A
8	8	\b	N/A
9	9	\t	&#9;
10	a	\n	&#10;
11	b	\v	N/A
12	c	\f	N/A
13	d	\r	&#13;
14	e	[SO]	N/A
15	f	[SI]	N/A
16	10	[DCE]	N/A
17	11	[DC1]	N/A
18	12	[DC2]	N/A
19	13	[DC3]	N/A
20	14	[DC4]	N/A
21	15	[SYN]	N/A
22	16	[ETB]	N/A
23	17	[CAN]	N/A
24	18	[EM]	N/A
25	19	[SUB]	N/A
26	1a	[ESC]	N/A
27	1b	[FS]	N/A
28	1c	[GS]	N/A
29	1d	[RS]	N/A
30	1e	[US]	N/A
31	1f		N/A
32	20		&#32;
33	21	!	&#33;
34	22	"	" "
35	23	#	&#35;
36	24	$	&#36;
37	25	%	&#37;
38	26	&	& &
39	27	'	' '

Continued on next page

TABLE A.1 CONTINUED: ASCII Character Set

Decimal	Hexadecimal	Character	XML Entity
40	28	(	(
41	29	)	)
42	2a	*	*
43	2b	+	+
44	2c	,	,
45	2d	-	-
46	2e	.	.
47	2f	/	/
48	30	0	0
49	31	1	1
50	32	2	2
51	33	3	3
52	34	4	4
53	35	5	5
54	36	6	6
55	37	7	7
56	38	8	8
57	39	9	9
58	3a	:	:
59	3b	;	;
60	3c	<	< <
61	3d	=	=
62	3e	>	> >
63	3f	?	?
64	40	@	@
65	41	A	A
66	42	B	B
67	43	C	C
68	44	D	D
69	45	E	E
70	46	F	F
71	47	G	G
72	48	H	H
73	49	I	I
74	4a	J	J
75	4b	K	K

Continued on next page

TABLE A.1 CONTINUED: ASCII Character Set

Decimal	Hexadecimal	Character	XML Entity
76	4c	L	&#76;
77	4d	M	&#77;
78	4e	N	&#78;
79	4f	O	&#79;
80	50	P	&#80;
81	51	Q	&#81;
82	52	R	&#82;
83	53	S	&#83;
84	54	T	&#84;
85	55	U	&#85;
86	56	V	&#86;
87	57	W	&#87;
88	58	X	&#88;
89	59	Y	&#89;
90	5a	Z	&#90;
91	5b	[	&#91;
92	5c	\	&#92;
93	5d	]	&#93;
94	5e	^	&#94;
95	5f	_	&#95;
96	60	`	&#96;
97	61	a	&#97;
98	62	b	&#98;
99	63	c	&#99;
100	64	d	&#100;
101	65	e	&#101;
102	66	f	&#102;
103	67	g	&#103;
104	68	h	&#104;
105	69	i	&#105;
106	6a	j	&#106;
107	6b	k	&#107;
108	6c	l	&#108;
109	6d	m	&#109;
110	6e	n	&#110;

Continued on next page

TABLE A.1 CONTINUED: ASCII Character Set

Decimal	Hexadecimal	Character	XML Entity
111	6f	o	&#111;
112	70	p	&#112;
113	71	q	&#113;
114	72	r	&#114;
115	73	s	&#115;
116	74	t	&#116;
117	75	u	&#117;
118	76	v	&#118;
119	77	w	&#119;
120	78	x	&#120;
121	79	y	&#121;
122	7a	z	&#122;
123	7b	{	&#123;
124	7c			|
125	7d	}	&#125;
126	7e	~	&#126;
127	7f	[DEL]	N/A

ISO-8859-1, Latin-1

The ISO-8859 standard defines a number of supersets of the basic ASCII character set. All ISO-8859 sets match the ASCII set for the first 128 characters and define additional characters for the range 128 to 255. The ISO standard actually incorporates a second control character block (C1) from 128 to 159 used in some terminals.

Unfortunately, unlike the C0 control characters, the characters in the range of the C1 characters are allowed within an XML document. This is because the Windows code page character set Cp1252 uses characters 128 through 159 for line-based graphics characters. Cp1252 is not actually an agreed character set within the XML standard, but some systems still allow you to introduce such characters into an XML document.

The Latin-1 standard (ISO-8859-1) is used under most Western operating systems. It consists of the ASCII set plus the accented characters necessary for most Western European languages and certain currency symbols. The full character set for Latin-1 can be seen in Table A.2. Note that Mac OS systems use the Mac Roman rather than Latin 1 character; see the next section in this appendix for more details.

TABLE A.2: Characters Supported by the Latin 1 Character Set

Decimal	Hexadecimal	Character	XML Entity
128	80	[XXX]	€
129	81	[XXX]	
130	82	[BPH]	‚
131	83	[NBH]	ƒ
132	84	[IND]	„
133	85	[NEL]	…
134	86	[SSA]	†
135	87	[ESA]	‡
136	88	[HTS]	ˆ
137	89	[HTJ]	‰
138	8a	[VTS]	Š
139	8b	[PLD]	‹
140	8c	[PLU]	Œ
141	8d	[RI]	
142	8e	[SS2]	Ž
143	8f	[SS3]	
144	90	[DCS]	
145	91	[PU1]	‘
146	92	[PU2]	’
147	93	[STS]	“
148	94	[CCH]	”
149	95	[MW]	•
150	96	[SPA]	–
151	97	[EPA]	—
152	98	[SOS]	˜
153	99	[XXX]	™
154	9a	[SCI]	š
155	9b	[CSI]	›
156	9c	[ST]	œ
157	9d	[OSC]	
158	9e	[PM]	ž
159	9f	[APC]	Ÿ
160	a0	[NBSP]	
161	a1	¡	¡
162	a2	¢	¢

Continued on next page

TABLE A.2 CONTINUED: Characters Supported by the Latin 1 Character Set

Decimal	Hexadecimal	Character	XML Entity
163	a3	£	£
164	a4	¤	¤
165	a5	¥	¥
166	a6	¦	¦
167	a7	§	§
168	a8	¨	¨
169	a9	©	©
170	aa	ª	ª
171	ab	«	«
172	ac	¬	¬
173	ad	[SHY]	­
174	ae	®	®
175	af	¯	¯
176	b0	°	°
177	b1	±	±
178	b2	²	²
179	b3	³	³
180	b4	´	´
181	b5	µ	µ
182	b6	¶	¶
183	b7	·	·
184	b8	¸	¸
185	b9	¹	¹
186	ba	º	º
187	bb	»	»
188	bc	¼	¼
189	bd	½	½
190	be	¾	¾
191	bf	¿	¿
192	c0	À	À
193	c1	Á	Á
194	c2	Â	Â
195	c3	Ã	Ã
196	c4	Ä	Ä
197	c5	Å	Å

Continued on next page

TABLE A.2 CONTINUED: Characters Supported by the Latin 1 Character Set

Decimal	Hexadecimal	Character	XML Entity
198	c6	Æ	Æ
199	c7	Ç	Ç
200	c8	È	È
201	c9	É	É
202	ca	Ê	Ê
203	cb	Ë	Ë
204	cc	Ì	Ì
205	cd	Í	Í
206	ce	Î	Î
207	cf	Ï	Ï
208	d0	Ð	Ð
209	d1	Ñ	Ñ
210	d2	Ò	Ò
211	d3	Ó	Ó
212	d4	Ô	Ô
213	d5	Õ	Õ
214	d6	Ö	Ö
215	d7	×	×
216	d8	Ø	Ø
217	d9	Ù	Ù
218	da	Ú	Ú
219	db	Û	Û
220	dc	Ü	Ü
221	dd	Ý	Ý
222	de	Þ	Þ
223	df	ß	ß
224	e0	À	à
225	e1	Á	á
226	e2	Â	â
227	e3	Ã	ã
228	e4	Ä	ä
229	e5	Å	å
230	e6	æ	æ
231	e7	ç	ç
232	e8	è	è

Continued on next page

TABLE A.2 CONTINUED: Characters Supported by the Latin 1 Character Set

Decimal	Hexadecimal	Character	XML Entity
233	e9	É	é
234	ea	Ê	ê
235	eb	Ë	ë
236	ec	Ì	ì
237	ed	Í	í
238	ee	Î	î
239	ef	Ï	ï
240	f0	∂	ð
241	f1	Ñ	ñ
242	f2	Ò	ò
243	f3	Ó	ó
244	f4	Ô	ô
245	f5	Õ	õ
246	f6	Ö	ö
247	f7	÷	÷
248	f8	Ø	ø
249	f9	Ù	ù
250	fa	Ú	ú
251	fb	Û	û
252	fc	Ü	ü
253	fd	ý	ý
254	fe	þ	þ
255	ff	ÿ	ÿ

Mac Roman

Mac Roman is not an officially recognized character set within either the XML or Unicode standard, but it is a standard for the typical character set defined within any given Roman font within the operating system. Mac Roman actually closely matches the Latin-1 set, albeit with some characters replaced with other alternatives and a completely different order.

Most languages support an encoding format that will allow you to convert a Unicode document to its Mac Roman equivalent for display. Obviously, because of a lack of certain characters, this will not be a perfect translation compared to Latin-1, but the majority of differences affect only symbols, not foreign letters.

Note, however, that you should not be storing XML documents in to the Mac Roman format; like Cp1252, it is not an agreed standard and therefore shouldn't be used. Instead, encode and decode your documents to/from the UTF-8 standard.

The decimal/hexadecimal and character equivalents for the Mac Roman set are listed in Table A.3.

TABLE A.3: Characters in the Mac Roman Set

Decimal	Hexadecimal	Character
128	80	Ä
129	81	Å
130	82	Ç
131	83	É
132	84	Ñ
133	85	Ö
134	86	Ü
135	87	á
136	88	à
137	89	â
138	8a	ä
139	8b	ã
140	8c	å
141	8d	ç
142	8e	é
143	8f	è
144	90	ê
145	91	ë
146	92	í
147	93	ì
148	94	î
149	95	ï
150	96	ñ
151	97	ó
152	98	ò
153	99	ô
154	9a	ö
155	9b	õ

Continued on next page

TABLE A.3 CONTINUED: Characters in the Mac Roman Set

Decimal	Hexadecimal	Character
156	9c	ú
157	9d	ù
158	9e	û
159	9f	ü
160	a0	†
161	a1	°
162	a2	¢
163	a3	£
164	a4	§
165	a5	•
166	a6	¶
167	a7	ß
168	a8	®
169	a9	©
170	aa	™
171	ab	´
172	ac	¨
173	ad	≠
174	ae	Æ
175	af	Ø
176	b0	∞
177	b1	±
178	b2	≤
179	b3	≥
180	b4	¥
181	b5	µ
182	b6	∂
183	b7	Σ
184	b8	∏
185	b9	π
186	ba	∫
187	bb	ª
188	bc	º
189	bd	Ω
190	be	æ

Continued on next page

TABLE A.3 CONTINUED: Characters in the Mac Roman Set

Decimal	Hexadecimal	Character
191	bf	ø
192	c0	¿
193	c1	¡
194	c2	¬
195	c3	√
196	c4	ƒ
197	c5	≈
198	c6	Δ
199	c7	«
200	c8	»
201	c9	…
202	ca	
203	cb	À
204	cc	Ã
205	cd	Õ
206	ce	Œ
207	cf	œ
208	d0	–
209	d1	—
210	d2	"
211	d3	"
212	d4	'
213	d5	'
214	d6	÷
215	d7	◊
216	d8	ÿ
217	d9	Ÿ
218	da	/
219	db	€
220	dc	‹
221	dd	›
222	de	fi
223	df	fl
224	e0	‡
225	e1	·

Continued on next page

TABLE A.3 CONTINUED: Characters in the Mac Roman Set

Decimal	Hexadecimal	Character
226	e2	'
227	e3	„
228	e4	‰
229	e5	Â
230	e6	Ê
231	e7	Á
232	e8	Ë
233	e9	È
234	ea	Í
235	eb	Î
236	ec	Ï
237	ed	Ì
238	ee	Ó
239	ef	Ô
240	f0	￿
241	f1	Ò
242	f2	Ú
243	f3	Û
244	f4	Ù
245	f5	ı
246	f6	ˆ
247	f7	˜
248	f8	¯
249	f9	˘
250	fa	˙
251	fb	˚
252	fc	¸
253	fd	˝
254	fe	˛
255	ff	ˇ

XML Character Set Names

Unicode itself really only supports two different character sets: UTF-8 and UTF-16. In addition, a number of different existing character sets ratified by the ISO also exist and are supported by most XML parsers. The exact list of character sets supported depends on your parser, but all should support the basic Unicode sets as well as the ISO-8859-1 set. UTF-8 and ISO-8859-1 match the ASCII set for the first 127 characters.

In essence, if you need access to a full range of characters from all languages, use UTF-16. If you are not concerned about the Eastern character sets of Chinese, Japanese, and Korean, use UTF-8. If you need only Western characters, use ISO-8859-1. Table A.4 lists the character sets supported by the XML 1.0 standard.

TABLE A.4: XML Character Set Names and Contents

Character Set Name	Contents
UTF-8	The default encoding for XML documents, unless another specification was made as part of the XML declaration at the top of the document. UTF-8 can be used for most Western documents, including those that contain a small amount of Chinese, Japanese, or Korean.
UTF-16	A 2-byte encoding format that supports the full Unicode 3.0 character set, including the majority of the Western and Eastern characters. In addition to the 2-byte character format, UTF-16 also supports a special format of 4-byte specifications working with two 2-byte pairs.
ISO-10646-UCS-2	The multilingual plane of Unicode; that is, the character set that incorporates all of the Unicode character set and is nominally identical to the UTF-16 format. The only difference is that the special 4-byte characters are not supported. Each character is specified in a 2-byte unsigned integer.
ISO-10646-UCS-4	The Unicode character set encoded with each character taking up exactly 4 bytes.
ISO-8859-1 (Latin-1)	ASCII plus the characters for most Western European languages such as Swedish, German, and Portuguese. This character set largely matches the sets used by most Western computers.
ISO-8859-2 (Latin-2)	ASCII plus the characters required by most central European languages such as Croatian, Hungarian and Polish.
ISO-8859-3 (Latin-3)	ASCII plus the characters required for Esperanto, Maltese, Turkish, and Galician. ISO-8859-9 (Latin-5) is preferred for Turkish.
ISO-8859-4 (Latin-4)	ASCII plus the characters for the Baltic languages: Latvian, Lithuanian, Greenlandic, and Lappish. Replaced by ISO-8859-10 (Latin 6).
ISO-8859-5	ASCII plus the Cyrillic characters used for Byelorussian, Bulgarian, Macedonian, Russian, Serbian, and Ukrainians.
ISO-8859-6	ASCII plus Arabic.

Continued on next page

TABLE A.4 CONTINUED: XML Character Set Names and Contents

Character Set Name	Contents
ISO-8859-7	ASCII plus modern Greek.
ISO-8859-8	ASCII plus Hebrew.
ISO-8859-9 (Latin-5)	Essentially identical to Latin-1, except that some Turkish characters replace less commonly used Icelandic characters.
ISO-8859-10 (Latin-6)	Covers the characters required for more Northern European languages, including Estonian, Lithuanian, Greenlandic, Icelandic, Inuit, and Lappish. Superseded by ISO-8859-13.
ISO-8859-11	Basic ASCII plus Thai.
ISO-8859-12	Previously reserved for Devanagari, now likely to be unused.
ISO-8859-13	Baltic set, essentially identical to Latin-6 but with additional Latvian and Icelandic characters.
ISO-8859-14 (Latin-8)	A variant of Latin-1 that includes letters required for Gaelic and Welsh.
ISO-8859-15 (Latin-9)	Essentially identical to Latin-1 but includes the Euro currency symbol; also replaces fractional symbols with some minor French letters and some punctuation characters with some additional Finnish letters.
ISO-2022-JP	The Japanese character as defined in JIS X-0208-1997, which uses 7-bit encoding. Used on web pages and in e-mail.
Shift_JIS	The encoding of the Japanese national standard character set JIS X-0208-1997 used under Windows.
EUC-JP	The encoding of the Japanese national standard character set JIS X-0208-1997 used by most Unix variants.

APPENDIX B

Resource Guide

F inding XML resources is a bit like looking for hay in a haystack—there is information everywhere, and typing "XML" into your favorite search engine is likely to keep you busy for hours. The real problem is sorting the wheat from the chaff. Finding good XML resources is more difficult.

In this appendix I've tried to collect together as large and comprehensive a collection of pointers as possible. Included here are details on websites, mailing lists, books, and any other resources, both generically on XML and XML-related technologies and with some language-specific and XML application–specific entries.

You can find a more up-to-date list of resources relevant to this book on the MCwords.com website.

Generic Resources

Listed below are some of the generic resources on computing and standards that you may find useful. Many of them have their own XML sections, and all of them are great places to visit periodically just to check out the latest news and information.

W3C (*http://www.w3.org*)

The World Wide Web Consortium oversees the specification and guidelines for numerous technologies on the World Wide Web and the Internet in general. The site is the best resource for information on a number of technologies including CSS, DOM, (X)HTML, XML, XLink, and XSL.

Unicode Consortium (*http://www.unicode.org*)

The Unicode consortium defines and manages the contents of the Unicode standard. You can find character set lists for the different Unicode tables at `http://www.unicode.org/charts`.

Internet Engineering Taskforce (*http://www.ietf.org*)

The IETF helps to agree on and design different standards for the Internet. Unlike W3C, which looks at web-specific technologies, IETF looks at generic Internet standards, including the core protocols and technologies such as SOAP. For those familiar with the documents, it's the IETF that now holds responsibility for RFC (Request For Comments) documentation, which forms the basis of many Internet standards, including FTP, SMTP, NTP, HTTP, and MIME.

ISO (*http://www.iso.ch*)

The International Standards Organization works with organizations around the world such as the American National Standards Institute (ANSI) and the British Standards Institute (BSI) to develop standards for different technologies, including systems such as HTML, XML, and Unicode.

OASIS (*http://www.oasis-open.org*)

The Organization for the Advancement of Structure Information Standards is an international group that creates specifications to promote open and interoperable communication. The standards are based on public technologies such as XML and SGML.

IBM DeveloperWorks (*http://www.ibm.com/developer works/*)

The IBM DeveloperWorks website is a combination resource site and article library. You can find information and background material on a host of standards and articles covering the theory and practice of developing applications for just about every topic. It primarily concentrates on open-source technologies, and there is a huge section on the use of XML.

Dr Dobb's Journal (*http://www.ddj.com*)

This is a huge and long-running site dedicated to news, reviews, and in-depth articles on all areas of computer programming. The site is also backed up by a paper magazine of the same name. You can go direct to the XML section using the URL `http://www.ddj.com/topics/xml`.

Developer Shed (*http://www.devshed.com*)

A useful article and news site covering nearly all of the languages we look at in this book, along with some of the other technologies related to the different programming languages and standards such as XML and HTML.

Meerkat (*http://www.oreillynet.com/meerkat/*)

Meerkat is a web-based RSS aggregator. Besides selecting and reading different RSS newsfeeds, you can also clip specific stories into a personal list of links, and you can group and organize your RSS feeds into different personal channels to make reading specific topics easier.

XML Resources

Here are some links and books covering XML, SOAP, XML-RPC, and other XML-related technologies.

XML.com (*http://www.xml.com*)

The O'Reilly XML resource page. Although it's primarily designed as a tool for finding O'Reilly's XML books, there is also a news section and loads of background information and articles on the XML standard and the use of XML in applications.

XML.org (*http://www.xml.org*)

The XML Industry Portal is a news and article site devoted to XML and related technologies. Along with the normal range of XML information, the site also includes a useful news page for information on the latest XML information and a searchable XML Registry for XML DTDs and other standard XML related standards.

XMLHack (*http://www.xmlhack.com*)

A great background and example resource for learning how to hack and program using XML.

Apache XML Project (*http://xml.apache.org*)

The Apache group, famous for its web server software, has been developing a suite of XML tools. The project consists of five main tools: Xerces, an XML parser in Java and C++ with Perl bindings; Xalan, an XSLT stylesheet processor (Java and C++); Cocoon, an XML-based web publishing environment (Java); Xang, a tool for rapid development of dynamic server pages, written in JavaScript; and SOAP, a suite for working with SOAP services, primarily in the area of SOAP servers that integrate with Apache.

SAX (*http://www.megginson.com/SAX/*)

Megginson Technologies posted a page devoted to the SAX parser, and it became such a success that the page is now a regularly updated part of the XML website matrix. The site is geared toward Java-based SAX parsers, but the same methods and techniques covered here can be easily migrated to other languages.

Microsoft's XML Site (*http://msdn.microsoft.com/xml*)

Microsoft has been a key player in the development of XML (its Office applications have used XML for some time) and related technologies such as SOAP. Although the site is heavily geared toward XML processing using Microsoft operating systems and developer tools, there's a wealth of background information to be found. Whether you like Microsoft or not, there are worse places to start looking for information.

XML-RPC.org (*http://www.xml-rpc.org*)

The home of the XML-RPC standard. The site contains standards information on the XML-RPC system, along with a regularly updated resource for XML-RPC implementations in all the different languages. It also provides a directory of XML-RPC services available for use with a suitable client. If you are looking for an XML-RPC solution for any language, start here.

James Clark's Expat XML Parser Page (*http://www.jclark.com/xml/expat.html*)

The home of James Clark's Expat parser. You should go here first for information on parsers and extensions for any language using the Expat system.

ActiveState (*http://www.activestate.com*)

ActiveState develop software and tools for using and creating applications with Perl, Python, Tcl, and technologies such as XML.

The XML Bible (Elliotte Rusty Harold, Hungry Minds)

A well-rounded book covering the mechanics of XML from basic document building to processing and many of the technologies, systems, and applications that have been built up around the XML standard.

Learning XML (Erik T. Ray, O'Reilly and Associates)

A terrific guide to the basic mechanics of writing and building XML documents and applications. Covers everything from basic XML document building to DTDs, Xlinks, and XHTML, and the development of XML documents using Docbook and other specialized formats.

XML Complete (Various, Sybex Inc.)

A great book covering all of the ins and outs of XML. It includes some of the chapters from this book as well as background information on XML, full details on the XML standard, and reference documentation for XML documents.

Perl Resources

Perl is and always has been a heavily web-supported programming language. Your primary point of contact should be the main Perl site, where you can find information for just about everything, including XML.

Perl.com (*http://www.perl.com*)

The O'Reilly-funded site for all things Perl. The site includes news, downloads, resource links, and a huge range of articles for processing all sorts of documents, including XML and related technologies.

Perl.org (http://www.perl.org)

The "free" site for Perl development that includes links to the local Perl Monger groups and meetings and general Perl resources.

CPAN XML Modules (*http://www.perl.com/CPAN-local/modules/by-module/XML/*)

The home of the XML modules on the Comprehensive Perl Archive Network (CPAN). You should be able to find all of the modules covered in this book and many more, which will help in your XML processing.

Python Resources

Python is heavily web based and like Perl has a central resource for most of its content.

Python Home (*http://www.python.org*)

The home of the Python language. Contains an extensive set of resources and information on the Python language, as well as download sections for the Python distribution and documentation. There's also a very handy search feature that will search all of the main sites for information.

Vaults of Parnassus (*http://www.vex.net/parnassus/*)

The Vaults of Parnassus is the Python equivalent of Perl's CPAN module. It contains links to most of the third-party modules available for Python.

Zope Corporation (*http://www.zope.com*)

Zope Corporation, formerly Digital Creations, is now the home of Guido van Rossum and the rest of the Python development team. Zope Corporation is also responsible for the Zope web publishing environment (`http://www.zope.org`), which can be tooled to work with XML documents directly as the source for content material.

Python XML SIG (*http://www.python.org/sigs/xml-sig/*)

The XML SIG (Special Interest Group) handles the development of Python-specific XML tools, including the XML modules that come as part of the standard distribution. The XML SIG publishes a more extensive collection of tools and modules that is available only from its CVS server. You can also join the XML-SIG mailing list. If you are serious about doing XML development with Python, you should consider joining the mailing list and downloading the new tools.

Python: The Complete Reference (Martin C. Brown, Osborne/McGraw-Hill)

An introduction and reference to everything to do with Python programming. Covers general *ML document processing as well as Unicode, regular expressions, and general data processing in Python.

PHP Resources

Listed below are the main PHP resources and some of the XML-specific tools available for PHP.

PHP.net (*http://www.php.net*)

The home of the PHP system. You can download the PHP distribution and search the online document for XML and other information.

PHP XML Manual (*http://www.php.net/manual/en/ref.xml.php*)

The XML manual for the core XML parser available in PHP.

PHPBuilder.com (*http://www.phpbuilder.com*)

PHPBuilder.com includes news and articles on using PHP, including a number of useful articles on PHP and XML. You'll also find an interesting article on using PHP, XML, and Apache's Cocoon project together to parse XML documents.

O'Reilly PHP-XML Mailing List (*http://www.onlamp.com/pub/a/php/php-xml-ml.html*)

O'Reilly has created a useful PHP-XML interest mailing list on which interested parties can discuss using PHP and XML.

REBOL Resources

Despite its heavy Internet focus and huge cross-platform support (27, at the last count), REBOL is not as well represented as older languages such as PHP, Perl, and Python.

REBOL Home Page (*http://www.rebol.com*)

The main focus for everything REBOL. REBOL is very well supported by the REBOL development team, so you should find everything you need to use REBOL and process XML documents.

REBOL: The Official Guide **(Elan Goldman and John Blanton, Osborne/McGraw-Hill)**

A good introduction to using and processing information using REBOL. Although it doesn't cover XML processing, it should give you basics.

Ruby Resources

Ruby is a relatively new language with a heavy object focus and a cleaner and simpler style than both Python and Perl, while still retaining much of the functionality of these and other languages. Ruby is written by Yukihiro Matsumoto.

Ruby Home Page (*http://www.ruby-lang.org/en/*)

The main focus point for everything Ruby. You should be able to find downloadable versions of the language and extensive examples and documentation.

Ruby Introduction (*http://www.ibm.com/developerworks/library/ruby.html*)

A good overview on using the Ruby language.

Programming Ruby (David Thomas, Andrew Hunt, Addison Wesley)

The first English guide to programming with Ruby contains everything from the basic structure and layout of the language to web programming.

Tcl Resources

The Tcl language has had something of a checkered history. Originally a Sun project, it then moved to Scriptics, a company devoted to the promotion and development of Tcl and Tk. In 2000, Scriptics was purchased by Ajuba, which in turn was acquired by Interwoven. The Tcl project now continues with the people at ActiveState, who also do Perl and Python development.

Scriptics (*http://www.scriptics.com* or *http://tcl.activestate.com*)

The main site for Tcl and Tk programming. Tcl and the Tk GUI are available for a number of platforms. Along with download links to the main installer packages, the site also includes articles and other information on using the Tcl and Tk languages.

TclXML (*http://www.zveno.com/zm.cgi/in-tclxml/*)

The home of the TclXML parser that we use in this book for processing XML documents.

XML-RPC for Tcl (*http://sourceforge.net/projects/xmlrpctcl/*)

The home of the XML-RPC extensions for Tcl. The site includes the main distribution and samples of programs using the system. Because it's hosted on SourceForge, you can also sign up for regular updates when new versions of the system are released.

AppleScript Resources

AppleScript as a technology is focused on the entirely operating system. It is available only for Apple's two operating systems: MacOS and MacOS X. Most of the AppleScript documentation is available only to registered MacOS developers, although this will likely change with MacOS X, which includes its own XML parser and SOAP interface.

AppleScript in a Nutshell (Bruce W Perry, O'Reilly)

A solid desktop reference for everything to do with AppleScript. As a reference rather than a learning guide, it concentrates on listing the documentation in a suitable format, but it can be a handy resource for double-checking your code.

XML Tools Scripting Addition (*http://www.latenightsw.com/freeware/XMLTools2/index.html*)

The core XML processing tools for AppleScript. The tools use osax to communicate with James Clark's ever-present Expat parser.

XML-RPC with AppleScript (*http://www.latenightsw.com/freeware/XMLTools2/xml-rpc.html*)

The home page for the XML-RPC implementation made available through the XML 2.2 Scripting Addition. This page provides a quick summary of how to use XML-RPC in Mac OS.

Making XML-RPC and SOAP Requests with AppleScript (*http://developer.apple.com/techpubs/macosx/Carbon/interapplicationcomm/soapXMLRPC/*)

The "book" that covers the use of SOAP and XML-RPC within MacOS X—now a standard capability of AppleScript.

XML Software

A huge amount of software is out there already using XML to do a lot of its processing and data storage. The following are some of the tools written in one of the languages featured in this book that either use XML as a storage or processing format or can be used to develop and write XML documents.

Amphetadesk (*http://www.disobey.com/amphetadesk*)

Amphetadesk is an RSS aggregator. You use it to download and read the outlines of various news stories from hundreds of different sites. The entire system is written in Perl, and the tool runs as a personal web server, downloading the content and providing an interface through which you can configure the newsfeeds or story outlines that you want to read.

Komodo (*http://www.activestate.com/komodo*)

Komodo is probably best described as a project development and editing tool. It doesn't go quite as far as a full integrated development environment (IDE), but it does provide project management tools and an editing environment that offers auto-formatting and completion of keywords and terms.

Komodo supports much more than just XML; it also supports Perl, Python, Tcl, HTML, and many others. Komodo provides formatting and completion facilities, making it an ideal tool for writing applications using one or more of these technologies.

Index

Note to the reader: Throughout this index **boldfaced** page numbers indicate primary discussions of a topic. *Italicized* page numbers indicate illustrations.

E

S

Z

TELL US WHAT YOU THINK!

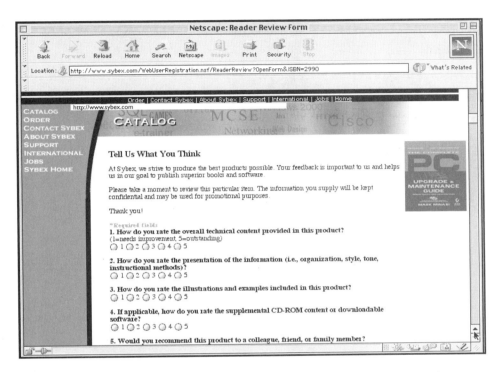

Your feedback is critical to our efforts to provide you with the best books and software on the market. Tell us what you think about the products you've purchased. It's simple:

1. Visit the Sybex website
2. Go to the product page
3. Click on **Submit a Review**
4. Fill out the questionnaire and comments
5. Click **Submit**

With your feedback, we can continue to publish the highest quality computer books and software products that today's busy IT professionals deserve.

www.sybex.com

SYBEX Inc. • 1151 Marina Village Parkway, Alameda, CA 94501 • 510-523-8233

The quotation on the bottom of the front cover is taken from the second chapter of Lao Tzu's Tao Te Ching, *the classic work of Taoist philosophy. This particular verse, from the translation by D. C. Lau (copyright 1963), asserts that there is always a connection between a thing and its opposite. For example, in order to understand the concept of "high," you also need an understanding of "low."*

It is traditionally held that Lao Tzu lived in the fifth century B.C. in China, but it is unclear whether he was actually a historical figure. The concepts embodied in the Tao Te Ching *influenced religious thinking in the Far East, including Zen Buddhism in Japan.*